HR Ready

Creating Competitive Advantage Through Human Resource Management

Steve Foster

© 2013 Steve Foster

All rights reserved. No part of this publication may be reproduced, stored in a retrieval system or transmitted in any form or by any means electronic, mechanical, photocopying, recording or otherwise without the prior permission of the publisher.

Steve Foster has asserted his right under the Copyright, Designs and Patents Act 1988 to be identified as the author of this work.

Published by Felden Business Books

ISBN 978-1-291-44702-6

Reference Edition 2013.0.2.11

CONTENTS

FOREWORD 5
INTRODUCTION 7
HR READY: AN OVERVIEW 10
PART I: THE SEVEN PILLARS OF HR READY 15
  1. HR SERVICE DELIVERY 17
  2. HR PRACTICES 52
  3. PERFORMANCE MANAGEMENT 74
  4. TALENT MANAGEMENT 91
  5. BUSINESS INTELLIGENCE 111
  6. FOCUS ON COMPETITIVE ADVANTAGE 135
  7. BUSINESS ENGAGEMENT 147
PART II: THE SIX TOOLS OF HR READY 163
  8. HR TECHNOLOGY (E-HRM) 165
  9. HR STRATEGY 205
 10. HR TRANSFORMATION 218
 11. BUSINESS PROCESS IMPROVEMENT 238
 12. BUILDING THE HR READY BUSINESS CASE .. 255
 13. MANAGING THE CHANGES 297
PART III: THE FUTURE OF HR 313
 14. HR: READY FOR THE FUTURE? 315
REFERENCES 333
INDEX 355
ABOUT THE AUTHOR 360

List of Figures

Figure 1: Seven Pillars of HR Ready 13
Figure 2: HR Service Delivery factors 20
Figure 3: Potential Shared Services Structure 27
Figure 4: Outsourcing HR – key actions 46
Figure 5: Scale of Social Technology Use 69
Figure 6: Impact of HR Practice Sophistication 71
Figure 7: The Performance Cycle 76
Figure 8: Organisational Perspectives on Talent 96
Figure 9: The Talent Cycle 99
Figure 10: HR Analytics Levels 120
Figure 11: Forms of Organisational Capital 139
Figure 12: HR Value Model 144
Figure 13: Three Legged Stool Model 155
Figure 14: HR System Structure 168
Figure 15: Human Capital v. Process Technology 169
Figure 16: HR Service Delivery Model 177
Figure 17: e-HRM Strategies 180
Figure 18: HR Technology Adoption Rates 181
Figure 19: Technology Adoption Lifecycle 182
Figure 20: e-HRM Strategy Linkages 190
Figure 21: Top 10 Design Principles 196
Figure 22: Outline HR Strategy Framework 216
Figure 23: Original Ulrich HR Roles Model 221
Figure 24: HR Maturity Levels 226
Figure 25: Process Levels 1 to 5 242
Figure 26: Process Framework 243
Figure 27: The e-HRM Value Model 261
Figure 28: Business Case Methodology 281
Figure 29: Reasons for Project Failure 300
Figure 30: Organisational Readiness Model 302
Figure 31: Change Management Top Tips 310

List of Tables

Table 1: Level 2 Example Metrics 122
Table 2: Level 3 Example Metrics 125
Table 3: Example Operational Benefits 266
Table 4: Example Productivity Benefits 273
Table 5: Example Strategic Capability Benefits 278

Foreword

The title of Marshall Goldsmith's 2012 book 'What got you here won't get you there' is as true for the HR function as it is for any other area of business - possibly more so. While it's a cliché to talk about change being the 'new normal', the last few years have seen the old Western economies face the combined challenges of low growth, austerity and difficult trading conditions, while new economies from the East and South America snap at their heels and force dramatic changes in the structure of the global economy. There is no going back; these new challenges bring about new ways of working, so that doing what always worked in the past is simply not a viable way forward.

In a rapidly changing world, every business function must find new ways to manage its costs and improve productivity, enabling the organisation to compete more effectively in its chosen market. HR functions are at the centre of these changes and must become more responsive and more adaptable to whatever happens in their business environment. For those prepared to rise to the challenge, it's an enormous opportunity to support and drive change, through a range of tools including leading-edge technology and service delivery options that contribute to achieving competitive advantage.

HR Ready organisations are well positioned to make their contribution.

Introduction

Textbooks in the HR or Payroll field tend to fall into two categories; the first type is aimed at the deep specialist, concentrating on 'how to...' (...design a job evaluation scheme, manage an employee disciplinary, define a competency model etc. etc.). These books often contain too much detail for a general audience and can be a difficult, 'dry' read. Others are aimed at explaining basic HR concepts to students but can be too simplistic and of little interest to the well informed reader. This book is boldly aimed at the middle ground – it deals with basic ideas for those that work in or around HR and need to demystify unfamiliar topics, as well as those interested in taking a more evidence-based, academic view of each subject. Its primary job is to provoke the reader into new ways of thinking about HR without getting too caught up in the mechanics of each topic. It also opens the Pandora's Box of some thorny HR issues – should Payroll be part of Finance or HR? ERP or Best of Breed? Should companies try to make people happy? Are highly talented people just smart people overloaded with confidence?

Shortly after writing my first book (*The Big Book of HR*), I (finally) completed a Professional Doctorate, based around HR's complex relationship with technology and how, in particular, HR makes sense of and justifies its investment in IT. The experience of several years spent studying the dark corners of academic HR research set my HR practitioner and consultancy experience in context and gave me a framework for exploration, removing a nagging suspicion that somebody out there had all the answers (it seems that nobody does and most of the time there is precious little agreement as to what even the most basic concepts mean!). It also highlighted to me that HR professionals and HR academics operate in quite different worlds and that they really ought to find some common language to enable them to communicate better with each other. After reading countless obscure, dull and often impenetrable HR articles, I came to the conclusion that much of what is published in academic journals is generally inaccessible to HR practitioners, despite some of the incredible value it contains. I'm convinced that HR people would benefit enormously from exploring and applying academic research as part of an evidence-based approach to Human Resource Management; it's not enough to base strategies on what comes out of conferences, internet searches and personal networks. Equally, academics need to work harder to make their research more open and practical. I have tried to straddle both worlds by providing as much theory as possible (based on almost three hundred research references) for those that want it and boxed it away for those that just want the key points.

The Big Book of HR was essentially a compilation of various articles and ideas that had been developed over a period of several years. This current book began life as a straightforward update of *The Big Book of HR*, an opportunity to improve on some sections I no longer liked or necessarily agreed with. Missing from the first book was a central defining idea to provide a framework for its content, which has now been addressed, with the central theme running through the book being the idea of **competitive advantage** (hence its subtitle), a concept often missing from academic and practitioner accounts of HR. The primary thesis is that this should be the ultimate objective of everything HR does; the simple question *"How does this help our business compete better in its market?"* should be asked regularly. HR Ready also raises questions about what HR organisations need to do to be fully prepared for a post-recessionary world that is unpredictable and uncertain. Like the 'HD Ready' theme from which it borrows (relating to future-proof televisions!), it alludes to future-proofing the HR function, being resilient, adaptable and helping organisations to compete better in their chosen markets. Because it draws heavily on academic material, the book is also a thesis, proposing and defending the HR Ready theme; like any good academic, I'm prepared to accept I may be wrong and may have missed something, so it's also the basis for a research model.

Finally, a couple of comments about language and terminology. I've always believed in the importance of plain English, despising clichés and management speak as substitutes for 'real' thinking by those incapable of expressing a complex idea in simple terms. A recent report in the UK Daily Telegraph (May 14, 2013) found that expressions such as 'Thinking outside the box', *'Let's touch base'* and *'Going forward'* were the most hated examples of management speak. I have therefore tried to avoid using 'buzz' words and meaningless phrases, although if sometimes the odd one slips through in error, I can only apologise. I was initially concerned that in many cases, it was apparently impossible to define many of the terms in common HR usage – whether it was talent management, performance management, HR technology or even the concept of strategy, time and again I discovered a multitude of contradictory definitions and explanations. It seemed that in many cases, there was simply no commonly accepted meaning for words that were part of everyday Human Resources language. I worried whether this was symptomatic of an HR function in turmoil, lacking in science and reliant on a series of half-baked ideas. I then discovered that most other professions have similar problems – it seems that psychologists cannot agree on what 'personality' means and biologists cannot agree on definitions for the words 'species', 'organism' or indeed, 'life'.

That made me feel much better.

Dr. Steve Foster
July, 2013

Special thanks to Jonathan Ellard, Julie Lock and Peter Yates for their valuable comments.

HR Ready: An Overview

HR should not be confined by what it does but by what it delivers – results that enrich the organisation's value to customers, investors and employees

David Ulrich, A New Mandate for Human Resources, 1996

In the mid 1990's, management guru Dave Ulrich opened his book 'Human Resource Champions' with a challenging question; *"Should we do away with HR?"*. His answer was simple and unequivocal – yes, if HR fails to deliver what the business needs. However, his next question *"How can HR deliver results and create value?"* is more useful and it is this topic that this book addresses.

Depending on your view of the economy, much of the world is currently either deep in recession, starting its recovery or on the verge of recovery; either way, changing economic conditions represent both a threat and an opportunity for HR functions. Some will emerge stronger, having helped their businesses to adapt to the challenges, introduce innovative solutions and find new ways of working. They will be leaner, fitter and ready for a period of growth. At the same time, others will revert to old ways, having abandoned their plans to be more strategic, settling into a more traditional role as an administrative support service. Tough economic times often have a Darwinian impact on business – success goes to those who can adapt in the face of new circumstances and they eventually mutate into a different kind of animal, while those that fail to adapt are marginalised and eventually become extinct. Whereas profitability in boom times often masks accounting realities, recessionary times have a way of highlighting flaws in the underlying business model at the organisational and functional levels. The past five years have seen the fortunes of some big corporate names (once thought to be indestructible), fade away. Think Woolworths, TWA, Borders and Saab, none of which any longer survive; it seems that every day we hear of new casualties. Likewise, many HR functions that have survived previous recessions have found themselves hit hard as organisations undertake deep dives into reviews of HR efficiency, asking difficult questions about the function's contribution. Some recent research (Roche et al, 2011) looked at how HR organisations are coping with the current recession, suggesting that there will be one of three possible outcomes for the HR profession as a result of economic turmoil:

- A 'cataclysmic' outcome for the HR function, where it fails to make any noticeable contribution to the business; organisations conclude that HR has little value and it ultimately withers and dies. In this scenario, the HR function faces a dramatic cut in numbers, while 'transactional' HR processes are increasingly relocated to low-cost countries.

- The second (which represents the dominant perspective among HR 'commentators') suggests that the recession will increase the stature and influence of the HR function and deepen the appeal and perceived value of HR practices. In this glorious future, HR finally proves its worth to the business and achieves the respect it craves.

- The third strand takes the middle ground. In this contingent scenario, changes are pragmatic, eclectic and incremental in nature, leaving continued doubts over the future of the function. Potentially, this represents failure, a kind of indecisive 'HR purgatory' where managers continue to lack respect and HR is rendered feeble and impotent.

One of the disappointing conclusions the study reached was that "*On the whole, there is a relative absence of reports of innovative HR approaches to the economic recession*" (p8). This is not good news for the HR function. It suggests that even in the face of deep recession, HR has generally continued to do what it has always done – cut training budgets, reduce bonuses, introduce pay freezes and pay cuts and take tougher negotiating positions....but not take positive steps to re-invent itself for a totally different world. Although not explicitly stated, it suggests HR is heading for the third option – hanging by a thread. HR Ready is an opportunity to prepare the function to cope with whatever is next, whether it's boom, bust or steady state.

The Seven Pillars of HR Ready

In recent years, there's been a debate about what constitutes 'good' HR. One difficulty is that the profession lacks a single, unifying theory against which to benchmark good practice. The problem is further compounded because the outcomes of HR are generally long-term and often intangible, with a multitude of economic and political factors potentially blurring the impact of HR initiatives. The result is that there's often no straight line connection between what HR does and bottom line business outcomes. It can take several years for an HR initiative to pay back - one of the objectives of HR ready is to make HR's contribution transparent and evidence-based so it can thrive.

The book is in three sections. Part One deals with the seven pillars of HR as shown in Figure 1, each of which is described from a practical and theoretical perspective, with appropriate evidence from the available research material and case study examples where they illustrate the key points. Why seven? Well, I have theology, history and mathematics on my side; seven is everywhere – seven hills of Rome, seven days of the week, seven wonders of the ancient world, seven deadly sins, seven ages of man, seven dwarves, seven samurai, seven brides for seven brothers, the Magnificent Seven, the Secret Seven and let's not forget James Bond as 007. In the ancient world there were seven known 'planetary' bodies – the sun, moon, Mercury, Venus, Mars, Saturn and Jupiter. The Christian Bible contains many references to the number seven (such as the seven virtues and the seven sacraments). Mathematically, seven is a Mersenne prime, as well as a Woodall prime, a factorial prime and a safe prime (Google that lot). Even Harry Potter thought that seven was a magical number.

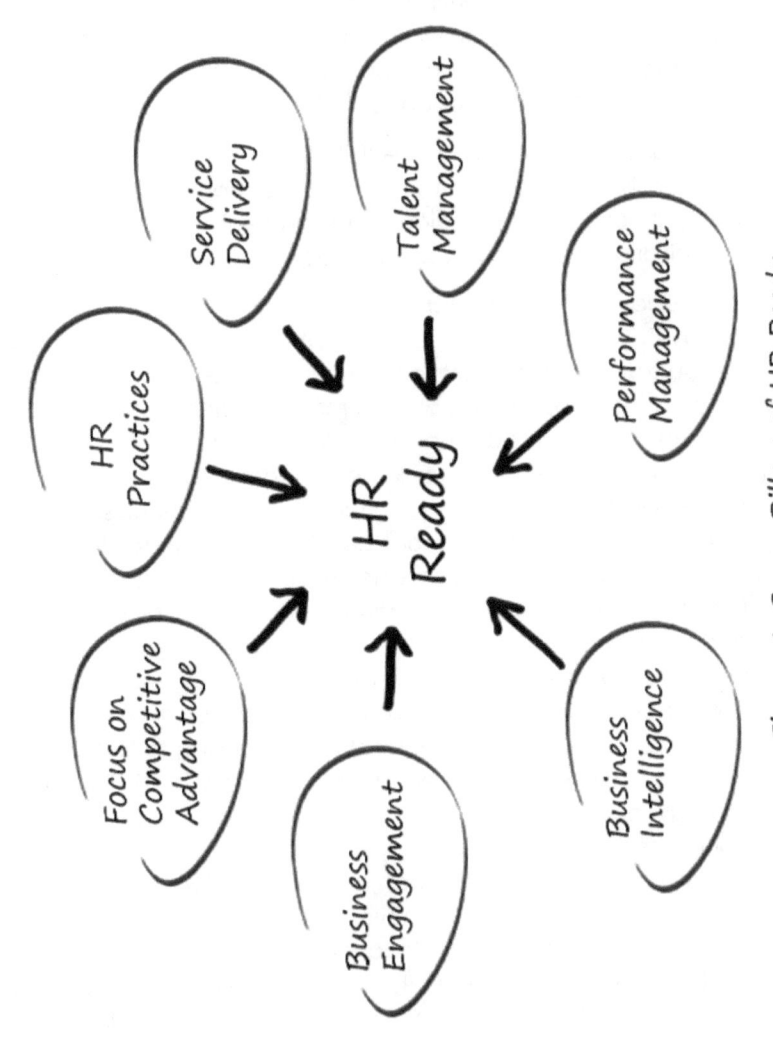

Figure 1: Seven Pillars of HR Ready

Part Two describes the six tools available to organisations to become HR Ready, such as the use of e-HRM technology, creating a business case and business process improvement. If there were seven tools, it would have given the book a certain poetic symmetry, but until a seventh tool is identified, you'll just have to live with the awkwardness. Six is much less interesting as a number and apparently in some cultures is considered unlucky, but I'll take my chances.

The final part indulges in a little 'futurism', exploring where the HR function is headed and the kind of economic, demographic, political and technological environments that HR Ready organisations need to be....well, **ready** for.

'HR Ready' is a simple term that's partly a test - 'Are you HR Ready?' - a benchmark against which the function can be measured. It also suggests a time context; being HR Ready goes beyond more than being able to meet the demands of today, it also stresses the importance of being prepared for what might happen tomorrow, next week, next month and beyond. If I can be allowed to indulge in just a little management speak, the essence of HR Ready is about building resilience for the future, future-proofing the function and making it infinitely adaptable. Fundamentally, it's a set of competencies that build resilience and adaptability, ensuring HR can thrive and grow whatever happens to the economy. HR Ready businesses are not complacent – they never believe they are ready enough and are always moving, testing their defences, trying to find different ways to stay ready. When an HR function is HR Ready, HR strategy becomes more responsive and more relevant, better connected to the business and better able to become an applied business discipline, not just a service function. Being HR Ready positions the HR function as an integral part of the business, where it would be inconceivable to think about driving the business forward without its involvement and perspective. But be warned - HR Ready is not an easy fix that can be quickly applied. It's about seeing the bigger picture and exploiting the unique insight that the HR function brings to the organisation, together with "A deep appreciation of what goes on and what really makes things happen, given its people, politics and culture" (CIPD 2011).

Part I: The Seven Pillars of HR Ready

1 HR Service Delivery

Why is Service Delivery Important?

In his 1997 ground-breaking book 'Human Resource Champions', Management Professor (and HR guru) Dave Ulrich set out a model for the operation of the Human Resource function that would influence a generation. One of the roles he defined for the HR function was the 'Administrative Expert', a role designed to cope with the vast range of back-office support services that ensure a business is compliant with statutory requirements and internal policy. HR typically delivers two distinct types of service:

- **Simple transactional services:** Administration arises as a direct result of employing people. It covers a vast range of processes – including issuing employment contracts, managing pay and conditions and maintaining personal data, all of which require effective administration. As a minimum, processes must meet basic legally requirements and ideally should also be cost-effective, efficient and of good quality. These activities are generally considered to be 'compliance' processes – they enable the business to operate within the law and its own policy, although they rarely provide any direct strategic capability or competitive advantage.

- **Transformational HR services** create value for the organisation through processes such as learning &

development, performance management, talent management and recruitment, leading to increased employee engagement and the creation of competitive advantage. These types of services tend to be delivered in organisations where the Human Resources model is relatively mature and where adding value is more important than policy compliance.

Providing HR and Payroll transactional services is expensive for an organisation, representing an overhead to the business both in terms of operational cost and managerial time. Anything that can be done to reduce the cost of delivering these services represents money the business could invest in other customer facing activities that could ultimately create wealth. As a result, there is often pressure on HR functions to meet the dual and sometimes conflicting requirement of reducing the cost of delivering service, while at the same time improving its quality. A key decision facing organisations is how best to structure the delivery of HR and Payroll services to meet these needs, a problem that remains just as much a challenge now as it did in the mid-1990s.

The HR Service Delivery Model

Planning an overall approach to HR service delivery requires strategic choices to be made about which HR and Payroll services the business needs, how they are delivered, how delivery should be organised and what technologies need to be in place. It involves a complex series of decisions based on the following factors:

- **Services and Processes:** What services and processes does the business need to provide, what additional services is it prepared to pay for and to what level of quality should services be delivered?

- **Organisation and Roles:** How will the HR function be organised in the future (centralised, decentralised, using a shared services model etc.) and what types of job roles are needed to operate services? How delivery be managed to ensure that service quality is maintained?

- **Governance:** How will service delivery be regulated, are accountabilities clear, what form should the service level agreement take and what metrics are needed to measure performance? Service contracts for outsourced services are often regulated through the use of Service Level Agreements that define expectations and Key performance indicators that monitor the quality of the service, although these tend to be less common for in-house services.

- **Location:** Where will service delivery be located – locally, nationally, internationally, multi-site, offshore, onshore? Organisations will need to assess the implications of moving certain processes away from the point where they are ultimately delivered.

- **HR/Payroll Technology:** How should the primary HR technology be designed to meet HR and business objectives, how will it support services and processes, how should the HR system be set up to ensure the most efficient services and the provision of good management information?

- **Service Technology:** What supporting technologies are needed to improve service delivery? For example, how should the organisation deploy self-service, case management tools, document management and increasingly social media technologies to support case management, recruitment and other processes?

- **Sourcing:** Will services be provided internally, through internal shared services, through a third party provider or through a mix of service channels? How will the organisation choose between these different options and will the decision be regularly re-visited to ensure it remains valid?

- **People:** What type of individuals are needed to deliver services, what skills will they need in the future and how will the organisation develop them and manage their performance? Where will the organisation obtain these skills – through a strategy of building them internally or from the open market?

Figure 2 illustrates the factors contributing to service delivery decisions.

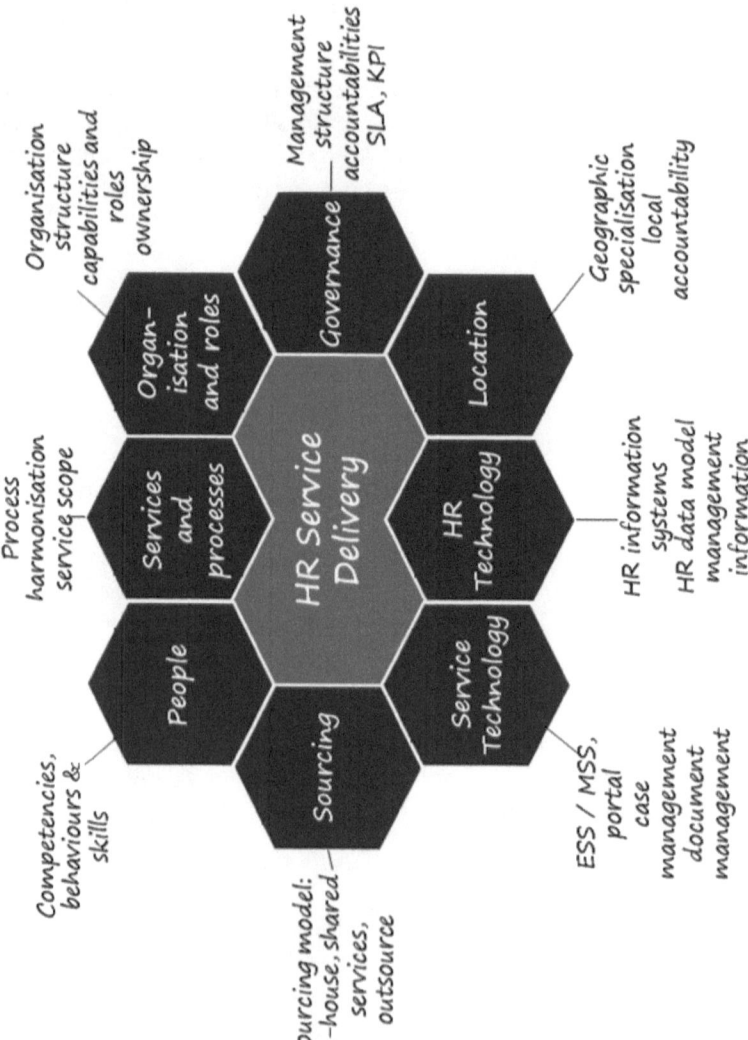

Figure 2: HR Service Delivery Factors

Service Delivery: The Theory

Research suggests that organisations generally lack confidence that HR and Payroll services are being provided as efficiently as possible; in one study, fewer than one third of organisations describe their internal HR function as 'very cost effective' **(Aberdeen Group, 2009a)**. There is also evidence that effective service delivery remains an important organisational priority – in one study, 46% identified economic uncertainty as a driver of cost reduction, to a point where it will force the organisation to operate more efficient 'back-office' functions **(Aberdeen Group, 2012)**. Research has increasingly recognised that HR needs to improve its customer orientation **(Bacon, 1999; Becker & Huselid, 1999)**.

Assessments regarding HR service delivery differ for transactional and transformational HR; the delivery of transactional HR services meet the administrative needs of end-users and business units, including timely and consistent HR service delivery, faultless HR administration and the standardised provision of transactional HR services **(Buyens & De Vos, 2001; Lepak, Bartol, & Erhardt, 2005)**. Transactional HR services are often viewed as a hygiene factor, that is, they do not increase end-user satisfaction once their quality exceeds a certain threshold, but they may lower satisfaction if delivered poorly. Transformational HR services involve higher level value creation, based on the client's *"Overall assessment of the utility of a service based on the perceptions of what is received and what is given"* **(Meijerink et al., 2013)**. Perceived value reflects the extent to which a service meets the needs of those who use it **(Priem, 2007)**.

Alleyne, Kakabadse, & Kakabadse (2007) and **Buyens & De Vos (2001)**, found that managerial satisfaction with HR processes and tools had an influence on satisfaction with the overall HR function. HR services are also thought to have an important influence on employee attitudes, so service quality is an important factor in employee and manager satisfaction. Studies have shown that satisfying the needs of managers and employee affects employee attitudes positively, such as increasing organisational commitment.

HR Delivery Structures

Once HR functions have reached a certain level of maturity (see Chapter 10 on HR Transformation), a wide range of options is available for structuring service delivery. The following summarises the main types:

a.   Service Centre

The starting point for many organisations is the introduction of a service centre (although at this point, it need not necessarily operate as a *shared* service model). A service centre regards employee issues as business problems and seeks to manage them through formal, highly structured business processes. Work is commonly divided into routine administration and specialist activity, with HR professionals often employed to deal with specific areas such as employment law, recruitment and payroll. In some cases, administrators are professionally qualified in administration methods, rather than being general clerical staff. The term 'service centre' is potentially misleading in this context, with connotations of a call centred filled with operators dealing with enquiries from distant employees. In practice, a service centre model describes the philosophy of the operation than anything to do with size, location or even technology.

For multi-site or multi-divisional organisations, one key question is whether HR services should be delivered centrally or on a decentralised basis:

- **Decentralised:** Each business unit has full control over HR activities and has the capability to provide the services needed to meet the demands of that business. Because of its proximity to the point of delivery, the decentralised model is potentially more responsive to customer needs and is able to provide better support for local variations in processes. However, there is a risk that certain specialist activities and processes will be duplicated by each business unit. There are few scale benefits.

- **Centralised:** In this model, business units join together for some or all services, creating economies of scale for delivery. Again, the service need not be provided from the same location, as centralisation refers to the underlying service philosophy – in some cases, centralisation can be virtual. Most Payroll and Pensions functions have traditionally operated as centralised services, providing a common service to multiple business units. The full centralised model simply extends this to include other transactional business processes such as recruitment, training and policy development.

In practice, multi-site or multi-divisional organisations operate a hybrid of centralised/decentralised models, where specific local processes are operated under a de-centralised model and common services are provided centrally.

b. Corporate HR

In addition to a service centre, shared services or outsourcing delivery unit, larger organisations typically operate a Corporate HR function that provides support and governance across multiple business units. Corporate HR tends to provide value-adding processes (as opposed to transactional services), centred around creating an identity and culture for the business, shaping HR programmes linked to the CEO's agenda, designing processes that link HR to common goals and being a hub for the movement of global talent. Corporate HR functions also frequently provide HR services to corporate level staff.

Corporate HR (like many other corporate functions) is often viewed with disdain by the rest of the organisation. One reason for this is that they are perceived to have a 'policing' role and ascbeing overly bureaucratic. There can sometimes be great tension between Corporate and Business Unit HR – Corporate sees the Business Unit HR as reluctant to comply with corporate policy, while Business Units see Corporate as interfering with local affairs, with no understanding of real-life issues. Of course, individuals that transfer between the two tiers find it very easy to adopt the opposite position!

c. Shared Services

HR Shared Service Centres (HR SSCs) have become widespread in response to a belief that they offer the best combination of centralised and decentralised models. While there may be some truth to this, a shared services operation is not necessarily the same as centralisation – in fact, it's possible to create a shared services model based on multiple locations, with specialist groups operating from different centres. Likewise, shared services are not the same as outsourcing, although an outsourcing arrangement is typically based around a shared service centre. There are two distinctive features of HR shared services:

- They are based on a common, i.e. **shared** provision of routine HR administration.

- They are **service-focused**, enabling the customers of the service to specify the level and nature of what is delivered.

Rather than duplicating activities within each business unit, a Shared Service Centre provides services to multiple business unit customers. Potentially, a Service Centre can serve every business unit, as long as it can take into account variations in policy and process across each of its customers. In a true shared services model, the service centre is operated as a separate business unit, with its own Profit and Loss line and the overall aim of providing services at the cost and quality levels required by its clients. Under this model, the customers of shared services choose the type, level and quality of services they want from the centre, at a price they are willing to pay. In principle, a centre could be operated on a 'menu' basis, where each customer defines the mix of services they want, although this is less common as the operation of multi-tiered processes typically presents structural and economic challenges and restricts the advantages of scale

Organisations operate a shared services model for a variety of reasons, including:

- **Reduce Costs and Eliminate Duplication:** There are often major economies of scale to be gained through reduced management overheads and shared technology, as well as rationalising facilities and accommodation. Streamlining business processes eliminates duplication of effort, simplifies services, smoothes out peaks and troughs in workload and helps to reduce costs through the creation of a 'critical mass' of delivery capacity. Shared services also offers the potential to exploit combined buying power, including standardising preferred suppliers such as recruitment agencies and training providers. Relocating an expensive location to an area where wage costs are relatively lower is a common technique for lowering the cost of service delivery.

- **Shared Specialist Knowledge:** In de-centralised structures, HR knowledge is often dispersed across several individuals and expertise may be hard to find. Shared Services allows the pooling and sharing of HR process knowledge across different parts of the organisation, rather than dispersing it across multiple locations. This leads to a better response and a more consistent approach to policy implementation.

- **Improving Quality of Service to Customers:** Efficient processes mean that timely, accurate information and advice can be given to customers, leading to a step change in the service quality. The sharing of services also helps to reduce competition and rivalry between different parts of the business.

- **Re-focus the HR Function:** By separating the administrative component of the HR service, HR is freed from its day-to-day routine activities, enabling the HR function to become more business-driven and better able to concentrate on enabling and supporting organisational change. Shared services are a way of both symbolically and practically making a statement about the role and activities of the HR function and how services are delivered.

- **As a First Step toward Outsourcing:** Once internal efficiencies are demonstrated, it can be easier to argue the business case for outsourcing the service to an external provider. Additional benefits can often by achieved through outsourcing, such as greater access to technology and further economies of scale.

- **As a Possible Profit Centre:** Successful HR Shared Service Centres may seek to use any spare capacity available to sell excess capacity to other organisations, effectively becoming outsource providers themselves. In practice, this can be a complex and expensive strategy and may detract from the focus on internal customers.

Building an HR Shared Service Centre therefore involves combining the most appropriate people skill sets with the right processes and the right technology.

> ### Shared Services: The Theory (1)
>
> The basic premise of shared services is that organisations optimise the benefits of both a centralised and decentralised delivery model **(Janssen & Joha, 2006).** Shared services has been defined as: "*A hybrid organisational model for centrally bundling resources in an HR shared Services that performs HR activities to be controlled by its end users and business units*" **(Meijerink, Bondarouk, & Looise, 2013, p85).**
>
> By balancing centralised and decentralised models, firms expect to reap concrete benefits such as rapid decision making, consistent implementation of policies, the creation of synergies, increased productivity, better management information, cost transparency and reduced administrative workloads **(Cooke, 2006; Janssen & Joha, 2006).** HR Shared Services are typically controlled by business units and end users; the focus of benefits evaluation is typically on improved customer satisfaction, service quality and HR effectiveness, including measures such as timeliness, responsiveness, customer focus and helpfulness **(Maatman et al., 2010).**

Key Principles for Shared Services

However, not every process is suited to be included in an HR Shared Service Centre and not every process can be successfully transferred to a shared service environment. The following sets out a number of key principles for establishing a shared service centre approach to HR and payroll services:

- **Organise Around Processes:** It's important that a shared services operation is organised around well-designed business processes with a clearly defined scope. Processes should be capable of being standardised, centralised and enabled by technology so that they can be run at high volume. It's important that accountabilities are clearly defined and communicated with no ambiguity. One study (Reilly, Tamkin, & Broughton, 2007) found that 55% of organisations identified boundary issues to be a major problem for shared services, including unclear accountabilities and poorly defined roles. Gaps in service provision (42%) and communication difficulties (37%) were also found to be major barriers to success. Those working in shared service centres also found themselves regularly getting drawn into the 'wrong' activities.

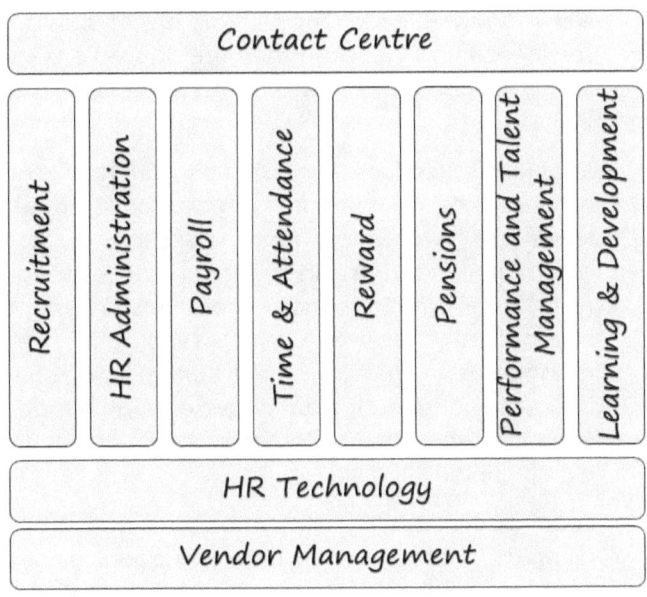

FIGURE 3: POTENTIAL SHARED SERVICES STRUCTURE

○ **Organise the Service in New Ways:** The introduction of shared Services is an opportunity to re-think how services are delivered and shift the focus from an inwardly looking, chaotic HR function to one where the customer is at the centre of work. In a shared services structure, the business should be focused on the customer; in theory the customer can have what they want as long as they are prepared to pay a non-standard (possibly premium) price for a non-standard service. However, any additional workload beyond the standard offering must be costed, planned, resourced and agreed - forecasting demand is an essential skill and the workload of a Shared Services Centre must be carefully planned and organised.

- **Manage Issues and Non-Compliance:** It's critical that customers perceive that their issues are being dealt with effectively and quickly. One of the biggest complaints about shared services structures is that they have an impersonal, call centre mentality that managers perceive is more difficult to deal with. There is some evidence that line managers experience low levels of satisfaction with service centres because they feel they are unnecessarily bureaucratic and a waste of management time (Cooke, 2006)

- **Regulate Relationships:** Shared services should be regarded as an in-house services provider with similar levels of governance that would be applied to an external provider. This includes Service Level Agreements (SLAs), Key Performance Indicators (KPIs), customer satisfaction reviews and strategic relationship management meetings, with close involvement from business sponsors. It's no longer enough to *'do the best you can'* when the customer is paying and the costs are highly visible.

- **Local Issues Matter:** It's impossible to ignore cultural diversity, whether it exists between countries or between locations within a country. For an international Service Centre, employing multi-lingual staff will be important, but even at a national level, people from different offices may have different policies, speak with different accents or have local ways of working; these need to be factored into service centre design.

- **Marketing and Reputation:** From time to time, Service Centres may need to engage in Public Relations exercise to remind its customers of the value and benefits of the service being provided. Some research has found that in a transactional environment, managers perceptions of quality are more influenced by cost than the actual level of services provided (Meijerink et al., 2013). Ensuring that

- **Seek continuous improvement:** Going live with a shared services operation is only the start – like any good provider, the shared services centre should have a spirit of continuous improvement, seeking better ways to improve processes and services and take advantage of technology. It's reasonable to expect that operating costs will go down over a period of time as new efficiencies are found.

Shared Services isn't for Everyone....

Shared Service Centres are sometimes thought to be an easy route to gain economies of scale and improve operational effectiveness. However, David Ulrich (2008) warns that other models "*Should not be abandoned.... unless the structure and strategy of the business mandates the choice*" There is a clear message here about not simply following fashion, but taking a considered view of whether the SSC model is appropriate for the business, based on all the available options – it should not be an automatic response to an inefficient HR service. There are several pitfalls of an internal Shared Services approach that need to be carefully considered. For example, Shared Services isn't a magic bullet: Implementing a Shared Service Centre in a disorganised company will not solve deeper problems. To be successful, an HR SSC needs to operate within a mature organisation, where line managers share the desire for service centres to be successful. Managers should be willing negotiate and work within Service Level Agreements, adopt and comply with processes and procedures and not attempt to work around the system by building their own delivery capabilities. In return, the Shared Service Centre must meet the Service Level Agreement and Key Performance Indicators at an acceptable cost.

It's also important to remember that technology cannot solve every organisational problem and new technology can create new types of challenges; for example. HR service teams will need to learn new skills and work with a range of technology solutions that provide multiple methods of communicating with customers (e-mail, web-chat, portals, Interactive Voice Response etc.). Introducing new technologies can sometimes be counter-productive if delivery teams are unable to make good use of them, and it may be better to build a scalable platform but initially restrict access to a single on-line channel (for example, telephone) and an off-line channel (e-mail). More sophisticated channels such as social media and chat areas can be introduced later.

Finally, shared Services takes time and it's often necessary to demonstrate the viability of the SSC concept through a series of 'quick wins'. One way to achieve this is to begin with a cluster of highly standardised business processes, then build on this by adding more complex processes later. Research suggests that successful SSCs develop and mature over time.

d.   Centres of Expertise

Centres of Expertise (CoEs) typically sit alongside Shared Service Centres and consist of technical experts in each area of HR practice. The major benefit of the Centre of Expertise model is that it allows the concentration of highly specialised skills, avoiding duplication across the business. However, Centres of Expertise are different from Shared Service centres in that, whereas Shared Services Operations primarily focus on transactions, CoEs mainly focus on HR policy and practices, with a greater focus on achieving business goals and implementing strategy. COEs are therefore *transformational* in nature rather than *transactional*. Centres of Expertise tend to specialise in the delivery of HR practices (see Chapter 2) including the following:

- **Compensation/Reward:** Pay for performance, job evaluation, performance measurement, reward and recognition programmes, bonus programmes.

- **Learning and Development:** Personal and career planning, performance management, executive training, diversity, organisational learning.

Shared Services: The Theory (2)

HR Shared Service Centres are thought to create value through the combination and exploitation of three forms of capital **(Meijerink et al., 2013; Ross & Dicker, 2000):**

- **Human Capital** - knowledge and skills (forms of intellectual capital) believed to account for significant variance in HR effectiveness (see also **Ulrich et al, 2008**).

- **Network capital** – the social relationships built up by HR Shared Services Centre members to exchange knowledge.

- **Organisational capital** – a reflection of the organisation knowledge that is codified, embedded or stored in knowledge 'containers' such as database, routines and IT.

The economic benefit of a shared service centre is maximised when all these forms of capital are put to use in the delivery of services.

Farndale et al (2009) argue that one of the key factors in achieving shared services success is that managers perceive that service centre staff have the appropriate competencies and skills. However, while this research found that the issue of customer-focus was paramount when establishing these new organisational forms, it also highlighted problems with lack of performance data on how well the centre is operating, despite the original aims of wanting to cut costs and improve service quality. It also revealed a larger degree of differentiation and 'fitness for purpose' against acceptable quality and cost-effective standards.

Other research suggests there is little evidence that Shared Services is an effective model, with little insight into how combined knowledge resources contribute to a low cost, high quality HR function **(Meijerink et al., 2013)**. They propose that the contribution of human capital to transformational HR value will be enhanced if it is combined with high levels of social and organic organisational capital.

- **Recruitment and Staffing:** Sourcing applicants, succession planning, career development, talent assessment, and screening.
- **Organisational Effectiveness and Change:** Process improvement, culture change, communications and transition, organisation design.
- **Employee Relations:** Trade union relationships, employee assistance, employee engagement.

Likewise, the types of people employed in Service centres tend to have administrative skills, while CoEs tend to be professionally qualified, consultancy focused individuals.

e.   Outsourced HR

Management Author Tom Peters once challenged companies to look at each of their internal functions and ask *"Are we good enough to sell this on the open market?"* He argued that if the answer is "No", the next question should be *"Why would we buy from ourselves that which nobody would buy from us?"* One of the critical service delivery choices for organisations is the 'buy or make' decision, that is, whether the organisation should develop an infrastructure to provide the services itself or buy from a specialist external provider. However, the traditional 'buy or make' decision oversimplifies the decision – the real question is *"How can we reduce the costs and increase the quality of our HR function?"*

True HR outsourcing came to the forefront of business activity in the early 1990s via the United States and slowly migrated to Europe, primarily as a means to achieve cost reduction. As companies increasingly began to recognise the value of concentrating on their core competencies, outsourcing non-core functions became a serious option.

Organisations have been using various forms of outsourcing for basic functions such as cleaning, catering and security for many years, often based around the performance of relatively low skilled work. However, these types of operation are effectively service contracts (sub-contracting) whereas true outsourcing has the following characteristics:

- **Greater Levels of Ownership:** The outsource provider has responsibility and ownership of people, processes and technology.
- **The Provider has an Increased Level of Risk:** The provider carries accountability for employees that work directly on delivering the service and carries risks and penalties associated with failure to deliver the service.
- **Length of the Relationship:** Large outsourced deals are often contracted for at least 5 years (and in some cases 10 years) requiring significant investment by the provider in terms of technology, people and resource.
- **Closer Integration with the Customer Organisation:** The provider is often so embedded within the organisation that customers are often be unable to tell whether the person they're dealing with is part of the provider's or their own organisation.

Why Companies Outsource the HR Function

While short-term cost savings are generally seen as the major reason for outsourcing, they are not the only reason. Academic research suggests the following drivers for HR Outsourcing (Woodall et al, 2009):

- **Influence from Elsewhere in the Business:** Organisations often explore outsourcing as part of a business-wide exploration of service delivery options, together with several other internal functions. For example, the organisation may have a parent company that encourages or requires an outsourcing strategy. Indeed, research indicates that the decision to outsource is often not driven by the HR team alone – there is usually pressure from fellow directors or other internal forces.
- **Cost Reduction:** The most obvious benefit of outsourcing is the removal of cost from the HR operation, achieved through streamlining processes and the introduction of leading-edge technology to support the delivery of new processes. Although (at least in theory) organisations could achieve a great deal of cost reduction through their own efforts, many lack the skills to bring about the transformation or do not have the right technology or scale to do so. For this reason, organisations often

conclude that it is much more cost-effective to use an external provider that has an established infrastructure in place and can bring expertise and experience to their customers. Outsourcing providers deliver services to a wide range of customers and are able to spread costs over a large number of employees, enabling them to achieve extensive economies of scale that would not be available to individual organisations. Outsourcing also reduces the cost of overheads involved in providing the service, smoothing out peaks and troughs in workload to ensure consistency of service delivery.

- **Moving HR up the Value Chain:** HR often sees administration as a barrier to working strategically – if the function can be freed from the burden of administrative work, there is more scope to operate at a higher level (this issue will be explored further in subsequent chapters). Even in organisations where the HR Business Partner model has been introduced, evidence suggests that organisations experience difficulties in breaking away from administrative tasks and seek transformational approaches that enable HR to concentrate on other activities (see Snell, Stuebner & Lepak, 2002). For example, Business Partners often find themselves pre-occupied by operational issues and are unable to diagnose and develop strategic HR solutions, becoming 'bogged down' in detail (Deloitte, 2009).

- **Risk Reduction:** All organisations have a legal obligation to comply with the requirements of local and national employment legislation. Employment legislation continues to become more complex (especially in Europe) and non-compliance can ultimately lead to legal action. A report by BusinessHR and MORI, which looked at UK SMEs and their attitudes towards staff attraction, retention and motivation found that 43% of managing directors experience difficulty in keeping up with growing employment legislation.

Outsourcing: The Theory (1)

Given the size of the outsourcing market and its history, it's perhaps surprising to find that definitions of HR Outsourcing tend to be fairly loose, ranging from descriptions based on long-term subcontracting to a fully independent service organisation. Even academics agree that there is a lack of consensus about what constitutes outsourcing. However, common to most definitions is reference to the role of the external provider.

One definition is *"The transfer to an external vendor, on a recurring basis, of HR activities that would normally be performed in-house"* **(Delmotte & Sels, 2008).**

A similar definition is *"The delegation of one or more business processes to an external provider, who then owns, manages and administers the selected processes based on defined and measurable performance metrics"* **(Gartner, 1995).**

Academic literature contains two different views of HR outsourcing. The first sees outsourcing as generating more time and resources for tactical and strategic HR contributions, allowing a stronger focus on core activities. The strategic driver mentioned most frequently in literature is the ability to concentrate on core activities **(Prahalad & Hamel, 1990).** This assumes that the outsourcing of transactional and operational HR activities benefits the strategic position of HRM **(Belcourt, 2006; Scott-Jackson, Woodall, Newham, & Gurney, 2009).**

The second view is based on Transaction Cost Economics, which considers outsourcing as a way of reducing operational costs based on reducing the number of HR staff (for example, **Williamson, 1975).** This view seeks to reduce HR activity to standardised, commodity processes which can be performed at a lower cost by an external provider which can create and exploit economic scale. Outsourcing is seen as a threat to the internal HR function but provides overall cost efficiencies to the organisation.

The risks are obvious – failure to comply with legislation can consume huge amounts of management time, while the cost to employers of defending a tribunal claim can be very high (in some cases, such as those linked to gender and disability discrimination, there are unlimited penalties). Bad experience of employment claims is often the trigger for exploring outsourcing options.

- **Service Quality Improvement:** Companies that want to improve the speed, quality and effectiveness of their HR operations face two barriers. Firstly, they lack knowledge of best practice processes and how to implement them and secondly, their HR teams are so entrenched in current ways of working that they find it difficult to make the transition to a customer-focused service centre approach. HR outsourcing service providers typically bring experience and knowledge of best practice processes, built through experience of working with a range of customers and technologies.

- **Increasing HR's Capacity to Respond to Organisational Change:** Outsourcing is a tool often used by smaller organisations during their early growth stage if they are not able or motivated to invest in an internal HR function. It can also be used by organisations that wish to transform HR but cannot see an effective way to change their service delivery structure without external intervention. Likewise, outsourcing is sometimes a response when one division of a company is sold (such as in the case of a management buy-out) leaving it with no HR infrastructure, as an alternative to establishing a new internal HR operation.

What HR Operations can be Outsourced?

As with Shared Services, research suggests that transactional HR activities that are standardised and highly repeatable are most frequently considered for outsourcing. In theory, all aspects of human resource management can be outsourced, including strategy, operations and administration, although in practice the processes an organisation chooses to outsource will depend on a series of factors unique to each organisation. These include its strategic goals, current HR capability, HR objectives, required cost savings and of course, its attitude to outsourcing.

> ## Outsourcing: The Theory (2)
>
> In principle, the decision to outsource is fundamentally economic in nature; studies have generally confirmed that the primary reason for outsourcing is cost reduction **(Cooke et al., 2005):**
>
> In classic economic theory, organisations assess the production cost and the transaction costs and will outsource where they can achieve lower costs externally than through building the internal capacity for a service **(Williamson, 1975).**
>
> The Resource Based View of the firm **(Barney, 1991)** suggests that organisations should focus on their core competencies and outsource peripheral work.
>
> Providers gain economies of scale by providing for many customers and lowering the cost per unit; activities that are high cost, asset specific and easy to measure are likely to be outsourced.
>
> Using this logic, it's argued that only the outsourcing of generic HR activities will be economic but not idiosyncratic or unique HR activities. Service quality is also a major factor in the outsourcing decision **(Beaman, 2004)** together with gaining access to specialist expertise, achieving flexibility, reducing risks and the opportunity to use otherwise expensive technology **(Scott-Jackson et al., 2005).**

Two models define contemporary approaches to HR outsourcing. The first is the MPHRO model (Multiple Process Human Resources Outsourcing), where organisations outsource a cluster of business processes such as payroll, benefits and general HR administration. In contrast, the SPHRO approach (Single Process Human Resources Outsourcing) is perhaps the longest established approach, typically based around Payroll but it could equally be another function such as Recruitment. Current HR outsourcing deals are increasingly focusing on MPHRO structures, including value-adding strategic processes that go beyond basic payroll and data management processes – in 2012, 59% of global outsourcing deals included a recruitment component, while 41% of deals included training and development and 31% included performance management (Everest, 2012). Data suggests that organisations are seeking the same things they have always looked for - cost reduction, improving the quality and effectiveness of the service provided and ensuring compliance - but that new expectations are being set beyond basic administration. For example, organisations are increasingly looking for Business Intelligence as part of outsourcing contracts, as a way of obtaining better metrics and analytics, combined with leading-edge technology tools to support management productivity and strategic outcomes.

Organisations often believe that undertaking an HR outsourcing strategy means they have to transfer **all** aspects of HR delivery to an external provider (that is, they need to enter into a full MPHRO arrangement). However, it's becoming increasingly common for organisations to outsource one or more discrete, defined processes on a phased basis, a strategy that allows them to experiment with each component before going further. There is also evidence to suggest that global organisations are starting their outsourcing strategy in regions with *lower* HR complexity, where risk is lower and easier to manage.

The following are examples of the Outsourcing services that can be delivered by external service providers:

1. HR and Payroll Administration

Payroll was one of the first HR related services to be outsourced and this continues to be a major component of most outsourcing deals. In addition to the traditional areas of payroll and time administration, a full range of workforce administration support services is available (often referred to as HR Administration or Workforce Administration). Using the latest technology, these services can reduce the cost and improve the service quality of transactional processes, for example:

- Producing contracts of employment
- Generating offer letters
- Dealing with a full range of 'life events' such as maternity/paternity processes, change of address and change of dependants
- Dealing with employee termination or retirement
- Managing exit processes
- Maintaining employee data in the HR system
- Continually updating employee files, often using scanning technology to maintain electronic files

2. Recruitment

Recruitment is another process that is commonly outsourced, and its growth has been so significant in recent years that it has become a branch of outsourcing with its own name – RPO (Recruitment Process Outsourcing). Again, it's important to differentiate between traditional service contracts and RPO arrangements: in a service (subcontracting) arrangement, the provider supplies individuals based on a person specification and job specification, but once the candidate is appointed, the agency tends to disengage. However, in a true outsourcing arrangement, the provider manages the process from start to finish, ensuring consistency throughout. Providers will often work directly with the line manager to create the job and person specifications, and in doing so develop a deep understanding of the company's culture, working arrangements and operations so they can act as the first layer of selection. Outsourcing providers often have expertise in a wide range of recruitment techniques such as assessment centres, psychometric tests and personal interviews and in many cases, providers also become responsible for taking up references and the induction, development and ongoing welfare of the new employee during the on-boarding (new joiner) process. This ensures the outsourcing provider has a stake in a successful outcome and is more likely to make a carefully considered decision, as it will have to manage any issues arising from an unsuccessful recruitment decision.

3. Learning and Development

Although the delivery of training via a specialist external company is common, most arrangements are effectively based on service contracts rather than true outsourcing. However, it is also possible to give responsibility for training strategy to an HR outsourcing provider, an arrangement that can provide the customer with certain advantages:

- The outsourcing service provider is involved in a long-term relationship with an organisation over a long period and has an insight into training needs
- The provider is in a unique position to evaluate the effectiveness of the solutions
- The provider remains fully involved with the client across all HR areas once the training solution has been provided and can follow up on specific issues raised by the training or development programme

4. Employee Relations

One of the top three reasons for an organisation deciding to outsource HR processes is to gain access to employment law expertise, ensuring that employment issues are handled professionally. An outsourcing provider will usually work with the customer to put HR policies and practices into place and then to train managers in applying the policies, reducing the risk of line managers becoming a point of failure. Where problems arise, outsourcing service providers will guide employers through employment tribunals (courts), redundancy and redeployment processes, disciplinary and grievance procedures and discrimination legislation. Typically, this service is provided as a telephone help service to line managers or where needed, as a direct face-to-face support service. Retaining an HR outsourcing provider to handle employee relations has distinct advantages over employing a legal firm – whereas an outsource provider aims to **prevent** problems happening rather than deal with legal processes after things go wrong. Outsourcers may also be able to provide indemnity cover, where organisations are effectively insured against any claims by employees.

Outsourcing: The Theory (3)

One underlying reason for any outsourcing is to improve organisational performance **(Lilly et al. 2005)**. The possession of key competencies defines what an organisation will do itself and what it will buy from outside. In theory, organisations that are more strategically focused will tend to gravitate towards outsourcing, given that outsourcing allows the HR function to re-focus on strategic activities that create competitive advantage **(Gilley & Rasheed, 2000). Klaas et al, (2001) and Lepak & Snell (1998)** suggest that as HRM becomes more strategic, there is also a tendency to opt for greater HRM outsourcing. However, some research suggests that this does not necessarily increase organisational performance.

Large organisations tend to outsource more processes **(Klaas et al., 2001)** although much HRM literature implies that smaller organisations have greater need for external expertise; nevertheless, smaller organisations which otherwise would find it difficult to create enough scale to justify an in-house HR function will also tend to use outsourcing services **(Sheehan & Cooper, 2011)** although research linking factors such as size and the decision to outsource are inconclusive. New organisations often bypass traditional approaches and move straight to an outsource service **(Gilley et al., 2004)**. Research suggests that older, more established organisations are more likely to outsource HR.

There is also evidence that organisations that have already started to cut the numbers of HR people are more likely to more towards outsourcing, perhaps because it reflects a long-term intention to cut costs. Certain Industries use outsourcing more than others, in particular those that place a higher level of importance on people management - chemicals, food, energy, metal and electronics have a higher tendency than the public sector and construction **(Delmotte & Sels, 2008)**. A final variable is 'HR Intensity' - organisations using a high number of HR Practices, especially those using scorecards, are more likely to outsource HR.

Offshoring

Once a service contract is in place, it's then up to the service provider to decide how best to deliver the service, including the location it is delivered from, how many staff are assigned to the work, what underlying technology will be used and so on. In theory, the entire service could be delivered as a 'black box', where the customer has no knowledge or understanding of how services are provided. In practice, potential buyers want to know much more detail about the kinds of people who will be working on the contract, their skills and experience, how they will work and where from. Even so, in recent years, there has been a rapid growth in offshoring, where some of the processes (or certain aspects of processes) supplied to a customer are performed in another country, typically one where labour costs are lower. The global offshoring market for all services has been estimated at $281billion dollars – a significant market (Fernandez-Stark, 2012).

Offshoring hot-spots for IT services in recent years have been India and the Philippines, together with Mexico, South America and Eastern European countries. It's a rapidly shifting market – as a result of inflation and strong economic growth, the Indian Information Technology sector has experienced a 10 - 15% wage growth in the early part of the 21st century. Consequently, there is a concern that India's operations are becoming too expensive in comparison with competition from other offshoring destinations, so India may soon need to offshore some of its work to lower cost regions!

Most offshored HR and Payroll related services are 'non-voice', that is, they involve only remote data entry, software development or processing work. In other cases, offshore call centres have been established to provide help desk and basic advisory services. However, offshoring is a highly controversial topic, spurring heated debate among economists and politicians. Some see it as benefiting both the origin and destination country by encouraging free trade, while others see job losses and wage erosion in the customer's home country as a negative outcome. For the buyer of outsourcing, offshoring potentially reduces service delivery costs by between 10% and 50% and allows the transfer of responsibility to the provider.

However, for any provider that uses offshore arrangements, there is often an overhead to managing the quality of services provided and there are many challenges involved in meeting customer needs while keeping costs low. In particular, where voice related services are involved, there may be issues of language – in some cases, customer perception of dealing with offshore call centres has not been good and this poor experience has encouraged many banks and insurance companies to relocate their call centres back onshore. Ironically, the ability to offer same-country based call centres has now become a differentiator in some markets.

Issues to Consider When Outsourcing

The following issues need to be taken into consideration when outsourcing:

- **Take a Strategic View:** Where an organisation has adopted a distinctive approach to certain HR activities that provide them with strategic advantage, some have argued that these activities' should not be outsourced (Klaas et al., 2001) as they are best performed internally. Likewise, some hold the view that outsourcing might limit the development of new strategic competencies (Ulrich, 1997).

- **Technology is Important:** Many organisations find that outsourcing their HR operations brings with it vastly superior technology, provided through the outsourcer who is able to spread infrastructure costs across many customers. This gives end customers access to tools such as manager and employee self-service that route work around the organisation quickly and efficiently. Likewise, case management tools allow individual employee issues to be tracked, escalated and re-directed to ensure they are dealt with effectively, while reporting tools enable better metrics on a range of people management issues.

- **Cultural Issues are Critical:** The outsourcing decision is emotional as well as rational and cultural issues can be a major barrier to outsourcing HR. Some organisations fear that by outsourcing HR to an external provider, line managers will react badly to the new service, especially where 'high-touch' services are important. I have seen several cases where the business case calculations looked extremely good on paper but HR leaders have changed their mind on the basis that they would not be able to manage the complexity of cultural change involved. This broadly translates into 'Our line managers would never accept it'. Others see that the best way to improve the delivery of HR services and make a contribution to the business is to hand it over to experienced external professionals, allowing them to concentrate on adding value through the remaining HR infrastructure. This is a critical decision for organisations.

- **Outsourcing is not a 'Magic Bullet'**: Outsourcing will not, by itself, solve organisational issues or make managers better. If HR processes are poorly defined, are not well understood or are overly complicated, then just transferring them to an outsource provider is unlikely to provide any benefit. Randal Tajer of UBS private banking expressed this as "Don't outsource what you don't understand", highlighting the need to be clear about what the organisation wants to achieve and ensure it understands the solution it is asking a supplier to provide. External suppliers need time to build up knowledge of the customer and understand their operations (Lawler & Mohrman, 2003).

- **People Management is Critical**: Outsourcing does not mean the organisation can forget about good people management. The most important people management relationship – the one between a line manager and their staff – must always remain an organisational responsibility. Even though the outsource provider designs and implements new policies and processes, the organisation must still make sure managers carry out their roles properly.

- **HR Leadership Retains Accountability**: The delivery of HR practices must ultimately be owned by the customer organisation. Although the outsource provider offers expertise in HR areas and operates the service, ultimately it is the customer organisation that carries the consequences of failure and is accountable for what happens (for example, in relation to external statutory bodies). The management of vendors is one of the hidden costs of outsourcing and customers must factor in time and resource to oversee contracts.

- **Business Partners:** This key organisational role must be developed to complement and support the service delivery structure. Even after outsourcing, there is usually a retained HR group of Business Partners or other specialists. Line managers will continue to use local HR professionals as the first line of support for queries and emergencies and processes will be needed for this, often developed with the outsourcing partner. At the same time, managers will need to be trained and proficient in the new processes (for more on this topic, see Chapter 7).

- **HR Career Paths:** One key issue identified in recent years concerns what happens to traditional HR career paths when it's no longer possible to gain an 'apprenticeship' in HR through an administrative route. Outsourcing may even have a detrimental effect on the HR function, as work eventually becomes de-skilled (Grugulis, Vincent, & Hebson, 2003).

Taking the decision to outsource the HR or Payroll function can be a major step for organisations. Figure 4 sets out some of the key actions that organisations need to take when exploring a potential outsourcing strategy.

Outsourcing the HR function – Key Actions

1) Get senior management support. Key stakeholders need to be involved in the decisions.

2) Understand where outsourcing fits into the long-term strategy of the business.

3) Define clearly which competencies need to be retained in-house and which can be outsourced.

4) Understand the current costs of delivering the HR service and build a business case for moving to a new HR service delivery model.

5) Review the alternatives to outsourcing – would a shared services model provide the same benefits?

6) Invest in the initial set-up and treat outsourcing as a long-term investment

7) Be honest with yourself, your service provider and your staff.

8) Define the key performance measures for assessing the provider and the service provided.

9) Communicate the changes to all staff.

10) Get the contracts right and ensure they address any concerns

FIGURE 4: OUTSOURCING HR – KEY ACTIONS

Making the Service Delivery Decision

Whether an organisation introduces Shared Services, moves to an outsourcing model or takes a hybrid approach to HR service delivery, several factors need to be taken into account:

STEP 1: Define and Understand the Problem

Any service delivery decision must be based on adding value to the business. A critical question to be asked is *"How will the service delivery decision help the organisation manage its business more effectively?"* Typically, companies find themselves asking the following questions:

- How to ensure compliance with employment legislation?
- Why are there so many complaints about HR and Payroll services?
- Why do we often face legal action over employment issues?
- Why are HR service delivery costs so high?
- How do we get access to leading edge technology?
- Why are we paying expensive HR professionals to do administrative work?

Organisations usually identify a gap in their ability to meet these needs, signalling a need to review their approach to service delivery.

STEP 2: Create the Business Case

It's important to understand the alternatives available and develop a well-thought out business case for each option. Unless there is a clear rationale and management support for the planned changes, changes to HR service delivery services will not be successful. Among the key questions that organisations need to ask are:

- Will the new solution (outsourcing, shared services etc.) achieve a similar level of quality (or better) for a more attractive price?
- Is there a clear financial benefit to outsourcing?
- What costs will be involved to make the changes happen?
- What other benefits will be gained? For example, will it lead to improved use of management time, improved efficiency or better management information?
- How will the success of the new solution be measured?

STEP 3: Review and improve HR processes

Simply pulling processes together into a single, central location is unlikely to lead to a more streamlined, customer-driven service. Moving either to an HR Shared Services Operation or outsourcing arrangement requires a fundamental re-engineering of HR processes to standardise processes and ensure that what is provided is as simple as possible. Chapter 11 addresses the topic of business process design in greater detail.

STEP 4: Clarify Scope and responsibilities

It's critical that that the range of services to be provided to customer (sometimes called the Service Catalogue or Statement of Services) is clear. Many outsourcing arrangements fail because assumptions are made on both sides about what will be offered and specifically, what services will **not** be provided and too many outsourcing or shared services arrangements encounter problems because incorrect assumptions are made by one or both sides. Customers will need a clear understanding of what processes are in scope, when each will be performed and how. It's also important to clarify and communicate the role and responsibilities of end customers (for example, line managers and employees). If the new model requires users to act differently (for example through the introduction of on-line self-service) they must be informed of the new processes and given appropriate support.

STEP 5: Contractual Issues

Outsourcing deals tend to be long-term (often five years and potentially longer) and are based on expectations about headcount, processes, scope, planned growth and business plans. Should any of these factors change during the life of the contract, either the provider or the customer may find outsourcing is no longer an attractive proposition. Outsourcing deals should therefore take account of a wide range of possible future scenarios. To a lesser extent, the same is true in a shared services arrangement where a nominal internal contract exists and in some cases there might be penalties for poor performance but in general these are less onerous than for an external provider.

Outsourcing contracts can be quite complex and it should go without saying that the involvement of legal experts is critical during outsourcing negotiation. Typically, there are two elements to a contract - a **transfer agreement** which governs how staff, assets and contracts will move to the service provider, together with a **service agreement** which sets out what services will be provided and the levels of service, standard of performance and costs to be provided. Some key aspects of contracts are:

- **Poor Performance Sanctions:** Poor performance is often penalised with service credits or even liquidated damages as compensation, for example, if key performance targets are missed. These often involve complex legal rules which may be difficult to understand, interpret and apply.

- **Governance:** The relationship between the customer and supplier is critical in outsourcing deals, and the terms of the relationship are often set out in the governance structure. Poor governance has been a major factor in many outsourcing contract failures, often leading both parties to a point where it is impossible to recover. It's important, for example, that there is a process for escalating and resolving customer problems. Regular reviews should take place as part of the supplier contract between operational service managers and strategic sponsors to ensure that the service provided is meeting expectations, both from the perspective of the organisation and the service provider.

- **Exit Management**: An outsourcing arrangement typically has a limited lifespan. Exit provisions that enable the customer to bring the service back in-house or to change the mix of outsourcing providers is important.

STEP 6: Define and Measure the Outcomes

Service Level Agreements (SLAs) should be put in place to demonstrate that processes are delivered to a specific quality standard. SLAs are not only used to track performance, but may also be the basis for increases in cost and to allow benchmarking against alternatives. Under an outsourcing arrangement, perhaps for the first time, HR delivery will be accountable and measured against a defined standard. It's essential that performance measures are agreed to ensure that services are being delivered to plan - service level agreements and Key Performance Indicators, together with a detailed Statement of Services, provide a framework for measuring the effectiveness of the service delivery, as well as ensuring continuous improvement.

STEP 7: Develop a Service Delivery Ethos

In a Service Centre operation, the focus should be on the employee/manager as a customer – it should be demand-led, not supply-led. Staff training is clearly important to this, together with a mind-set that supports the idea. Non-standard processes or ad-hoc requests drive up costs and culturally it will be a challenge to refuse to process certain types of work. New charging mechanisms may have to be put in place to deliver specific work and it's possible to apply premium pricing to certain activities.

Summary: HR Service Delivery

Getting HR service delivery right remains a challenge for many organisations; however, unless basic service delivery is effective and efficient, HR functions will not earn the right to make a more strategic contribution to the business. Many options are available, including multi and single process outsourcing, in-house shared services, Centres of Expertise and various hybrid combinations; a key priority for organisations becoming HR Ready is to understand these options, create a business case and make a meaningful change to the way services operate.

Service Delivery: Are You HR Ready?

- [?] How often do you review the HR service delivery model and the viability of shared services, outsourcing and other delivery methods?

- [?] What services do your customers (managers, employees etc.) want HR to deliver?

- [?] What are customers prepared to pay for HR services – do they expect to pay the lowest rate possible in return for a simple service or would they pay a premium price for a value-adding service?

- [?] What is the business case for improving service delivery?

- [?] What do customers say about the quality of service?

- [?] What opportunities are there to introduce greater levels of technology to improve service delivery?

- [?] Is service delivery a barrier to HR development?

2 HR Practices

Defining HR Practices

HR Practices have a major impact on the creation of competitive advantage. In this chapter, we'll explore the growing evidence suggesting that when organisations design effective practices and execute them in a way that is unique or difficult for others to replicate, they will tend to gain an advantage over their competitors.

HR practices are typically non-transactional activities that have the potential to create enormous value for an organisation. They define how new people are brought into the organisation, how they are rewarded, their personal and career development, how their performance is managed and how the organisation builds pools of talent for the future. HR practices are closely linked to HR strategy and organisational culture and they have high visibility within and outside the organisation - they not only shape the way that HR and the organisation are perceived, but they also influence how employees and managers relate to each other. Because they can make a real difference to people management, HR practices are sometimes thought of as 'proper' HR – the meaty, value-adding activities that professionals aspire to spend more time doing and why they went into HR in the first place. This contribution to competitive advantage, earns HR Practices a place as the second pillar of HR Ready.

Historically (mostly in the 1990's) HR Practices were generally known as High Performance Work Practices (see Huselid, 1995) because of their influence on and relationship with improving business performance. However, in recent years, the term 'High Performance Work Practices' has tended to be used in the context of employee engagement practices rather than in the more general sense it's being used here (Stone, 2011).

To understand the nature of HR practices, we need to set them in the context of the full range of activities performed by HR to support the organisation they serve, ranging from basic administration to complex strategic processes. These can be categorised as four types of activity, as defined by Ulrich & Brockbank (2005):

- **Flow of People:** Regulating how people move in, through, up and out of the organisation.

- **Flow of Work:** Defining and regulating who does what work, the scope of their work, how work is done and where it's done.

- **Flow of Performance and Rewards:** The standards and processes that link people to work, how people are measured and what rewards are associated with work, including pay and conditions.

- **Flow of Information:** Ensuring people know what is happening and why, including communications and business intelligence.

These activities are generally managed through a series of business processes that are known by more familiar names such as recruitment, reward, employee relations, learning and development, performance management, talent management and employee engagement. Together these practices provide the organisation with capabilities that go beyond administrative compliance.

Within each of these categories, organisations must make critical strategic choices about how best to deliver each practice; for example, within the 'Flow of People' category, organisations can buy, build or borrow resources, but may also need to 'bounce' them out of the organisation. Practices must also provide support to 'bind' organisational talent as well as 'boost' opportunities for people to improve their career opportunities.

Because of the central importance of performance and talent management to competitive advantage, these practices have been given their own pillars in HR Ready and are dealt with in separate chapters. The following sections deal with each of the main HR practices in turn.

HR Practices: The Theory (1)

HR practices have been the subject of much academic research in recent years and studies have attempted to identify causal relationships between HR practices and business results, based on the premise that performing certain practices well (and better than the competition) will result in improved shareholder return, higher profits, and higher levels of productivity. Some academics believe that HR Practices will become a source of competitive advantage when an organisation implements policies more effectively than its competitors **(Barney, 2001; Becker & Huselid, 2006)**.

Mark Huselid (1995) in one of the most significant studies in this field, assessed the simultaneous use of multiple HR practices and identified a strong correlation with turnover, productivity and financial performance. Similar research **(Pfeffer, 1994; Patterson et al., 1997)** examined the impact of specific people practices on bottom-line financial measures and enhanced firm performance.

Employee satisfaction is also thought to lead to a bottom-line increase in customer satisfaction **(Rucci et al., 1998)** with a positive linkage between people management and business performance **(Wright et al., 2005)**.

Despite much early academic interest into areas such as training and information sharing, research is inconclusive in terms of defining whether specific practices create more value than others, or whether certain practices interact and have a complementary effect. Research into HR practices has divided into two schools of thought; the first suggests that a single, universal configuration of HR practices leads to higher performance, while an alternate, opposing view is based on a 'best fit' approach, proposing that HR Practices are contingent on internal and external variables and must be uniquely structured for every organisation. Many now question whether the study of HR practices actually represents a useful way forward for HR **(Purcell, 1999; Gerhart, Wright, & McMahon, 2000)**.

HR Practices: The Theory (2)

Lepak & Snell (1998) suggested that HR practices could be categorised as core, traditional, peripheral, or idiosyncratic. *Core* practices are those that are not widely available in industry and whose use is instrumental for achieving strategic benefits. Similar to core practices, *traditional* HR practices are important for a firm's success. However, these traditional practices do not help differentiate the firm from the competition. *Peripheral* HR practices are those that are fairly generic and contribute little, if anything, to firm competitiveness. Finally, *idiosyncratic* HR practices are those that are unique to the firm but do not directly add value.

Examples of a link between good people management and business outcomes are:

Bartel (1994) established a link between the adoption of training programmes and productivity growth.

Becker et al. (1997) Training programmes were shown to be positively related to organisational performance.

Yeung & Ulrich (1990) found that alignment between HR and business strategy had an impact on organisational performance. Performance evaluation and its linkage to compensation schemes were identified as contributors to increased business profitability **(Borman, 1991).**

Investments in HR activities such as incentive compensation, staffing techniques and employee participation resulted in lower turnover, greater productivity and increased organisational performance **(Huselid, 1995).**

Arthur (1994); MacDuffie (1995); Delaney & Huselid (1996) found that HR practices that focus on enhancing employee commitment (e.g. decentralised decision-making, comprehensive training, salaried compensation, employee participation) were related to higher performance.

Purcell et al (2003) concluded that there is a clear link between business performance and the quality of people management. Meaningful improvements in HR management were shown to produce a 10-15% in business performance.

a. Recruitment

Poor recruitment processes create the conditions for poor performance. The price of a bad hiring decision can be high - for example, the replacement cost of a poor sales hire can be around $30,000 (Aberdeen Group, 2012). For this reason, some academics (for example, Taylor & Collins, 2000; Ulrich & Brockbank, 2005b) believe that recruitment is the most important part of HR work, as it determines who ultimately works in the organisation, as well as shaping candidate and employee perceptions about how effective other HR practices are performed by the organisation. It's much better to hire someone who is a close fit against the organisation's requirements than to solve the problem later through performance management and expensive training. There's a great story about Sam Walton, founder of the giant Wal-Mart retail chain, who was asked why his employees were always so helpful, positive and resourceful and whether he had any special training techniques. He replied "*I don't make 'em that way, I hire 'em that way*".

Recruitment: The Theory

Recruitment "*Includes those practices and activities carried out by the organisation with the primary purpose of identifying and attracting potential employees*" **(Breaugh & Starke, 2000 in Parry & Wilson, 2009),** with the main objective being to draw human capital into the organisation. Good recruitment involves having clear recruitment processes, starting with effective job design and job evaluation, linked to a clear person specification, well defined job and person spec and a clear selection criteria. There must also be a linkage to reward and benefits that ensure the role attracts the right applicants in a competitive market. There has been a trend in recent years to develop 'Accountability Profiles' rather than job descriptions that focus on what gets done rather than what people do **(Taylor, 2008).**

Effective recruitment now involves a large subset of HR practices, requiring skills in advertising, testing, screening and interviewing, as well as maintaining relationships with applicants throughout the recruitment cycle. The skillset of recruiters has changed considerably in recent years - recruitment increasingly involves using social technologies such as Facebook, Twitter and LinkedIn to advertise jobs and any recruiter without knowledge of these technologies will be at a profound disadvantage. Other skills involve building relationships with applicants and prospective applicants, building the external employer brand and maintaining communications throughout the process. Some innovative organisations are successfully building recruitment campaigns on technology platforms such as SecondLife and creating communities of interest to develop future talent pools.

In many countries, applicant referencing has become a complex activity, as increased legislation and regulation has forced organisations to think carefully about how jobs are advertised, what can be discussed in interviews and how to avoid the potential for discrimination on grounds such as gender, race, religion, sexual orientation and disability. Recent years have seen increasing emphasis on the 'people checking' aspects of the recruitment process, to ensure that recruits not only have the legal right to work, but that they have no criminal record and in some cases have not belonged to certain affiliation groups.

There is now an entire industry devoted to checking that people have the qualifications they claim, have worked where they say they have worked and possess the skills needed to do the job. A recent UK newspaper article (Daily Telegraph, 2013) claimed that one in five people have lied on their CV/Resume and that an increasing number of graduates are attempting to fake the level of their degree. One negative aspect of social technology is that it has given applicants many new opportunities to lie about themselves, with the risk that they be discovered and exclude themselves out of good jobs during the people checking process. According to research by CareerBuilder (2012), 65% of recruiters have used social technology to check whether the candidate presented himself/herself professionally; over half use it to test whether the candidate is a good fit for the company culture. However, having looked at candidate's online posts, they found that:

- 49% posted provocative and inappropriate photographs and/or information
- 45% posted information which talked about them drinking and/or using drugs
- 35% 'bad mouthed' their previous employers
- 26% made comments on their profiles that were discriminatory
- 22% lied about their qualifications

Other surveys have found that up to 35% of companies that had checked up on applicant's social media sites had changed their opinion on an applicant as a result of what they found (Grasz, 2009, cited in Brown & Vaughn, 2011). Nevertheless, recruiters find that using social media gave them a good feel for a candidate's personality and offered a useful additional channel for checking that the information given was supported by professional qualifications. The use of social technology for recruitment decisions clearly raises many ethical questions about the boundaries between private and organisational life and what is regarded as acceptable intrusion into applicant's personal lives. The HR profession is divided about where the boundaries lie and there is no doubt that these topics will feature in debates for many years. In any case, the effective use of these tools for recruitment is now an essential HR practice, even though many ethical and legal issues are yet to be addressed (as with other aspects of the internet). HR Ready functions will need to ensure they put good practices in place to protect themselves in these areas.

> **Recruitment Case Study: London Olympics**
>
> The organising committee for the 2012 London Olympics (LOCOG) needed to hire a large volunteer army of 'games makers' to support the games. The unpaid volunteers would eventually become one of the key factors in the success of the Olympics. An early challenge was how to secure the help of up to 250,000 people, who would be working for no pay or expenses.
>
> A 'values driven' web-based selection tool was developed to screen applicants. Around 3,000 selection event volunteers were identified and trained, with the job of screening and interviewing all applicants. Many of the selectors had no prior interviewing experience (although many were professional recruiters. Recruitment practices were defined to ensure that selection was made on the basis of well-defined competencies, with a clear journey as to where they were in the process. In total, 70,000 volunteers were appointed; the overall cost was around £9k per volunteer **(Maclachlan, 2012)**.

b.   **Reward**

Reward (or Compensation & Benefits / Remuneration & Benefits as it's sometimes known) is a highly specialised field. Like other HR practices, it involves a mixture of economics and psychology to determine what will motivate and engage staff to join, stay with and ultimately perform at their best for their employer. It's essential that reward strategy is linked to the values and strategy of the organisation, rewarding those aspects of individual performance and behaviour that the company wants to encourage. It's been said that organisations get the behaviour they tolerate and the behaviour they reward (the same is true when parenting children!) so, if innovation is important to the business, this should be the focus of the reward strategy. If Sales staff are rewarded for bringing about a quick sale that is potentially loss-making for the company, then it is probably the reward strategy that is at fault, not the Sales people.

Reward is one of the central tools that organisations have available to encourage employees to release their 'discretionary performance', that is, the effort they choose to withhold but can still be considered competent at their job. A basic assumption of Strategic Human Resource Management (SHRM) is that each person brings a blend of job-relevant competencies and capabilities to the organisation, as well as a desire to invest their skills and expertise in the work of the organisation. Although some employees will choose to make only the most basic contribution, it's assumed that most people go to work to do a good job and play their part in achieving business objectives.

Good reward practices include the development of effective pay structures, bonus plans, incentives and benefits, closely linked to job design, job evaluation and performance management, each of which is a highly specialised area, beyond the scope of this book. However, as well as financial benefits, reward can also take the form of recognition, career opportunities and improved quality of work life. A number of techniques are available to organisations to support their reward strategy:

- **Recognition:** This is a powerful reward, based on providing feedback and public recognition to raise self-esteem. It need not involve an 'employee of the month' scheme, but could simply be immediate constructive feedback from a manager to increase employee confidence, motivation and status.

- **Career Development / Career Opportunities:** Offering employees ways to improve their skills and enhance their career can be as powerful as a pay rise, especially for those that are not generally motivated by pay. Clear career paths and opportunities to move to new roles are an important aspect of this.

- **Work-Life Balance:** Many employees value a good work-life balance, especially at different stages of their life, where the opportunity to take time for family duties and flexible working is becoming important.

- **Total Reward:** Employees receive a range of rewards for their employment, not just basic pay. This can include pensions contributions, allowances, and other benefits. Making clear the full range of benefits available can be a powerful retention and recruitment tool. Employers are increasingly using total reward statements to demonstrate the value of non-salary items in their employment packages.

- **Flexible Benefits:** Many employers are moving towards a flexible benefits scheme, allowing employees to choose what combination of benefits they take, although there are typically minimum levels of take up required (for example, employees can sometimes buy or sell holiday/vacation time but only up to a certain level to ensure legal compliance with minimum holiday requirements.

- **Other Forms of Reward:** Certain forms of employee benefits are also considered to be reward, such as subsidised membership of a pension plan, paid holidays, child care vouchers, life assurance schemes and enhanced family benefits such as maternity, paternity and parental leave.

Case Study: Apple

Apple's reward package is very basic when compared to those of Google, Facebook, and Microsoft. Compensation is largely tied to the company's valuation rather than through base salary, so most employees at Apple get periodic stock grants and cash bonuses of up to 30% of their base salary, sending a clear message that individual accomplishments are important only if they directly contribute to the overall success of the company. This approach, coupled with the firm's famous "product focus" keeps everyone targeted on product success rather than individual results and individual rewards **(Sullivan 2011).**

Reward: The Theory (1)

A reward strategy is *"The alignment of the reward policies and practices with the business and human resource strategies of the organisation, its culture and its environment, providing a set of goals and declaration of intent as to what the organisation wants to reward, and how critical reward issues will be addressed"* **(CIPD, 2005)**

Much reward theory is linked to the psychology of motivation, or *"The degree to which an individual wants and chooses to engage in certain specified behaviours"*. Employees have a certain amount of discretion over how they perform and employers tend to want to release higher levels of performance from employees. Contrary to early views on motivation (such as those promoted by **FW Taylor** in his 1911 *Principles of Scientific Management*, which suggested that workers were entirely motivated by money, later research such as the Hawthorne experiments and **Abraham Maslow's** 1943 hierarchy of needs suggested that this was overly simplistic and other factors are involved in motivation.

Frederick Herzberg's 1959 research into motivation changed the way organisations looked at job enrichment and led to the two factor theory – that there are motivating factors at work such as achievement, recognition and responsibility as well as 'hygiene' factors which must simply be met at a basic level (for example, minimum salary levels and safe and pleasant working conditions.

Modern academics such as **Scase (2007)**, argue that simply being paid for attending work is not enough of a motivator to release discretionary performance - employees seek an employment relationship where they regard themselves as a stakeholder in the long-term success of the organisation.

As a result, pay for performance will only work if employees can see that the reward is an adequate incentive and where they feel they are capable of achieving the goal set. If neither of these conditions is true, pay for performance programmes may actually decrease workforce productivity by alienating or de-motivating employees **(Schaubroeck et al., 2008)**. This simply underlines the point that reward as an HR practice is complex and needs professional expertise.

c. **Employment Relations / Employee Engagement**

Historically, workplace relations have fallen under the category of 'industrial relations' or 'employee relations'. This category of HR practice was traditionally focused on regulating relationships with trade unions, with little emphasis on non-trade union staff. However, in recent years, trade unions have endured a period of decline in many countries, through a combination of state deregulation and a shift away from collective bargaining to individual contracts. In part, this has been driven by a rise in social legislation in Europe which offers new levels of protection for workers which (some have argued) has removed the need for a strong trade union to protect the interests of workers. Employment relations are based on three main frames of reference:

- **Unitarist:** The organisation is perceived as an integrated and harmonious whole, where management and the workforce all share a common purpose. In this perspective, trade unions are deemed unnecessary, since the loyalty between employees and organisations is considered mutually exclusive - there cannot be two sides of industry.

- **Pluralist:** The organisation is made up of powerful and divergent sub-groups, each with its own legitimate loyalties and with their own set of objectives. The role of management is less about enforcing and controlling and more concerned with persuasion and co-ordination. Trade unions are deemed to be legitimate representatives of employees and conflict is resolved by collective bargaining, although individual relationships with employees are equally important.

- **Radical:** This focuses on class conflict and challenges to the capitalist order. There is a fundamental division of interest between capital and labour; workplace relations take place against this background. Inequalities of power and economic wealth are seen as having their roots in the nature of the capitalist economic system.

It's been argued that employment relationships are becoming increasingly pluralist in nature; as a result, workplace relations have evolved from an organisational focus on industrial relations to the relatively new concept of employee engagement, first described in the early 1990s. Although similar ideas (for example, the concepts of employee motivation, job satisfaction and employee commitment) have been around for much longer, the advent of the knowledge worker and increasing emphasis on individual talent management needed a term to describe an individual's emotional attachment to the organisation, their co-workers and the job itself.

> ### Employee Engagement: The Theory
>
> Employee engagement has been defined as *"The harnessing of organization members' selves to their work roles; in engagement, people employ and express themselves physically, cognitively, and emotionally during role performances"* **(Kahn, 1990, p.694).**
>
> Research has demonstrated the relationship of employee engagement and positive work outcomes, such as low attrition, high performance and positive business results **Hallberg & Schaufeli, 2006; Saks, 2006.** Findings from **BlessingWhite, 2005** showed a clear correlation between engagement and employee retention, with 85% of engaged employees indicating that they planned to stay with their current employer. The positive outcomes of employee engagement include better financial performance and profitability **(Gibbons, 2008; Schaufeli & Bakker, 2004).**
>
> Research by the UK **CIPD (2011)** suggests that the extent to which an employee is engaged with their work is based on many factors, including job security, compensation/reward structures, line managers, colleagues, culture and relationships with customers outside the organisation. However, engagement not only changes over time, but also varies in its intensity and depth. Perhaps not surprisingly, the form of engagement most strongly correlated with performance was found to be the job itself or 'task engagement'. Quite simply, people engage most strongly with the actual content of the work they do, with factors such as manager and colleague relationships being lower level indicators. This has important implications both for how jobs are designed and how people are matched to the right jobs to ensure they are sufficiently interesting, motivating and challenging.

d. Learning & Development

Every organisation possesses a unique blend of skills and knowledge; one important role for management is to ensure that these are collectively harnessed and used to give the organisation competitive advantage over its rivals, whether it is based on a differentiation, innovation or low cost strategy (see Chapter 6). The term 'Learning & Development' has replaced what was once simply known as 'Training', recognising the shift in emphasis from training events to broader development programmes. As a consequence, Learning & Development is now a critical HR practice for HR Ready organisations. Learning & development encompasses several different ideas, for example:

- **Learning:** Changes which occur in an individual's skills, knowledge or attitude. This can be achieved through placements, secondments, job rotation, coaching, e-learning, or a range of informal learning opportunities.
- **Development:** Longer-term changes which take place as a result of training and learning.
- **Training:** Usually instructor led aimed at developing a particular skill or specific knowledge.
- **Education:** Formal approaches to learning sponsored by the employer over a long period of time, usually resulting in an externally recognised qualification.

The speed and manner in which people learn is often a key indicator of the effectiveness of the organisation and its potential to innovate and grow (Garavan, 1997). In recent years, the idea of becoming a 'Learning Organisation' (Senge, 1992) has been embedded in many HR strategies, with the ambitious aim of creating communities where continuous individual development and improvement are part of the culture. However, academics are divided as to whether a Learning Organisation can be 'designed in' to the fabric of an organisation (and if so, how?) or whether it is a metaphor to describe an aspect of organisational culture (and if so, what does this mean?). Of course, organisations do not learn (people do), so either way, the learning process must be translated into an HR practice of some form.

One critical organisational competence is the ability to identify individual needs and decide which combination of the above approaches is the most appropriate to achieve the required results. Training needs may change as the organisation's culture, products or services change and one important aspect of an organisational approach to talent management is to ensure that training is closely aligned to business plans, succession plans, career development, skills requirements, productivity changes and other inputs.

An important aspect of this HR Practice is the need to stay up to date with new ways of delivering Learning & Development. The traditional concept of employees attending classroom training courses or watching an e-Learning video is being challenged. In a 'Wiki' world, knowledge is increasingly stored in the cloud and learning often comes from colleagues rather than formal training (see the British Telecom Breakout Box). Learning techniques based on technology such as gaming style platforms, simulation learning, augmented reality and knowledge sharing portals are a long way from traditional classroom style learning and eLearning.

> **Case Study: British Telecom**
> BT set up Dare2Share, a YouTube style portal enabling staff to post podcasts, blogs, videos and advice, after a survey showed that 78% of employees said they learned most from each other. Within one year, it saved 10% of the formal training budget and one in ten staff now contributes content.
> Source: **(Personnel Management, April 2013).**

It's also highly important to evaluate the outcomes of Learning & Development, in particular to assess its return on investment. This is one of the most complex areas of HR, since many of the outcomes of Learning & Development are not immediate. The outcomes of long-term development programmes such as management development can be very difficult to measure because initiatives may not pay back for ten years (if at all), by which time it is very difficult to attribute success to any single activity.

When properly implemented as an HR practice, an organisation should be able to defend spending on Learning & Development programmes; it may even choose to spend **more** in a difficult economy as an investment in the future. Ideally, it should be possible to relate learning outcomes to bottom line performance outcomes and quantify the benefit. However, activity is often **reduced** when times are challenging, perhaps reflecting the lack of good data to demonstrate added value. Some organisations dislike spending money on training in case it encourages employees to develop skills at their expense, then use the knowledge to further their careers elsewhere. However, there is an old saying *"It's better to train them and have them leave, than not train them and have them stay"*.

e.   **Social Technology**

In the 2009 book, *'The Big Book of HR'*, social technology (often referred to as social media) was included in the 'Future of HR' section. Although social technology is not fully mainstream yet, in just a few short years, its expansion has been so great that it now deserves a place as a central HR practice. It's linked to the massive growth in connected devices such as smartphone and tablet PCs, as well as the rapid expansion of social media sites. Most people immediately think of Wikipedia, Facebook, Twitter, My Space, LinkedIn and You Tube as social technologies, but it's by no means limited to these applications. Social technology includes a vast range of applications, including social-networking sites, knowledge sharing forums, video sharing, wikis, blogs, podcasts, RSS feeds and information aggregation (mash-ups).

Many organisations have already found creative ways to use social technology and others are already considering extending it beyond sharing content and communications into more interactive applications. Analysts Gartner found that 11% of companies now use social networks, predicting that by 2015, more than 40% will have a corporate Facebook presence (Gartner, 2011). A recent study by Silkroad (2012) found that almost 70% of organisations are using or planning to use internal social networking technology, although the hype is so great that three-quarters believed themselves to be lagging behind what they *thought* other organisations were doing.

As well as the recruitment and Learning & Development applications previously mentioned, organisations should consider the opportunity for collaborative online learning, threaded discussions, knowledge management and employee opinion tools (online surveys, etc.). Potentially, social technology offers the potential for everyone to contribute to the generation and evaluation of ideas. Because social technology does not follow traditional hierarchies and works by gathering input from across the organisation rather than through formal channels, it encourages different ways of working and may produce better ideas which are not filtered out through the reporting structure.

Collaboration also includes the idea of 'crowd sourcing', based on soliciting ideas or content from an online community, where each person or group contributes a small portion of a solution to create a significant result. In case we get too carried away by this vision of an inter-connected future where everyone participates and ideas are rapidly spread, many organisations are resistant to even its most basic use. For some, it's a great opportunity (see Breakout Boxes); others have 'demonised' social media, banning employees from using it at work and in some cases, preventing employees from loading career details into sites such as LinkedIn for fear that staff will be poached by competitors.

Likewise, some organisations are concerned that employees might use social technologies in a way that might have a negative impact on their customer and employer brands. There have even been high-profile employee dismissals in recent times as a result of opinions expressed on social networking sites by unhappy employees, that clearly distort the boundaries between personal and work life.[1]

---

[1] "Dixons staff insult customers on Facebook", Personnel Today, September 8, 2009

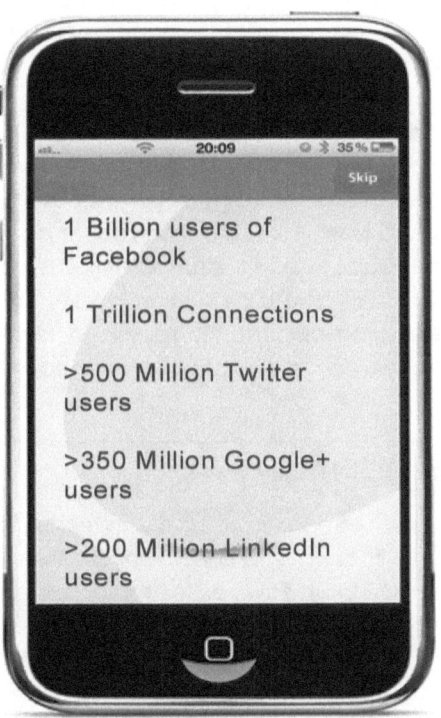

FIGURE 5: SCALE OF SOCIAL TECHNOLOGY USE

Perhaps the biggest fear of social media is the concern that if left unchecked, employees may use technology to challenge the traditional authority of management. The response of HR has often been conservative, more concerned with limiting access to social networking sites (which just looks like people having fun), whereas perhaps the question should be "*How do we exploit their intuitive appeal and creatively make good use of these new tools?*" A typical response is to block access to these sites, yet the line between business and personal technology is being blurred and arguably, it's irrational to restrict their use, especially when employees have equal access to the tools at home as well as at work. In some cases, employees are finding and using non-corporate systems to share knowledge with co-workers because their employers have failed to provide suitable organisational tools that meet their needs.

What's clear is that the use of social technology (together with more traditional forms of eHRM technology as set out in Chapter 8) is an important HR practice, potentially as valuable to the organisation as a good reward strategy and its presence or absence says much about a company's values. However, using social technology demands more than simply switching it on – as with all forms of technology, it's about how it's used, implemented and how value is perceived. It needs a champion and some early successes to demonstrate its value as well as providing a convincing Return on Investment to business leaders. There is an emerging opportunity for HR to take a lead role in using social technology and exploit its 'connective' nature.

> **Case Study: TGI Friday's**
>
> TGI Friday's had suffered from under-investment in the 1990s and wanted to find ways to allow employees to express their personalities, which it saw as a major differentiator in a crowded restaurant market. An analysis revealed that the average age of team leaders was 22. TGI Friday's developed a teamwork tool based on social networking, using a dedicated blog site called 'Fridoids' where staff could start sharing experiences, charity work, parties etc. The site currently gets more than 30,000 hits per month and has been developed as a full employer proposition, linking to external recruitment sites to draw in new recruits, who now self-refer.

HR Practices – Why More is More

HR practices do not stand in isolation from each other and there is a danger that organisations may simply focus on improving each practice in turn. However, one of the key aspects of HR practices is that the separate components must be tightly integrated so that they mutually support each other and are sufficiently internally consistent to form a 'system'.[2] Successful

---

[2] 'System' as used in this context does not refer to HR technology, but to an integrated set of HR practices operating in a systemic way

organisations are those that match organisational needs to individual needs; there is no point in recruiting highly talented, qualified, ambitious staff and having them perform dull, dead-end jobs, or in designing jobs that empower supervisors without ensuring the individuals are capable of taking on the roles.

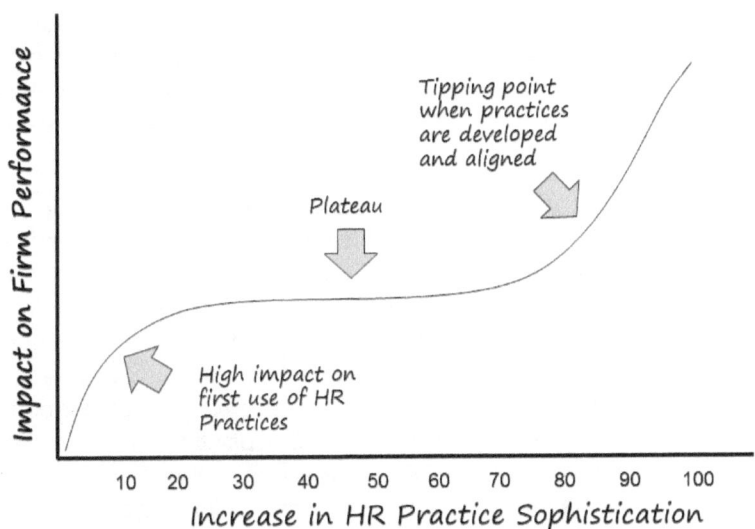

FIGURE 6: IMPACT OF HR PRACTICE SOPHISTICATION

Unfortunately, research confirms that the way HR practices are implemented in organisations is often fragmented, incomplete and based on faulty assumptions (Schein, 1987). It's also important to improve HR Practices sufficiently so that they make a meaningful difference. In one study, HR practices were correlated with financial data across more than 2,400 firms; where there were previously no prior HR practices in place, the organisation responded well to introducing a small number of HR Practices, with a significant effect on business performance. However, where there was some previous experience of HR practices, adding a small number of additional HR practices or focusing on getting one or two working well had only minimal impact on firm performance. There then follows a long plateau period where additional development of practices has only a small impact on outcomes, where it can feel like a waste of time.

There is then a 'tipping point' when enough practices are developed that there is again an impact on business performance (Becker & Huselid, 1999). Figure 6 illustrates the way that firm performance responds to the introduction of increasingly sophisticated HR Practices.

This reinforces the message that simply 'tinkering' with HR practices is unlikely to have much impact (unless there are no current HR practices in place) - the greater the number of variables, the greater the multiplicative effect in achieving success. Failure to implement enough strong HR Practices may lead the organisation to think that all practices are flawed, whereas in reality what is needed is a critical mass of practices.

To be effective, HR Practices need to be aligned to the organisation's strategy, so that each HR practice supports the development of the key capabilities that the organisation needs. For example, if new skills are required, the recruitment, learning & development, talent and performance practices should reflect how skills will be acquired and developed. HR practices need to work together - one of the main reasons for HR transformation failure is when the individual elements appear to work well but they are not fully integrated. Making only small improvements against one HR practice may not create sufficient benefit.

Organisational practices change all the time and HR Ready organisations make sure they are aware of the latest developments in methods, techniques and technology; they find out what their competitors are doing and ask whether they could learn from them, adopting them to their own business requirements.

Summary: Transforming HR Practices

The evidence presented in this chapter suggests that HR Practices can make a powerful contribution to competitive advantage; however, many organisations fail to do enough to develop and improve their HR practices, both in terms of the level of improvement of each practice and the number of practices receiving attention.

HR Practices: Are You HR Ready?

- [?] Are your HR practices delivering value?

- [?] Which HR practices give you a competitive advantage?

- [?] Are your HR practices aligned to HR and business structure?

- [?] Which HR practices need improvement and development?

- [?] Is there a business case for improving some or all of your HR Practices?

- [?] Is there an opportunity to use technology to improve HR Practices? For example, applications include flexible benefits, compensation management and job evaluation?

3 Performance Management

Overview

Unfortunately, recruiting and selecting high-quality people does not automatically guarantee that those individuals will then perform to the best of their ability. As Ed Lawler pointed out, having talented individuals on the payroll is one thing; leveraging their capabilities to secure competitive advantage is quite another (Lawler, 2009).

'Performance management' is a term that potentially has many meanings, depending on its context. For example, it can be used to describe the performance of an organisation, a department, an employee, or even the control processes needed to manage the manufacture of a product or service. Indeed, a Google search on 'Performance Management' brings up over 300 million search results! In the sense that it is being used here, performance management relates to establishing a framework in which human performance can be directed, monitored, motivated and refined, with the purpose of encouraging, supporting and sustaining high levels of individual, team and organisational performance. The difference between a high performing worker and a low performing worker can account for as much as 40% of salary, which means a poorly performing employee earning £50,000 is only as productive as one earning £30,000.

As a concept, performance management is not new – throughout history, managers have always devised ways to set tasks, ensure they are carried out, measure how well people are doing and fine-tune the outcomes, whether the work involves winning a battle, building a pyramid or running a complex business project. For this reason, the performance process is inherently strategic, because it seeks to link individual, group and departmental objectives directly to the organisation's goals. It can also be an important motivational tool (see Theory Breakout Box 2). As noted in Chapter 2, Performance Management is, strictly speaking, an HR practice, but like talent management, it is of such critical importance that it deserves its own pillar within HR Ready.

The Performance Cycle

One of the key roles of line managers is to set targets, manage and monitor the performance of employees and provide regular feedback. Organisations often stress to their managers the importance of performance management as an ongoing, continuous cycle that includes informal as well as formal activities; the central message is usually that the annual performance review should be a continuous process, not just discussed once or twice a year. But there lies the challenge for most organisations – how to take an activity something that everyone recognises is the 'right' thing to do and make it part of everyday organisational life, rather than it being seen as a burdensome task once or twice a year. Yet, many managers struggle to do give sufficient time and attention to this activity, mainly because day-to-day operations are seen to get in the way.

Most models depict performance management as a cycle with linked events that follow each other in sequence (see Figure 7). The cycle shown here is an amalgamation of the types of models frequently found in text books – while many variations exist, it is a reasonable (idealised) representation of how most organisations work. Each step in the cycle raises questions about how it will be performed, what documents are used, how it will be implemented, what knowledge is needed and the specific processes that support it.

In theory, there is no formal starting point for the performance management process as it is effectively a continuous cycle; one year's performance year end is the start of another performance year, a never-ending loop, as the following model shows:

FIGURE 7: THE PERFORMANCE CYCLE

Setting Objectives

The starting point for any performance management process should be a clear organisation strategy with well-defined business objectives. This approach stems from Peter Drucker (1954), who stressed the value of Management by Objectives (MBO), an important element of which is the measurement and comparison of the employee's actual performance against the standards (objectives) set. It stresses that when employees themselves have been involved with goal setting and choosing the course of action to be followed, they are more likely to fulfill their responsibilities.

In most organisations, corporate objectives are cascaded through the organisation's structure to departments, teams and individuals and in theory there should be straight line connection between business strategy and every individual objective. However, This 'waterfall' approach to creating and cascading objectives represents an idealised view of how objectives are actually created; in practice, some individual objectives are formed as a continuation of the previous year's objectives, some are formed on the basis of what work is anticipated and some constantly change throughout the year to adapt to changing business conditions. To add further complexity, cascaded objectives may not always appear at the very start of the performance cycle, as the CEO and Board may not have fully defined the business strategy at that point – in some organisations, there can be a delay of several months between the performance cycle starting and getting agreed business strategy. Even then, adapting the strategic objectives for every level of the organisation is likely to require some form of negotiation and validation, where senior managers may not accept defined targets and additional discussion is required. However, research has identified that 'operationalising' the link between strategic and individual goals is often difficult and that most organisations struggle to do this effectively. Many managers experience difficulties in translating broad strategic objectives into individual objectives; by the time they have filtered down the organisation, it can be very difficult to see the thread that connects an objective to the overall strategy. It can be made more complicated because organisational goals and strategies change regularly and sometimes only 'emerge' in response to the market or other factors. Likewise, some organisational objectives may even be contradictory or competing, with financial targets being inconsistent with customer service and productivity targets. Performance objectives often ignore the inherent conflicts in organisational life, so that success in meeting formal objectives is sometimes achieved at the expense of individual pride in skill and job satisfaction.

Nevertheless, in general, most employees are keen to be involved in determining their own goals and objectives given the company's strategic objectives and their personal needs and capabilities (Schaubroeck et al, 2008). Unfortunately, the inherent complexity in many organisational strategies means that many employees admit to not understanding what they are supposed to be doing in their jobs and what their priorities should be, leading to a sense of dis-engagement from their employers.

Performance Management: The Theory (1)

According to **Saiyadain, (1998),** the basic purpose of performance appraisal is to judge the relative worth or ability of an individual employee in performing his/her tasks. If objectively done, appraisal can help to identify a better worker from a poor one. It has been observed that employee motivations to perform, to develop capabilities and to improve future performance are strongly influenced by the performance appraisal system **(Landy et al, 1978; Kanfer, 1990).** However, definitions of performance management are often confusing, focusing only on narrow aspects of the process such as the appraisal review or the measurement and setting of objectives. Although these activities are important, it's critical to see performance as a more holistic activity.

Performance management has been described as a complex process, one which is often misunderstood and seen as difficult to implement **(Latham et al., 2007).** Although there is no single accepted definition of performance management among either practitioners or academics, the following are useful:

"Performance management contributes to the effective management of individuals and teams in order to achieve high levels of organisational performance. As such, it establishes shared understanding about what is to be achieved" **(Armstrong & Baron, 2005).**

"A continuous process of identifying, measuring and developing the performance of individuals and teams and aligning performance with the strategic goals of the organisation" **(Agunis, 2009).**

Performance management also acts as a communication tool and a means of engaging employees with the organisation's goals **(Murton et al., 2010).**

Performance theory suggests that people work best when they are set a relatively small number of concrete goals they can easily focus on.

Measuring Performance

An effective performance management process should ensure there is continuous observation and monitoring of individual performance, including gathering both formal and informal evidence, feeding into a formal review or appraisal.

Assuming the organisation has been able to identity what performance measures are to be included, it must then decide how best to measure those dimensions. Some have suggested that what gets measured is not necessarily what is most relevant, but that in practice, organisations tend to measure those items that can be most easily measured (Fowler, 1990). Performance measures tend to be either quantitative or qualitative in nature:

1. *Quantitative Measures*

Most organisations use some form of quantitative (i.e. numerical) indicators to assess whether goals are being achieved. These may include meeting financial targets against budgets, sales figures, output and productivity. Measures of performance are often cascaded down from the top of the organisation (the 'waterfall effect'), so a CEO might, for example, set a target based on a 10% increase in revenue, which then ripples down the organisation where it is converted and adapted by individual areas; so, some areas might be asked for 15%, some 5% but together they aggregate to a single figure.

Although quantitative measures appear to be robust and straightforward to measure, they are sometimes more arbitrary than they at first seem. For example, profitability measures can easily be changed and interpreted according to how the organisation chooses to treat costs or recognise revenue at any point in time; however, as long as comparisons can be made at the start and end of each cycle, they will serve their purpose. The biggest risk in relying on quantitative measures is that they overly emphasise financial measures, without necessarily taking into account the impact of other measures. In some circumstances, this may encourage managers to distort short-term financial measures to suit their own purposes (for example, getting a large bonus). Organisations have used techniques such as Balanced Scorecard to remove the emphasis on purely financial measures (see Breakout Box on p.129).

2. **Qualitative Measures**

Some aspects of performance are harder to measure and quantify because they are not readily converted to hard numbers. Monetary or output based measures are much easier to define than measures of customer satisfaction, team work and innovation. Even so, in most cases by using a little creativity, it's possible to translate qualitative measures into some form of quantitative metric - so, for example, customer satisfaction can be measured by numbers of complaints or correction costs; innovation can be measured by the implementation of successful new ideas; effective policy implementation can be measured by the results of evaluation surveys. In general, the quality of any performance measure will depend on whether it is both valid and reliable; **validity** refers to whether the indicator actually measures what it is meant to measure and **reliability** means that similar results will be discovered if the same measure is used by different people at different times (it is repeatable). Nevertheless, by their nature, there will always be a higher degree of subjectivity when qualitative measures are involved. Many organisations now use competency measures to support the performance appraisal process, focusing on behaviours that indicate not just what has been achieved, but how it has been achieved,

Managing individual performance

The basic criteria for any performance management system are:

- **Accountability:** Employees must be accountable or their performance and individual and team behaviours should be tied to clear goals.
- **Transparency:** Ensures that financial and non-financial rewards are clearly understood.
- **Completeness:** Performance management practices cover the full range of behaviours and goals.
- **Equity:** Ensures those who perform better and produce more are better rewarded.

The appraisal of performance can take several forms including the following:

- **Downward appraisal:** Conducted by the immediate line manager, often combined with self-assessment.
- **Upward appraisal:** The employee appraises their manager, often anonymously.
- **Self-appraisal:** The individual assesses their own performance.
- **Peer Assessment** and **360° appraisal:** Ratings from colleagues other managers, subordinates and colleagues (see Breakout Box).
- **Customer appraisals:** Feedback is provided by customers sometimes anonymously.

Of course, the ultimate purpose of the performance process is not for managers to complete a form; a good performance management strategy should improve both individual and organisational performance and ultimately provide the organisation with competitive advantage. Any approach to performance management must be designed and implemented within the context of the organisation, its needs and its culture, and for this reason, it's often difficult to buy a performance approach 'off-the-shelf', adapt them from a text book or borrow them from another organisation. Attempting to do so risks throwing away an important component of competitive advantage.

The formal appraisal process is strongly linked to talent management processes, so it is often accompanied by an assessment of personal potential and readiness for future positions, together with consideration of long-term career aspirations. The outcome of the overall performance process should be an assessment of training and development needs, including formal training courses coaching, mentoring, work shadowing, on-the-job training and distance learning. Many organisations use personal development plans to maintain a record of what action needs to be taken.

> ### Case Study: Tesco
>
> Retailer Tesco has over 6,000 stores in 14 countries and total group revenue of £70bn. To manage its 380,000 global employees, Tesco created a performance management framework to outline its key strategic objectives, which they called the Corporate Steering Wheel, covering twenty corporate objectives across five perspectives. The perspectives are arranged in a circle around the central philosophy of 'Every Little Helps' and the value of 'No one tries harder for customers'. The Steering Wheel is a powerful way of communicating key strategic objectives strategy to all staff. Tesco has adapted its Steering Wheel in line with a shift in strategic objectives **(Advanced Performance Institute, 2009).**

Problems with Performance Appraisal

Despite its potential to be a highly value adding HR practice, extensive studies have found the performance management process to have significant shortcomings. One of the main problems with appraisals is the potential for distortion in assessment and some question whether appraisals can ever be a reliable means of assessing employee performance, because they are inevitably subjective and liable to social influences (Arvey & Murphy, 1998). For example, if the appraiser and appraisee do not have a good relationship, this will inevitably cast a shadow over the ability to achieve a meaningful, fair performance review. Other factors can also cloud the issue - for example race, gender and other variables are known to interfere with the process and lead to bias.

Some organisations use a forced approach to performance ratings against a pre-defined statistical standard, for example, where only 10% of the population can be in the highest category and 10% must be in the lowest category, creating a normal distribution (bell curve). This is a controversial subject and could be the subject of an entire chapter in itself – some academics have argued that forced distribution can encourage higher performance, but it can also lead to high attrition rates and extreme job dissatisfaction among employees (especially those in or close to the bottom 10% - Chattopadhayay & Ghosh, 2012).

Some organisations (such as General Electric's use of the famous 'vitality curve') have routinely used the normal distribution to force the bottom 10% of employees out of the business, although this assumes that people are replaced with fresh, higher performing talent. It also potentially masks poor job design, poor management and weak organisational structures.

> **Performance Management: The Theory (2)**
>
> Two theories in social psychology are especially relevant to performance management:
>
> **Goal Setting Theory:** This states that specific and challenging goals and appropriate feedback contribute to higher and better task performance. The willingness to work towards attainment of a goal is the main source of job motivation. Clear, specific and difficult goals are greater motivating factors than easy, general and vague goals, leading to greater output and better performance. Goals should be realistic and challenging, giving an individual a feeling of pride and triumph when they are attained, ready for the attainment of their next goal **(Edwin Locke, 1968)**.
>
> **Expectancy Theory:** This states that an employee's motivation is an outcome of how much an individual wants a reward (Valence), the assessment that the likelihood that the effort will lead to expected performance (Expectancy) and the belief that the performance will lead to reward (Instrumentality). Expectancy is the faith that better efforts will result in better performance and is influenced by factors such as possession of appropriate skills for performing the job, availability of the right resources, the availability of crucial information and getting the required support for completing the job **(Victor Vroom, 1964)**.

360° Performance Appraisal: The Theory

360 performance feedback has been defined as *"The systematic collection and feedback of performance data on an individual or group, derived from a number of the stakeholders in their performance"* **(Ward, 1997).** Many organisations now use this technique to support the performance appraisal process. There are several potential benefits of this approach - including offering a broader perspective and greater self-awareness for participants that allows employees to *"Hold a unique mirror that enables an individual to see, perhaps for the first time, how his or her actions are understood and interpreted"* **(Handy, Devine, & Heath, 1996, p.13).**

In general, participants generally find the overall experience of the 360° review a positive one; goal-setting theory indicates that managers will set goals for self-improvement if they realise that other people's perceptions of them differ from their own, although it may be that those most in need of developing their self-awareness would avoid it **(Handy et al, ibid.)** 360° feedback appears to be more useful when it focuses on task level commentary rather than challenging individual self-concepts **(Morgan, Canna, & Cullinane, 2005).**

Some research has challenged the value of the 360° process, arguing that the feedback provided may not raise self-awareness because what is being said is largely "nothing new" and it simply reinforces participants' understanding of the need to improve, encouraging them to modify weaknesses that they are already aware of **(Morgan, Canna, & Cullinane, 2005).**

The 360° process also carries political risks - in some highly political organisations, an individual may use the process to sabotage perceptions of their colleagues and gain a career advantage by giving negative or distorted feedback on them, or by only seeking feedback from positive sources. Smart technology allows line managers to control which colleagues are nominated to participate and spread feedback across multiple contributors.

The following are common problems when evaluating performance (Grint, 1993, cited in Murton et al., 2010)

- **Halo Effect**: Where one specific criterion distorts the assessment of others, for example, where an employee has a specific strength but is weak in other areas.
- **Crony Effect:** Caused by a close personal relationship between the appraiser and the appraisee. The impact of favouritism is potentially very demotivating for others in a team.
- **Doppelgänger Effect:** Where the appraiser and appraise have similar personalities and the appraiser projects positive characteristics onto the appraisee. In this situation, the appraiser is really conducting a warped form of self-appraisal!
- **Veblen Effect:** The problem of central tendency, where appraisals are reluctant to rate individuals at the extremes of the rating scale and tend to rate towards the middle.
- **Recency Effect:** Where recent events and influence the assessment disproportionately and historic events are ignored. This happens where a strongly positive or negative event towards the end of the performance year become the focus of the evaluation.

Perhaps the biggest problem in the performance management process is that it is both relative and absolute – it is **relative** in the sense that employees are measured in relation to the performance of others in the organisation and to their own previous performance, but is also **absolute** in that the formal objective setting process means that employees are measured against a defined standard based on objectives.

This raises many questions; for example, if an individual raises their performance level against a previous period, but so does everyone else in the organisation (say the business has a very good year), should that individual be rated higher than before or rated as staying relatively the same compared to the wider organisation? Arguably, in any performance cycle, organisations should seek higher relative performance from everyone, otherwise continuous improvement would not be possible. Likewise, if an employee is promoted, it's reasonable to expect a higher level of performance from them, so that their initial performance in a new role will drop relative to their old role and the performance expectation should be recalibrated at the point of promotion. So, should performance be relative to that of the previous incumbent or relative to their performance in their old role? Equally, if an employee consistently exceeds their personal objectives, should they be promoted to another role, or should 'stretch' objectives be set so that meeting them is more difficult? It is this confusion of absolute and relative measures that sometimes leads to problems and can tie managers (and many HR functions) in knots.

> ### Performance Management: The Theory (3)
>
> Several academic theories exist to define the components of performance. For example, **Blumberg & Pringle (1982)** proposed that performance is a function of capacity, willingness and having the opportunity to perform. The AMO theory **(Appelbaum et al., 2000)** attempts to explain the link between human resource management and performance, concluding that employees perform well and use their discretion when they have the ABILITY to do so through skills and knowledge (A); they are MOTIVATED to do so (M) and they have the OPPORTUNITY to do so through their work environment (O)
>
> **Where P= f(A,M,O)**
>
> Although the exact relationship between these variables is not known, all three have been demonstrated to impact on employee performance. Of course, the components of AMO are abstract concepts which are difficult to prove empirically, but AMO model is intuitively strong and invites debate. Its applications extend beyond business and could equally apply to sports or any endeavour.

Technology and Performance Management

Performance appraisals can be time-consuming and often involve a great deal of form filling and paperwork, considered by many managers to be an administrative burden that gets in the way of the real purpose – measuring performance and seeking ways to bring about an improvement. Many organisations are now moving towards electronic forms of performance management (e-PM) to reduce the administrative components and allow managers to focus on the strategic and development aspects of performance management. Technology supports performance management processes in several ways:

- **Objective Setting:** Providing an online format for the capture and distribution of objectives. This is particularly useful in organisations where objectives are cascaded several levels down the organisation or where large groups of people share common objectives.

- **Staging:** Leading edge systems allow 'staging' of the process, so that managers can set objectives in draft form, then publish them to individuals when they are ready. This allows a central HR function to monitor how far managers are through each stage in the review process.

- **Self-Assessment:** Employees can complete a self-assessment of their performance against objectives and immediately share it with their manager, supporting a two-way discussion. Maintaining performance documents in electronic form means documents are never lost.

- **Range:** A range of assessments can be performed during the performance review, for example, competencies, behaviours, standards and attainments can be assessed and updated.

- **Integration:** e-PM links the review of objectives and competencies to the next stage in the process, the creation of development plans, career development plans and training plans. The most sophisticated systems will suggest training paths to close the gap between standard competencies for the post and the individual's evaluated level.

- **Reporting:** e-PM generates summary data for performance measurement, allowing the generation of statistics on the performance process and supporting the calibration of performance ratings.

Challenges of e-PM

Despite its many advantages, organisations have mixed views on using technology and its introduction can sometimes raise objections to the use of e-PM technology. One of the main concerns raised is that technology may introduce a barrier between the appraiser and appraisee, with the risk that it may de-personalise the process. Managers initially fear that conducting an appraisal from behind a laptop screen has detrimental impact on the face to face nature of a performance review, forcing them to make handwritten notes then re-type them into a system. The secondary impact of this is that it reduces the effectiveness of the Performance Management process, leading to a greater distance and decreased trust between manager and employee. In short, *"Technology can divide managers from workers and instil an adversarial climate"* (Cardy & Miller, 2005, p.162). Of course, paper based approaches also create similar problems where managers become so involved in completing paperwork that the process becomes merely a mechanical exercise. The answer to this challenge is to see technology as a tool that supports the face-to-face process, rather than being the process itself and find ways of adapting to the technology.

Another issue often presented by organisations resistant to the use of e-PM is that line managers may lack the technology skills to make the process work, a problem common to all forms of e-HRM. In this case, proper training of line mangers prior to the roll-out of technology is essential; it's likely that aspects of the performance process will change as a result of introducing technology, so training and coaching will ensure that everyone is comfortable with new ways of working. If the organisation is genuinely concerned about line management responses to e-PM technology, its introduction should be delayed until the business is ready.

What to Look for in e-PM

There are many options available in the market for electronic performance management. The following are some of the functions organisations should look for in selecting performance management technology:

- There should be a high level of integration with the HR platform to remove the need for constant synchronisation of data across databases. Performance cycles often last 2-3 months so it's highly likely that employees will switch departments, functions and managers during this period, which can make keeping track of employees very difficult. A central system means that these changes are easy to track and happen in real-time.

- It should allow objectives to be set at a high level, then cascaded down the organisation and amended, if required, skipping levels in the organisation.

- It should allow 'staging' of key steps in the process, so that managers to create an initial performance appraisal then push it out to employees in a staged way, as well as allowing employees to conduct their own performance review.

- It should not only allow managers and employees to rate against performance objectives but also against competencies, attainments and skills.

- It should allow individual competency levels to be compared against the standard requirements for a post and provide recommend learning paths that might help the employee bridge the gap.

- It should link with the talent management processes and provide the basis for assessing potential to create a 9 box grid.

- It should contain pre-defined reports for analysis of performance

Performance Management: Are You HR Ready?

- [?] Could more employees be covered by the performance management process?

- [?] Do line managers take the performance process seriously or is it seen as an administrative burden?

- [?] Are line managers capable of supporting the performance process?

- [?] Does performance management genuinely lead to higher levels of performance?

- [?] How can technology support your performance processes?

- [?] How will line managers respond to the use of electronic approaches to performance management?

- [?] Is the technology infrastructure capable of supporting e-PM?

Talent hits a target no one else can hit; Genius hits a target no one else can see

Arthur Schopenhauer (1788 - 1860)

The Rise of Talent Management

Talent management is an idea that's been around for a long time, although there has been renewed interest in the topic in recent years. Its roots go back to when consultancy firm McKinsey first coined the phrase *'the war for talent'* in the 1990s, spawning a plethora of research papers, management conferences and strategy papers, leading to 'talent management' entering the HR lexicon.

Although talent management is essentially an HR Practice, like performance management, an effective talent strategy is considered to be so important in its own right that it forms the fourth pillar of HR Ready. Some would argue that the true test of an organisation's leadership is how it builds the next generation of leaders; under this philosophy, the primary purpose of the HR function is to ensure a flow of talent through the organisation - everything else is secondary to that purpose. This chapter attempts to define what talent is, to assess some of the challenges of managing it, and to explore how technology can support talent processes. It also examines some of the inherent flaws in defining people as 'talent'.

What is Talent Management?

Unfortunately (like so many of the topics in this book), there appears to be very little agreement among academics, consultants and HR professionals as to what talent management actually is. As Ross (2013) notes, definitions of talent often lack clarity and become entangled with references to what makes a great leader, leadership success, high potential, high performance and whether talent is innate or can be developed. As a result, the term 'talent' is frequently abused and mis-used. One study concluded "There is a disturbing lack of clarity regarding the definition, scope and overall goals of talent management" (Lewis & Heckman, 2006), while another pointed to "An alarming lack of theoretical development in the area" (Collings & Mellahi, 2009). Even the Economist concludes that "Companies do not even know how to define talent, let alone manage it" (2006, p4. As Carole Tansley puts it "Some definitions of talent are so vague that one is forced to ask "What is the point of using the term 'talent' at all" (Tansley, 2011). The Breakout Boxes in this chapter provide some alternative definitions as to what talent is, but it's fair to say that they are inconclusive.

There is also widespread disagreement as to whether talent management represents anything distinctively new. Proponents of talent management believe it represents a paradigm shift away from more traditional models of human resource management, with a focus on gaining competitive advantage through the development of people and recognition of the complexities of working in a knowledge-based global economy. Once again, not everyone sees the world in this way; for some, talent management is simply 'old wine in new bottles', a re-badging of the traditional processes of 'recruit, retain and reward'. Those subscribing to this latter view would argue that because talent management ultimately represents nothing new, the term is effectively redundant, in which case all that remains is 'Strategic Human Resource Management' or just plain 'people management'.

If, however, talent management represents a new way of approaching these subjects, then it's important to be clear about precisely **what** is different.

What is Talent? One for the Historians...

A 'Talent' originally referred to weight and later monetary units. It was approximately the mass of water required to fill an amphora (whatever that is). Even the ancient world disagreed about talent - a Greek talent was 26 kilograms, a Roman talent was 32.3 kilograms and an Egyptian talent was 27 kilograms. The talent as a unit of value is mentioned in the New Testament in the Parable of the Talents since the 13th century it started to mean an inclination or disposition, later coming to mean aptitudes and faculties. Modern dictionary definitions typically define talent as a natural ability to do something well, a special aptitude or a higher mental or physical ability **(Tansley, 2011)**.

Until recently, talent was mainly used in the context of the entertainment industry – the Hollywood movie industry still refers to on-screen performers as 'talent' and of course we're all familiar with TV shows such as 'Britain's Got Talent' (the format now extends to 39 countries from Albania to Vietnam that have 'Got Talent'!). Talent in this context means a specific skill or attribute that is valued and appreciated by others, although much of the entertainment value comes from watching those with delusions of talent.

Use of the word 'talent' is common in other areas – for example, the sports industry employs 'talent scouts' to seek out the next generation of sports stars. It's also used in the fashion industry and one UK Model agency can be found at www.TalentManagement.com, a URL which potentially distorts any online search into this topic! Finally, 'talent' is often used colloquially to describe an attractive person, clearly referring to specific physical 'talents'.

The way in which an organisation conceptualises talent is critical. Lewis & Heckman (2006) identified three organisational perspectives on talent management, each of which, as a philosophical position, leads to a very talent management strategy. The first perspective sees 'talent' as a select group of special people, the chosen few that have been sprinkled with corporate fairy dust, those with the potential to be future CEOs and CFOs. This approach is based on an assumption (perhaps it should rightly be called a strategic position) that organisational success is directly tied to the capabilities of a limited number of talented individuals (Cheese, Thomas, & Craig, 2008). Talent management assumes a causal relationship between talent and success, with the implication that the most successful people are those with the most talent (see also the section 'Is Talent a Flawed Concept?' later in this chapter). Under this approach, the job of management is to ensure that talented people are nurtured, retained and developed for future leadership roles and organisational talent is carefully managed and aligned to the plans of the organisation. This perspective often takes a competency based approach to talent, based on the identification of the core competencies that define individual talent and lead to organisational success.

However, this view of talent is potentially damaging for two reasons; firstly, it is potentially divisive and splits the world into 'talent' and 'non-talent', as well as creating an obsessive search for specific characteristics that indicate talent - Goffee & Jones (2006, p.10) summarise this as a process through which *"Beleaguered executives are invited to compare themselves with lists of leadership competencies and characteristics against which they are always finding themselves wanting. Attempts to imitate others, even the most successful leaders are doomed to failure"*.

The second perspective is that **everyone** in an organisation has talent, not just a select group of people. The implication is that organisations should not restrict their planning to a sub-set of the employee population, but should cast their corporate net wide and aim to maximise the value of all forms of human capital. In this case, the job of management is to discover talent in all its forms, bring it into the organisation, develop it and point it in the right direction to meet business needs. This more pluralist, egalitarian view is more socially acceptable to some organisations, as it removes the need to be seen giving special treatment to certain individuals. However, it carries with it the risk that those in need of special development may be ignored. Under this perspective, talent management is simply another label for traditional HR management.

A third view places talent acquisition as the defining feature of the talent cycle. It proposes that organisations should aspire to employ **only** high-performing, talented people and the focus of talent management should be to remove non-talented people (poor performers) from the organisation, using tools such as forced distribution for performance management (partly discussed in the previous Chapter).

Collings & Mellahi (2009) add a fourth strand to this debate, arguing that the primary role of talent management is the systematic identification of key posts rather than key people, with key posts being those with the potential to impact the competitive advantage of the firm. The emphasis of talent management is finding suitable people to fill key posts, not simply finding talented people. It's a subtle difference, but one which highlights that matching talented people to the right position is critical - badly matched talent can be damaging both to the person and the organisation. These perspectives are shown in the diagram in Figure 8.

In either case, the way that an organisation defines talent will inevitably shape people strategy and policy, as a result of which, the definition of talent is critical - narrow definitions of talent risk ignoring layers of people who are essential to the running of the organisation; broad definitions can lack focus and result in little getting done. Regardless of the strategic position that drives talent management, organisations must ensure that there is a common internal understanding as to the definition of talent management – without this, there will be confusion about intentions and approach. Ultimately, talent management should be about creating a culture where everyone believes in the value of hiring the right people, developing them, rewarding them appropriately and managing their performance effectively.

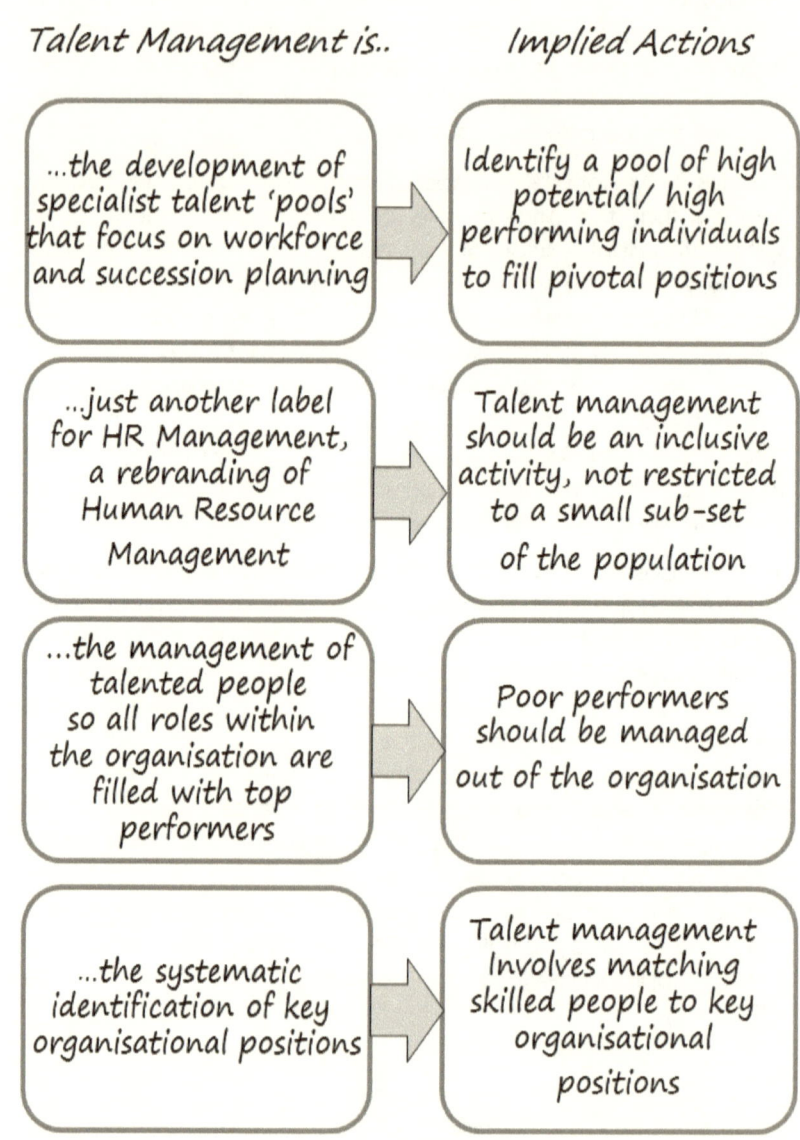

FIGURE 8: ORGANISATIONAL PERSPECTIVES ON TALENT

Talent Management: Definitions

Human Capital Management theory proposes that human capital is of little value unless it can be deployed in the implementation of the organisation's strategy Human Capital Management theory proposes that human capital is of little value unless it can be deployed in the implementation of the organisation's strategy **(Becker & Huselid, 2006).** Modern definitions of talent tend to focus on the notion of differentiation according to greater ability and the relationship between that greater ability, increased success and results for the individual, in comparison to others.

Gagne (2000) defines talent as *"The superior mastery of systematically developed abilities and knowledge in at least one field of human endeavour"*, while **van der Sluis (2008)** defines talent as the *"Sum of knowledge, experience, skills, behaviour, career, ambition, values and personality aspects that a person exhibits in his work"*. Strategic Talent Management is defined as *"managing the organization and employees with specific talents so both can develop in the most efficient and effective way, in line with the strategy of the organization and the ambitions of its employees"*.

Collings & Mellahi (2009) define talent management in terms of *"Activities and processes that involve the systematic identification of key positions which differentially contribute to the organisation's sustainable competitive advantage, the development of a talent pool of high potential ... and the development of a differentiated HR architecture to fill these positions"* (p.304).

Ross (2013) argues that because definitions of talent are complex, ambiguous and incomplete, there can never be a "one size fits all" approach. She argues that, as models, frameworks and criteria for defining and identifying talent evolve, rather than enabling a more effective approach, organisations are overwhelmed with complexity, conflicting opinion and an ever growing list of attributes for benchmarking talent.

The Talent Equation

Ulrich & Smallwood (2012) define talent as a mathematical formula rather than a strategic definition, proposing that talent can be reduced to:

Talent = Competence x Commitment x Contribution

The 'talent equation' has the following components:

- **Competence:** Competence is generally defined as the knowledge, behaviour, skills and values required to perform a job, task or role. Organisations often define 'competency frameworks' as a way of defining the critical behaviours and aptitudes that drive high performance, including features such as leadership and communication skills. Once defined, a competency framework can be used as a selection tool as well as a way of identifying those with high potential.

- **Commitment:** This is also an important component in the talent equation because being competent is irrelevant if employees are not prepared to work hard and release their 'discretionary performance'. Commitment involves concepts such as a sense of belonging, a sense of excitement about the job, and engagement with the task.

- **Contribution:** From an organisational perspective, competence and commitment has to make a difference to the organisation in terms of business outcomes. For example, a hard-working, highly skilled copy typist in a modern office would not have a high impact on the business because these skills are no longer required in a digital age.[3]

The Talent Equation defines talented people as those that have high levels of competence and commitment and through these attributes are able to make a contribution to business outcomes. Ulrich & Smallwood stress that in the talent equation, the three

---

[3] There may well be some areas of publishing that still use these skills so apologies if I inadvertently offend anyone.

terms are multiplicative, not additive. If any single component is missing, higher levels of the other two will not replace it. Of course, such a simple formula masks even further levels of complexity, because it deals in abstract concepts which are equally variable in their meaning and interpretation. For this reason, the Talent Equation should not be used literally – however, it's useful to think of the role of each of the three elements.

Developing a Talent Management Strategy

Although organisations frequently refer to 'talent management', this often specifically refers to the talent review process, where top talent is identified, a succession plan is created and individual career plans are prepared. However, the true talent management process is potentially very broad and can best be seen as a continuous cycle (see Figure 9) - a never-ending loop that follows the employee life-cycle, starting with recruitment and including the key elements of performance management, succession planning, personal and career development and Learning & Development.

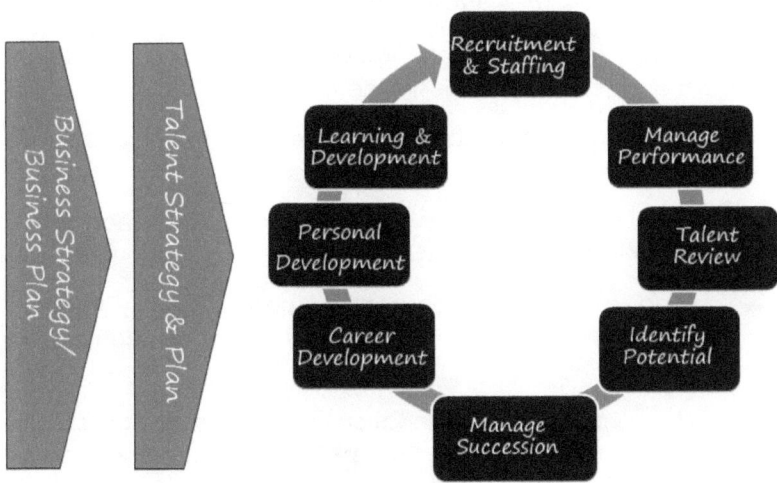

FIGURE 9: THE TALENT CYCLE

Talent Management cannot exist in isolation from the full set of HR practices as described in Chapter 2 and as stressed, the biggest impact arises when a range of practices is in place. One of the key tasks of any organisation is to put in place good work practices, technologies and processes that ensure it gets the best from talented individuals - simply employing talented individuals is not enough.

A talent management strategy should answer the following important questions:

- How does the organisation define talent management and which of the perspectives set out earlier is closest to the organisation's view?

- How does the organisation 'socialise' an agreed view of talent management, that is, to make it part of the culture of the organisation and ensure there is a consistent understanding of what it means?

- What is the relationship between talent management and other HR initiatives, such as succession planning (and is there any difference)?

- What labour market issues will impact on talent management activities in the future?

- What are the main challenges the organisation is facing in developing a talent pipeline?

- Can the organisation benchmark talent meaningfully against other organisations?

- What technology tools can be used to identify the right talent, assess potential and support employee engagement?

- How should the organisation train those responsible for talent management to ask serious questions about performance and potential?

- How can the success of the overall talent management process be measured?

Talent Management: Best in Class

Research by the **Aberdeen Group (2008)** found that those organisations considered to be 'Best in Class' on talent management were able to increase employee retention by 31%, employee performance by 27% and capacity utilisation by 23%, far ahead of average organisations and substantially superior to laggards. 'Talent' processes are therefore critical to economic growth, both at the organisation level and for the wider economy as a whole.

Best in class organisations understand how talent impacts on the organisation, hold the business accountable for talent decisions and are better able to provide accurate data to stakeholders for measuring and monitoring talent management **(Aberdeen Group, 2012).** The research identified that 'Best in Class' organisations operate talent processes differently than competitors. For example, they work harder to ensure that talent strategy is aligned to business strategy, spend more time identifying gaps between workforce skills and customer demand and use HR Analytics to produce data that drives a talent culture. The results of this show up in significantly improved customer satisfaction, retention and revenue per FTE compared with average organisations.

Research has found that high performing organisations following a talent pool strategy are more likely to recruit the best people and are more effective at finding matching positions for them **(Stahl et al., 2007).**

Challenges of Talent Management

Research by Hewitt (2008) reveals that 86% of senior leaders agree that 'talent' is increasingly a top priority for organisations. Despite the importance attached to it, inevitably, there are a number of barriers to implementing a successful talent management programme. For example, more than three quarters of practitioners participating in a 2011 World Trade Group poll believed that talent management is not delivering as effectively as it should (Coulson-Thomas, 2011). About half thought that important opportunities were being missed and that organisations were over-complicating talent management, leading to unnecessarily expensive approaches to recruitment, development and performance management.

One fundamental problem, according to Cranfield University research, is that 39% of UK companies don't have a written HR strategy, let alone a formal talent strategy, a factor that clearly limits the ability of the HR function to put talent strategies in place and develop a business case for investing in people management. The problem is compounded because line managers tend to have a short-term focus when it comes to people issues such as recruitment, managing performance, succession and career development. Recruitment and development is often cut back when business growth slows down, creating problems that divert management attention away from talent management and towards short-term activities.

One of the key challenges for an organisational talent management strategy is that of ownership - the Economist Intelligence Unit (2006) reports that many CEOs believe that talent management is too important to be left just to the HR function. This is not necessarily a reflection of the capability of the HR function – it simply reinforces the idea that to be effective, people management activities must involve line managers in the activity and hold them fully accountable. Certainly, talent management will not be a success if it's seen purely as an HR initiative – HR functions have a tendency to make the talent process overly bureaucratic, with the result that managers feel alienated from the process.

Talent management therefore shares a common problem with performance management – senior managers want it, HR wants to make it happen, managers know it's the right thing to do but operational issues get in the way of doing it well. Tragically, the phrase *'too busy chopping down trees to sharpen the axe'* aptly describes the situation many organisations find themselves in with regard to talent planning. To be truly effective, talent management needs not just senior management buy-in, it will require support from a range of groups across the organisation and a commitment to make it a priority.

Case Study: Apple

Not surprisingly, Apple has a slightly alternative approach to talent management. Apple wants employees to take full responsibility for their career movement and doesn't actively create career paths because it doesn't want its people to develop a "sense of entitlement" and think that they have a right to continuous promotion. Apple believes career paths weaken employee self-reliance and indirectly decrease cross-departmental collaboration and learning. Without a career path, employees actively seek out information about jobs in other functions and business units. Automatically moving employees up to the next functional job may also severely narrow the range of internal movement within the organization, which could reduce the level of diverse thinking in some groups **(Sullivan, 2011).**

Technology and Talent

Many organisations currently conduct their talent processes using a mix of technologies, ranging from spreadsheets to sophisticated talent management systems, which are often quite primitive and ineffective. The market for talent technology is growing rapidly - according to one analyst, the annual market for talent related technology is worth more than $3 billion (Bersin & Associates, 2011). Technology offers many opportunities to automate talent management decisions, for example:

- Capturing performance and potential ratings to create '9 box grid' analysis as the basis for talent planning and strategy formulation. A 9 box grid plots individual potential against performance to enable organisations to see high potential/high performance individuals and make plans for their future development.

- Creating 'dynamic' succession plans that ensure the organisation is constantly aware of the status of every key post and has a succession plan for every key post. Regulations in some industries (such as nuclear power and airlines) dictate that certain key roles must have a succession plan.

- The development of a career plan that defines what future posts the employee might hold over a given timescale.

- Linking the talent plan to individual learning and development plans, suggesting potential learning paths to help the development of certain competencies.

- Allowing employees to develop an 'aspirational' career plan to indicate specific future posts they are interested in, or even general areas of work that are appealing. This is a highly effective way of gathering data on what individuals want from the organisation and ensuring alignment between the aspirations of employees and the likelihood of them meeting their needs. This approach carries risks such as setting unrealistic expectations but on balance, these are better addressed early rather than set false hopes.

However, talent management software does not in itself deliver talent management – it can only support the organisation and requires the development of a talent strategy, good design of talent processes, effective change management and the continuous monitoring of these processes. Talent management is also strongly related to Business Intelligence – ultimately, talent management is about the capture and analysis of a range of qualitative data and interpreting them in a manner that provides insight into the individual and the organisation. Talent data is not like payroll data – it is not absolute and precise, and typically depends on a range of (often subjective) assessments about individuals, their performance, potential, career horizons and development needs. Even performance reviews contain a mix of objective and subjective measures – they are not a precise science. This means talent data is rich in meaning and open to interpretation, so that managing the talent process requires some of the skills of an academic researcher - seeking evidence, challenging assumptions and interpreting data.

One of the biggest challenges of applying technology to talent management is a lack of integrated data. The Bersin and Associates report (ibid.) found that sixty percent of companies possessed two or more separate talent management systems *in addition to* the central HR platform or employee data warehouse. Not surprisingly, most organisations report that the sharing of data between their systems is poor or non-existent, with the result that it is practically impossible to get clear data on the state of organisational talent. The ability to manage all talent related data in a single database seems to be a defining factor in making talent management successful. Having a single 'source of the truth' consistent across all technology platforms means that organisations are better able to analyse, share and manipulate talent data and make informed strategic decisions. Once again, best in class organisations behave in very different ways from average organisations when it comes to using technology. For example, 63% of best in class organisations give their managers direct access to talent data, while only 48% of average performing companies and 32% of laggards do so. The same research found that organisations that are able to integrate their talent data have a richer perspective on their employees and their aspirations and can analyse it much faster than those using separate systems. The Aberdeen Group (2012) also found that around half of all organisations are dissatisfied with their current talent software.

Is 'Talent' a Flawed Concept?

Talent management strategies work on the reasonable assumption that the most competent people should be given greater levels of responsibility in line with their ability. However, because human ability to identify and interpret talent is often flawed, organisations can sometimes wrongly assess talent. Recent research evidence suggests that organisations need to be wary of making talent judgments without careful consideration. This section highlights some of the potential errors that can be made when answering the question "*Who's got talent?*"

(1)   Competence v Confidence

Recent research from the University of California (Cameron & Brion, 2010) suggests that individuals in high status positions often have far greater levels of overconfidence than everyone else. 'Overconfidence' is more than simply being confident - it involves levels of confidence escalated to the point where others might describe that person as 'arrogant', 'audacious', 'conceited' or 'egotistic'. Some of this confidence is simply a result of high status (naturally, success tends to make people more confident) but it seems the reverse is also true – higher levels of confidence can actually lead to higher status. Essentially, those people who strongly believe in themselves tend to be more successful in organisations and are more likely to be regarded as 'talent'.

Spotting good talent is a minefield. It seems that highly confident people emit more 'competence cues' – they're louder, more outspoken and more self-assured and these attributes are often (wrongly) mistaken for actual ability. The California research found that overconfident individuals are perceived as being highly competent but their confidence often masks the reality - for every three percentage points of overconfidence, a person is perceived as one percentage point more able than they really are. So, if someone with average ability considered themselves to be better than 80% of their colleagues, people in the organisation would rank them as being in the top 40% in terms of competence. The sad reality (or a hot tip) is that if you think you're more competent than everyone else, others will start to believe that you actually are!

Organisations often seek out talent from competitors when they identify a deficiency in their own, but hiring people perceived to be high performers from outside can be expensive and highly risky - a star in one context may not do so well in another (Groysberg et al, 2010). An examination of Wall Street analysts suggests that individuals identified as very talented in one organisation often fail to perform at the same high levels when lured elsewhere by increased salaries. This highlights an important point - simply recruiting people is only one aspect of the HR Practice 'cluster' and once hired, people need to be properly managed through performance systems. Paying for talented people will make little sense for organisations that cannot harness, capture and share what they do differently.

Anyone who's watched TV shows such as The X Factor or The Apprentice will be familiar with the over-inflated sense of self-belief displayed by participants, sometimes bordering on delusional. On TV, the delusion is quickly shattered - those claiming to be great singers or sharp business people are often revealed to be highly untalented. For many viewers, the gap between arrogance and reality is highly entertaining and modern TV audiences have learned to be cynical about these misplaced levels of overconfidence. The problem is that uncovering the delusion is more difficult in an organisational setting – while the talent gap can be revealed by 10 seconds of bad singing, a claim to be a great business leader can take a year to be disproved.

This is the paradox of talent management - it's not always the most competent who take charge, and talented individuals that lack confidence can sometimes remain at the bottom of the hierarchy simply because they do not give out the necessary competence cues. The California researchers suggested that organisations become dysfunctional because its members lack the ability (or are too lazy) to seek out evidence of actual talent, instead believing exaggerated claims of competence.

The effect of this mis-attribution can be significant and may cause multiple organisational problems. Higher status breeds even more misplaced overconfidence *("I got the job so I must be good"*) and worse still, over-confident bosses employ like-minded subordinates, with the possible result that entire layers of over-confident management will be hired and 'groupthink' sets in – a condition where risks are unchallenged and irrational thinking occurs.

Yet, you exclaim, surely eventually, the overconfident, over-promoted bosses will get found out, reveal their mediocre ability and be demoted or even fired like those no-hopers on TV? Not necessarily. Overconfident individuals tend to choose more risky strategies, while those with a more realistic self-perception tend to be more rational and take fewer risks. And here's the real paradox – when over confident people fail, their level of perceived competence is such that failure is attributed to other factors such as market conditions, bad luck or incompetent colleagues, whereas success tends to be attributed directly to the individual.

(2) Individual v Organisational Talent

Employers often assume that the future of the organisation is in the hands of a few highly talented individuals, in the belief that they are one of the 'chosen few'. These individuals are then given accelerated career progression and enhanced development opportunities, reinforcing the idea that these individuals are 'special'. However, in certain cases, it's possible that success is not due to an individual, but to the collective efforts of a strong team or perhaps even the organisational culture which enables the individual to perform. In football[4], a great goal by a talented striker usually relies on a great pass from another equally talented team-mate - but who gets the credit? This is another example of a fundamental attribution error – we believe people possess special talents, when in fact their success is a result of the combined talents of others.

There are lots of examples of how "talent" (or lack of it) is wrongly attributed to individuals:

- Football coaches often appear successful at one club, only to fail miserably when they move to another (or vice versa).

- Great sports people often experience a downturn in performance when they are no longer working with equally talented team-mates.

- Successful TV presenters or musicians sometimes attempt a solo career, but become less successful without the creative skills of those around them to support their individual talent.

- When investment bankers change firms, their performance often plummets, revealing that their apparent individual success was actually linked to wider organisational factors or support from co-workers (Groysberg, 2010). Even when entire teams transfer, the new environment or culture may limit successful performance.

- The performance of surgeons improves significantly the more frequently they perform a procedure at a given hospital, yet it doesn't appear to significantly improve

---

[4] For North American readers, please read soccer

when they work at other hospitals. This suggests that surgeon performance is not fully transferrable across hospitals and that the surgical team as whole influences success rates.

What looks like individual skill might therefore be the product of wider organisation and team factors. Indeed, some forms of talent may be so dependent on collaboration with others that it may effectively be non-transferable. Anyone thinking about leaving their current organisation might wish to consider that their own performance may actually be sustained by the work of others around them.

These ideas have important implications for HR professionals when considering talent processes. Firstly, the recruitment process is critical as a way of filtering out misplaced confidence and should include mechanisms for seeking evidence to support extraordinary claims of great achievement. As described in Chapter 2, it's apparent that some applicants tend to exaggerate their resumes / CVs, but mis-placed self-belief is a dangerous thing. This applies equally to the performance management process, where delusional thinking may require a strong challenge from managers to help the individual keep their performance in perspective. Finally, many reward and career development programmes are highly focused on individuals, with the risk that employers might put too much emphasis on personal rather than team development, rewarding individuals for what they perceive to be individual "talent".

Talent Management: Are You HR Ready?

- [?] Are you clear about what 'talent' means to everyone in your organisation?

- [?] Does the organisation have a talent management strategy that is linked to organisational objectives?

- [?] Does the organisation know how to identify talent and develop it appropriately?

- [?] Is there a plan for developing those in the organisation that are not superstars but are critical to organisation success?

- [?] Is the right technology in place to support the talent strategy?

- [?] How do you validate 'talent'?

5 Business Intelligence

What counts can often not be counted - and what can be counted often does not count.

Albert Einstein

Reporting v Business Intelligence

Several years ago, I was working with the Global Head of HR of a large industrial organisation, who lamented to me that although his company employed around 40,000 people, this was only an estimate and there could actually be 2,000 more employees around that he simply did not know about. He explained that he felt like he was flying a plane without the instrument panel switched on – he didn't know (metaphorically) his altitude, how much fuel he had on board or whether he was about to crash into a mountain. He wanted better data and the ability to predict future skills requirements, staffing levels and to be able to experiment with numbers using 'what-if' scenarios. Because he had experienced good systems in a previous company and found that the ability to experiment with data in this way really switched on his strategic thinking, he now missed being able to work in this data-driven way. He knew that some of his current problems were about the lack of a global HR system and poor data definition, but his biggest challenge was the lack of a *business intelligence* strategy for HR, that would include performance indicators, metrics, measures and tools for HR Analytics.

This chapter explores the importance of Business Intelligence as a pillar in HR Ready and how using it effectively enables HR functions to deliver better value and create competitive advantage. It's important to make a distinction between true Business Intelligence (BI) and what I will refer to as 'traditional business reporting' or just plain 'reporting'. Although in common usage the two terms are often interchangeable, in practice they mean very different things. Traditional business reporting typically involves creating formatted output on a regular periodic basis, generally consisting of lists - employees, departments, location, headcount, sickness, gender, ethnic group and so on, grouped and summarised but essentially static[5]. Because the list looks the same every week or every month, reports are not immediately useful unless further analysis is performed – raw data are often dumped into spreadsheets to enable manipulation through pivot tables and charts to turn data into useful information. However, if new queries or reports are needed (such as adding a simple field) it usually requires IT involvement, leading to user frustration and higher costs.

Traditional approaches to reporting have several disadvantages:

- They provide only a rear-view mirror perspective on what has happened (who has left, who has joined, who attended a training course etc.) but they lack the ability to predict and forecast.

- They are often heavily reliant on the use of spreadsheets, an inelegant solution to storing and managing data. These are often updated infrequently, filled with errors and inaccuracies and not always understood by other users. If the spreadsheet owner leaves, they often take the secret of the spreadsheet with them (not just the password).

- Although a range of software tools is available to support a more sophisticated form of Business Intelligence, many organisations lack the technical and data analysis skills to get the best from these tools.

---

[5] There's an old joke – "*I want a list of everyone in the organisation broken down by age and sex*". It's not that funny but it keeps HR people amused.

- Reports often use pre-defined, static formats that are difficult to change. In many cases, they were originally designed to meet the requirements of a previous HR structure with simpler needs.
- They are not well-suited to users who need to directly interrogate or interact with data[6] such as those that want further analysis or to ask 'what if' questions.
- Reports are often created to act as checklists to ensure data has been entered properly, so are often used in conjunction with highlighter pens rather than as a tool for information analysis.
- Reports fail to provide the self-service, responsive, user-driven insight business leaders demand to run their business.

As a result, many organisations are moving towards an approach based on Business Intelligence rather than traditional business reporting. One key feature of HR Ready organisations is their focus on using data to drive their HR and business strategies; quite simply, Business Intelligence is a key pillar in supporting an HR Ready organisation. Good Business Intelligence reveals not only how well the HR function is delivering its services, but also how successful the organisation is managing its investment in people.

What is Business Intelligence?

The term 'Business Intelligence' was first used in a 1958 IBM article where it was defined as: *"The ability to apprehend the inter-relationships of presented facts in such a way as to guide action towards a desired goal"* (Luhn, 1958) suggesting a focus on using data to plan for future action. In the mid-1980s, the term began to be used to describe software deployed so support decision making and planning; however, it wasn't until the late 1990s that

---

[6] Strictly speaking, data is a plural word, with datum as the singular. Therefore, to retain strict grammatical logic, it sometimes appears as 'data are…' which looks odd but is correct!

the term came into widespread use to describe sophisticated software that allowed the deep analysis of data.

What differentiates traditional business reporting from true Business Intelligence is the 'intelligence' part – it refers to the ability to provide **insight**, revealing patterns, trends and exceptions as the basis for action. Business intelligence also provides an indication as to future trends - it's the 'what-if' part of what my Global Head of HR wanted, sometimes known as predictive analytics. Business Intelligence is based on three central concepts:

- **Information Provides Competitive Advantage:**
  Although organisations ultimately compete on cost, products and service, they also compete on information; the old adage 'knowledge is power'[7] is relevant. Predictive analytics – the ability to exploit patterns found in historical and transactional data – allows organisations to identify risks and opportunities, to model future scenarios (what might happen) and to improve the ability to plan ahead. Knowing the current status of your own business, as well as being able to benchmark against others in the market and predict business changes ahead of the competition allows an organisation to see opportunities and find better ways to use its resources. Business Intelligence is inherently strategic.

- **There's no Management Without Measurement:**
  Once a business strategy has been created, relevant measures are need to provide the organisation with a view of how well it is performing against the strategy. It requires appropriate measures to be established that track the right things, allowing the business to fine-tune its actions as the strategy is implemented. Business Intelligence should help to answer the central strategic question *'What do we do next?'* As well as highlighting key areas for action, it should provide the evidence

---

[7] This frequently used phrase is often attributed to Francis Bacon (*scientia potentia est*) but it's more likely to have first been used by Thomas Hobbes in the 17th Century

required for continued investment in HR programmes, by demonstrating that current approaches are working.

- **It Requires the Integration of Disparate Data:**
  True Business Intelligence is not function specific – rather than being restricted to the HR function, it should provide a 'big picture' view of the whole business, which may involve merging data across disparate systems. Tools such as data warehouses enable the integration of data and provide further levels of analysis. For example, HR systems contain masses of information about people, while Finance systems tend to contain lots of numbers relating to invoices, costs, revenue and investments. By combining data from multiple sources, it would be possible, for example, to gain a richer insight into issues such as the cost of sickness absence or employee performance that would not be available through the individual systems.

Research indicates that organisations taking a Business Intelligence approach operate at a more strategic level and are able to create a strong business case for making an investment in appropriate tools (see Breakout Box).

The Failure of HR Business Intelligence

While many business functions have made great strides in improving their Business Intelligence, an overwhelming amount of research data suggests that HR functions are generally failing to make good use of the data they hold. Many find it hard to get beyond the type of traditional reporting described earlier, even though they have access to a great deal of data – they are Data Rich, Information Poor (DRIP). Having the basic data is not the problem - most organisations have headcount and pay data[8], but many struggle to extract and manipulate even the most basic statistics relating to turnover, hire source and reason for leaving (Adecco, 2006). Indeed, many HR managers are unable to provide basic people related data such as headcount, turnover and sickness absence; according to the UK

---

[8] Sizing estimates indicate that a typical HR and Payroll system for a 5,000 employee organisation holds around 500gb of reportable data

CIPD (CIPD, 2007b), only around 10% of employers can effectively calculate their labour turnover costs.

> **Business Intelligence: The Theory**
>
> Effective Business Intelligence provides a number of strategic benefits:
>
> - HR Organisations that can use data to show the business impact and effectiveness of HR programmes are more likely to be strategic partners **(Lawler, Levenson, & Boudreau, 2004).**
>
> - Research consistently points to the positive outcome of using data to drive people-based decisions. For example, "*When HR uses fact-based decision making – instead of intuition or best guesses – the group becomes a more credible partner to the business it serves. Fact-based decisions help HR improve HCM practices, recruit and deploy the right talent, cut costs, contribute to business performance and provide evidence of those contributions.*" **BusinessWeek Research Services.**
>
> - Organisations that place a high value on using data are believed to operate at a higher level of performance. There is a significant link between 'analytic orientation' and competitiveness **(IDC, 2010).**
>
> - Organisations with more than the average number of BI applications in place have higher year 1 & 2 sales growth **(CedarCrestone, 2012a).**
>
> - Studies show that *organisations that have matured their business intelligence and analytics capability ..... and put that capability into the hands of managers, outperform, with 12% higher sales per employee than with other delivery approaches* **(CedarCrestone, 2012, p.22).**

Even when organisations are using leading-edge Business Intelligence technologies, many still fail to establish effective reporting strategies that demonstrate the effectiveness of their investment - according to one survey of US employers (CIPD, 2007b), more than half do not measure the return on their talent investments and of those that do introduce measures, 71% still use spreadsheets. Less than half are in a position to use data to forecast future workforce needs, even though the underlying data exists in their systems. This may sound familiar to readers - many HR professionals often cite difficulty with source data as the most common problem for not being able to track workforce metrics.

It's no surprise that most studies produced in the last ten years conclude that HR needs to become more data driven and better able to create meaningful Business Intelligence (for example, Boston Consulting Group, 2008; Aberdeen Group 2009). Research by Bersin & Associates (2011) reveals that only around 6-7% of HR organisations claim to have reached a deep level of expertise in the use of HR analytics, while almost two-thirds rate themselves as "poor." Although not all organisations can operate like Google (see Breakout Box), it's clear that there are compelling reasons for HR to focus on producing high quality, strategic, relevant information that is linked to performance outcomes.

There are many possible explanations for HR's lack of expertise in providing strategic HR information. At its simplest, it may be that organisations simply do not have the necessary skills in analysis, database management and business consultancy to turn data into meaningful information. Some have even argued that HR functions should hire teams of specialist 'data geeks' to implement software tools and develop metrics as part of an investment in an HR analytics strategy. However, consultants McKinsey forecast a shortage of 180,000 "data analysis" experts in the US alone over the next three years. Because Business Intelligence usually requires an investment in technology, many will cite lack of investment funds as a reason for lack of good data; however, as Chapter 12 on 'Building the HR Ready Business Case' Chapter makes clear, a good Business Intelligence strategy can pay for itself and this should not be an obstacle.

A more cynical view is that many HR professionals simply do not understand the need to develop relevant people metrics other than at the most basic operational data level. This view is often based on a (misguided) view that the HR profession shouldn't be distracted by metrics and analysis, or even that it's too difficult - some may even claim that "*I didn't go into HR to deal with numbers*".

The harsh reality is that most business decisions are based on hard financial data and people decisions are no different – HR is now at a point where it's no longer acceptable to base decisions on intuition and guesswork. Good, evidence-based metrics support decision making, planning and development and it's clear that unless HR professionals become skilled at manipulating and interpreting people data, as a profession it will appear to be most un-business like in its approach.

Perhaps the biggest challenge for any HR organisation is to establish a Business Intelligence strategy that underpins people-related decisions and provides insight into not just what has happened in the past, but offers some capability to predict what might happen in the future. Whether this is called Business Intelligence, HR Analytics, HR Metrics, Key Performance Indicators or some other term is much less important than being hungry for information and using it to steer the business.

Developing a Business Intelligence Strategy

The approach set out below for creating a Business Intelligence strategy for HR is based on building up a series of layers of information, each of which adds more sophisticated data (see Figure 10). It's essentially a maturity model, where each additional layer becomes richer in the depth and breadth of information and each level of data provides more insight into people management. The base layer is Level 0, which is simply implementing a basic infrastructure to store and manage data. Levels 1 and 2 build on this infrastructure layer by providing a basic reporting capability – even so, for some organisations this will represent a major leap forward and will provide valuable organisational information.

Levels 3 and 4 are based on the organisational impact of better decision making, providing better management awareness and a greater focus on employee performance. At these levels, managers will have more information on which to base action; faster/better access to information enables managers to see trends, expand revenue or savings opportunities and avoiding risks.

> ### The Moneyball Analytics Story
>
> This 2011 movie starring Brad Pitt, is based on the book by **(Michael Lewis)** (*The Art of Winning an Unfair Game*). It tells the true story of a struggling baseball team, the Oakland A's; the central premise is that decisions about buying new players were mostly based on highly subjective views generally held in the sport about what drives strong performance. Historically, talent scouts had used measures such as batting average, speed and ball contact to determine whether to hire new players. Teams would spend millions of dollars buying in those skills that were perceived by most teams to be rare and valuable.
>
> Using computer based analysis developed by a Yale economics graduate, The A's could define the *actual* player characteristics that drive strong performance, based on evidence from data. One key metric – on-base percentage – was seen to be a central driver of performance, a characteristic that was significantly less expensive to buy in the market. From this, Oakland developed a system for finding value in undervalued players and set about restructuring the team. This approach turned the team around and brought the A's to the playoffs in 2002 and 2003.
>
> The lessons for HR are obvious – question standard assumptions and what you intuitively believe about people and performance and use evidence-based data to drive decisions.

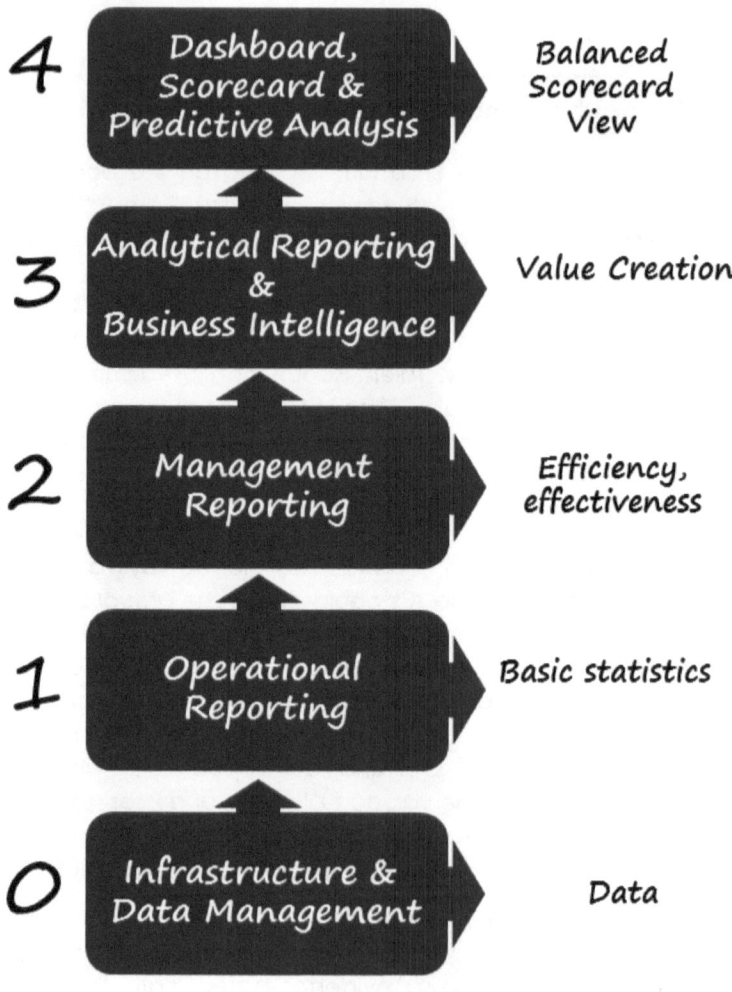

FIGURE 10: HR ANALYTICS LEVELS

Level 0: Infrastructure & Data Management

A prerequisite of any HR Business Intelligence framework is the creation of a database containing employee and organisational data. Most organisations now have a basic Human Resources Information System in place containing HR and Payroll data; a well-designed and maintained position management hierarchy that defines the structure of jobs, posts and relationships will ensure data consistency and provide a framework for analysing data. However, at this point the infrastructure does little more than create a repository for data.

Level 1: Operational Reporting

The Human Resources database provides the basic workforce composition and biographical data needed for operational reporting. Level 1 requires software tools to manage, manipulate and compile data then produce reports such as:

- **Personal Employee Data**: Gender, nationality, length of service, time in post, ethnic group/diversity, age, qualifications, career history, recruitment source, reason for leaving.

- **Job Data**: Job title, job family, post, location, grade, terms and conditions,

- **Organisation Data**: Manager and subordinate details, hierarchy data.

- **Pay Data**: Remuneration, additional pay and reward, effective dates, temporary data.

Ideally, data should be available on a 'like-for-like' historical basis, so that over a period of time, organisations build a valuable resource of historic data and enable comparisons to be made. The ideal approach to producing Level 1 data should be based on an integrated HR/Payroll system which is identified as the master source of people data. Although data is often shared with a Finance system through an interface, it's not unusual to find data in different systems become unsynchronised. Over time, data stored in the HR system should represent the 'truth', becoming a trusted source of data, rather than raise questions about which system is accurate. At some point, this may involve a policy decision about who owns people data – for example, HR, Finance or IT – but unless this basic data is in place, it will be impossible to move towards sophisticated measures beyond this level.

As a principle, Level 1 data should be captured as a result of basic business processes – for example, employee biographical data should be gathered while setting up new employees on the HR system or when changing their posts, or ideally through a self-service approach which ensures it is accurate at its source. A well thought-through position management hierarchy is invaluable to ensure data consistency.

Level 2: Management Reporting

Once basic data is established at Level 1, organisations should become more ambitious and explore more complex analysis. This usually involves creating relationships between different types of data through statistical analysis and techniques such as ratios analysis. This data may originate within the HR system or perhaps even be brought in through interfaces from other organisational systems such as Finance. Typical types of data that are included at this level are shown in Table 1 below.

CATEGORY	DEFINITION
Labour turnover	Leavers against the base employee population, including an analysis of reasons for leaving, by department, location, length of service, gender, etc.
Sickness and absenteeism	Length, type of absence by service, location, department etc.
Recruitment	Cost of hire, source of recruits, stability of recruits by source
Vacancies	Number of vacancies, time to fill vacancies
Number of positions in job family	By location, department, gender, ethnic group etc.
Number of promotions, transfers, secondments	By location, department, gender, ethnic group etc.
Training / Development	Training spend per employee
Performance appraisals	Number of appraisals completed

TABLE 1: LEVEL 2 EXAMPLE METRICS

One good example of Level 2 data is absence and attendance data, where management reporting can have a significant impact on business performance and support increased productivity. The analysis of absence data is usually a valuable exercise; according to the UK CIPD, two-thirds of working time lost to absence is accounted for by short-term absences of up to seven days and over one fifth is caused by long-term absences (four weeks or more). In the UK, The average level of employee absence is now 6.8 days per employee per year, although this varies around the world and by business sector (see Breakout box). On average, the reported cost of UK absence per employee has stopped rising and is falling back to levels reported in 2010 (2012 median: £600; 2011 median: £673; 2010 median: £600).

Although UK sickness absence levels are generally falling, fewer than half of all employers monitor the cost of absence, with the public sector and larger organisations being most likely to do so. However, it's not enough to simply measure absence rates – data must form the basis for strategies to deal with absence, which may include management training in handling absence cases. The continued measurement of data will assess its impact on absence. It's also important to measure what actions managers are taking in response to absence data to assess the success of strategies.

Level 2 reporting typically contains data on retention and motivation, size and composition of the workforce, skills, competencies, training, remuneration, leadership and succession planning. Data at Level 2 still remains largely focused on the performance and efficiency of the HR function.

> ### When is a Sickie not a Sickie?
>
> Across Europe, more than 800 million days are lost each year due to sickness **(Aon Consulting, 2010)** However, of these, more than 120 million days a year are actually for personal reasons rather than illness. A study of 7,500 European workers surveyed in Belgium, Denmark, France, Germany, Ireland, The Netherlands, Norway, Spain, Switzerland and the UK found that 15% of employees were feigning illness when they last took a day off from work as sick leave. Additionally, 10% of people took their last sick day in order to look after a family member.
>
> Spanish employees are the most likely to admit having taken a fake 'sickie' (22%), followed by UK and Irish workers (both 21%) and the Dutch (20%). Danish (4%) and Norwegian employees (10%) are the least likely to have taken a sick day from work under false pretences.

Level 3: Analytical Reporting & Human Capital Management

While Level 2 data is often used to demonstrate the efficiency of the HR function, it reveals little about how value is being created by the organisation. True Business Intelligence is ultimately about enabling business performance – it's fundamentally about measuring the contribution of people and the creation of value.

At Level 3, data should consist of more than simple lists and ratios - they need to provide an insight into the business outcomes of people management at the Human Capital Management level. Level 3 metrics involve searching for patterns in data – it might involve tracking high performing employees against the recruitment source, their career development history and even which managers have managed them. It may require that key roles are identified and tracking the stability of employees in these roles, or calculating how long it takes to fill a vacancy. True Human Capital measurement emphasises people data in the context of business results, so organisations should focus on measures such as those shown in Table 2:

CATEGORY	DEFINITION
Revenue per full time equivalent head (FTE)	Revenue / income received divided by the number of FTEs creating the revenue/income
Fully loaded costs per FTE	Total cost of employment in addition to basic salary, e.g. taxes, benefits, rewards, pensions
Average profit /EBITDA per FTE	Total profit (or alternatively Earnings Before Interest, Taxes, Depreciation and Amortization) earned by the business divided by the number of FTEs needed to create the profit
Wealth created per FTE (added value)	Total value added divided by the number of FTEs needed to create the added value
Average remuneration per FTE	Total remuneration divided by number of Full Time Employees
Average training investment per FTE	Total cost of training divided by number of FTEs
Proportion of employees performance managed	Total number of employees performance managed divided by total number of employees
Proportion of employees covered by the employee engagement survey	Total number of employees covered by the employee engagement survey divided by total number of employees
Key employee stability rate (those occupying business critical roles)	Number of key employees staying in the business over a rolling period (key employees are those occupying business critical roles)
Employee stability index	Number of employees staying in the business over a rolling period (key employees are those occupying business critical roles)
Key Employee hire rate	Number of key employees hired over a rolling period
Recruitment acceptance rate	Number of accepted offers as a proportion of offers made

TABLE 2: LEVEL 3 EXAMPLE METRICS

> **Case Study: St. Vincent's University Hospital**
>
> St Vincent's University Hospital (SVUH) is a major academic teaching hospital, located in Dublin, Ireland, which provides an accident and emergency service, medical care to inpatients and outpatients and employs 3,000 staff.
>
> The hospital introduced a new HR and Payroll system to improve its business processes. The integrated system provided the Hospital with opportunities for both efficiency and improvement, based on the principle of "one touch" data entry and a single employee record. Management reporting on HR activity such as absenteeism and headcount was previously highly time consuming and took up considerable resources; reports were generally out of date when published.
>
> An investment in Business Intelligence provided a big improvement in reporting capability," says John McPhillips, HR Director. *"It's now much easier for us to generate reports for the Group CEO and the Senior Management team on a number of HR metrics including absence, headcount, turnover and overtime."* Management Reports are now run in a matter of seconds with complete accuracy, including a suite of Management reports for the Senior Management Team and Line Managers. It has allowed the Hospital to continuously improve and enables both strategic and operational decision making in relation to all areas of HR activity across the Hospital.

At Level 3, performance indicators may be partly qualitative in nature and are potentially less straightforward to define and measure but they should become a baseline against which to set targets and measure improvement. There are a few principles which need to be established for these types of measures:

- They should be easy to understand and free from jargon.

- Where possible, they should be supported by a clear pictorial representation of figures in a consistent format to help understanding.

- The measures should be regularly reviewed to ensure that they remain valid.

- Avoid the trap of measuring the same things, year-in and year-out, even when they become irrelevant.

Level 4: Dashboards and Workforce Scorecards

Level 4 represents the ultimate level of Business Intelligence maturity; whereas the previous three levels added increasing levels of complexity to data analysis, Level 4 provides users with the ability to manipulate, model and analyse data, often using real-time data which is pushed to end-users based on their individual needs. By reporting only on an exception basis through a user 'dashboard', users can focus on what's important, rather than having to wade through to find the single data point they are interested in. This ability to personalise reporting and relate it to the objectives of each user makes applications that deliver data in this format very powerful.

However, while Level 4 Business Intelligence offers real-time, exception based reporting, it also demands new skills in managing and interpreting relationships between data. At this point, organisations often create 'workforce scorecards' (Huselid, Becker, & Beatty, 2005) to structure data and provide greater insight, based on the Balanced Scorecard concept (see Breakout Box). Workforce scorecards are a sophisticated way of analysing people-based data into the key drivers of organisation success, taking the principle that *managing* workforce success involves *measuring* workforce success. At this level, any metrics must answer important strategic questions and provide insight into whether HR practices are working effectively – they are far removed from the operational data provided at Levels 1 and 2. For example, training measures should describe success in the development of workforce competencies and skills, not just the volume of people being trained. Two final principles are critical; firstly, workforce measurement is not just HR's responsibility - line managers should want scorecard data and put value on it. Finally, there should be a focus on the 'vital few' – the critical metrics that make a difference and influence strategy. In this case, less is more.

The Balanced Scorecard

The concept of the Balanced Scorecard was originally proposed by Robert Kaplan and David Norton in the 1990s as a way of moving performance management away from a single-minded focus on the bottom line. **Kaplan & Norton (1996)** proposed three perspectives in addition to financial measures – customer satisfaction, internal business processes and learning & growth. Kaplan and Norton did not directly include Human Resources and performance management in the Balanced Scorecard, perhaps because of the difficulties in measuring outcomes. However, both internal processes and Learning & Growth often include elements of performance management.

Big Data? What About Small Data?

There's been much media attention given to the idea of 'Big Data' recently, defined as *"Large pools of data that can be captured, communicated, aggregated, stored, and analysed"* **(McKinsey Global Institute, 2011)**. Big data arises from the volume, velocity and variety of data produced by modern organisations and the need to respond more quickly to operational and strategic questions. The data sets involved are so large and complex that they can't be processed using traditional database management tools. It could be the kind of data supermarkets collect about shopping habits, the results of clinical trials or crime patterns.

In HR terms, big data could involve analysing what is being said about the company as an employer on social media, the analysis of time recording data or interpreting historical performance results. However, most HR systems contain around only 500 gigabytes of data for an organisation of 5,000 employees, including several years of history, based on industry standard data storage sizing calculations. Yet, even with a relatively small amount of data, there is a great opportunity for HR to create valuable Business Intelligence for the organisation.

> **Google: HR Built on Analytics**
>
> Google claims to be the world's only data-driven HR function, with a goal to *"Bring the same level of rigor to people-decisions that we do to engineering decisions."*
>
> The People Analytics team reports directly to the VP of HR and has a representative in each major HR function. It provides many tools for the business, including employee surveys (non-anonymous) and dashboards. It seeks to identify insightful correlations on behalf of the business and to provide recommended actions. Analytics has led to:
>
> - A retention algorithm - to proactively predict which employees are most likely to become a retention problem
> - Predictive modelling – to continually improve Google's forecasts of forthcoming people management problems and opportunities
> - Improving diversity – by identifying the root causes of weak diversity recruiting, retention, and promotions
> - A hiring algorithm – to predict which candidates have the highest probability of succeeding after they are hired
>
> The use of analytics means that business change plans are based on data and actions are grounded in evidence
> Source: **www.tlnt.com** (Sullivan, 2013).

There's no Accounting for People....

Most assets of a business are routinely measured, using well-established accounting practices, many of which are effectively enshrined in company law. Formal rules about how to measure the value of physical assets such as buildings and equipment and depreciation formulae are applied; sales, costs and profits are measured, analysed and presented to senior management. Modern accounting ensures that everything has its price and everything has a cost; if you were to ask an average Finance Director to tell you the value of the stock held in warehouses, they could tell you in great detail when it arrived, what it costs, the value it will add to products, when it is due to be used and the impact of any of it being defective.

However, ask most Finance Directors about the people employed by the organisation and they will struggle to tell you much about the skills they possess, the true cost of replacing them or the impact of someone leaving the business. Of course, they could tell you what people cost in salaries, wages and benefits and possibly something about the revenue they earn, but very little about what they are worth and the value they create.

The problem is partly historic - since the invention of modern accounting techniques in the fifteenth century, accountants have had limited mechanisms for measuring the value people create. Of course, it's possible to measure the *cost* of people based on what they are paid in salaries and benefits, and we can assess their *price* in the labour market, but understanding the *value* they create for an organisation is more elusive (see Chapter 12 for a more detailed analysis). Although the accounting profession has made several attempts to develop suitable models, current techniques generally struggle to put a value on the contribution of people – they are generally regarded as an overhead, a cost to be minimised. Despite people being a major factor in creating intellectual capital, almost the only mechanism the finance function has to recognise people value is 'goodwill'. Under current accounting practices, there is effectively no way to recognise the impact that human capital has on an organisation. This topic is explored in greater detail in Chapter 6, but it's raised here because there are important implications for the kinds of measures that an organisation puts in place to measure the contribution of people.

However, the problem is also one of attitude and mindset. Just because the Finance Department can't measure an aspect of organisational performance doesn't make it unimportant for HR to try (see the quote from Albert Einstein at the start of this chapter) and just because something is hard to measure, it isn't necessarily irrelevant – it's important that HR functions make some attempt to put a value on the people contribution. If not, how can senior management and external stakeholders properly assess the value that is being created by the people who work there? And if they can't make an accurate assessment, how do they know whether the organisation is doing the right thing?

Nevertheless, financial analysts are keenly aware that traditional measures of business success such as revenue, profitability and share price don't always reflect the value of the business in the market, which explains why businesses are often valued and sold for many times the face value of their non-human assets. Some economists have estimated that up to 75% of the difference between the market and book value of an organisation can be attributed to intangibles, including people (John Hand and Baruch Lev 2003). It's no surprise that investors and analysts see human capital as a key indicator of future business performance. Some years ago, I spoke about this idea to a conference audience consisting of mostly Finance Directors, the conference theme being *"If you can't value your people, you can't value your business"*. There appeared to be healthy level of interest in finding better ways to recognise the value of human capital and there were some enlightened viewpoints – however, interest appears to be mostly from a small group of academics rather than from a significant section of the accounting profession.

Accounting for People: The Theory

History fans (and accounting geeks) will know that in 1494, **Luca Pacioli** published his famous book Summa de Arithmetica, Geometria, Proportioni et Proportionalita (The Collected Knowledge of Arithmetic, Geometry, Proportion and Proportionality). One section, the Particularis de Computis et Scripturis, described double-entry accounting, also known as the Venetian Method, which became the basis for all modern accounting. It revolutionised economies and business and made Pacioli a celebrity (that's right, a celebrity accountant!), ensuring him a place in history, as "The Father of Accounting." Unfortunately, as far as we know, Pacioli said nothing about recognising the value of people, a tradition accountants have followed for more than five hundred years....

A Statutory Framework for Human Capital Measurement?

Some organisations have started to issue a 'Human Capital' report alongside their statutory accounts for use by external investors, as a means of demonstrating their commitment to employees and their investment in this asset. These include traditional measures such as the number of employees and staff turnover, together with output measures such as the investment in training, added value per employee, succession planning, retention and the cost of turnover, as well as data on innovation and employee engagement. Although currently voluntary, in recent years, there have been moves in some countries to set standards for the measurement and reporting of Human Capital data, so that various stakeholders can compare organisations and their human capital investment. One reason for this is to meet the requirements of a range of stakeholders:

- **External stakeholders** (investors, journalists, competitors, governments) are interested in confidence, benchmarking and compliance.

- **Internal stakeholders** (senior management and line managers) are interested in comparative performance and performance improvement. To be useful internally, people measures must be linked to performance and be relevant to specific groups.

Human Capital reporting is currently a voluntary initiative and as such, organisations will tend to report only on those items they are pleased to report, avoiding those that they would prefer to hide. Although widespread interest in a statutory requirement for Human Capital reporting has waned in recent years, it's likely to return at some point in the future, particularly in a post-Enron, post banking-sector collapse world where investors need to know that organisations are being well managed. For this reason, it's likely that there will eventually be a requirement on companies to report on people issues.

Until that time, there is an opportunity for organisations to develop a range of Human Capital metrics (based on Business Intelligence) to understand more about how their business operates. Human Capital reporting therefore raises a number of important questions:

- How to recognise the value of people and find a way to quantify it for comparison purposes?
- How to set up a framework of people-related measures that will form an intrinsic part of an organisation's performance measurement system?
- How to quantify the value – financial and non-financial - that is added through the people that we have?
- How to ensure that value is increased, and not lost, when organisations merge and restructure?

HR Goes Mobile

The growth of mobile technologies now means that there is growing demand for data 'on the go' to enable users of data to see dashboard data whenever and wherever they need it. According to **McKinsey (2011)**, more than 4 billion people (60% of the world's population), use mobile phones, of which 12% are smartphones, with penetration growing at more than 20% pa. There are currently 4 billion mobile internet users and one billion PCs with internet access available in the world, suggesting hugely changing patterns of information access and device availability. This growth in technology mobility is driving a desire for Business Intelligence to be available whenever and wherever executives need data, not just when they are a desk. Mobile solutions mean information is available remotely, whether in meetings, working from home etc. Employees are increasingly using their own devices to access information, such as tablet technologies, in a move termed 'Bring Your Own Device (BYOD). Although this presents major security issues for corporations, the trend will see a push for more data to be available.

According to the **Aberdeen Group**, organisations are rapidly introducing mobile Business Intelligence because of market pressures such as the need for higher efficiency in business processes, improvements in employee productivity, better customer service and the need to make 'real-time' decisions anytime and anywhere. A Business Intelligence strategy should include provision for how the organisation will deliver metrics and whether there is scope for mobile solutions.

Summary: Business Intelligence

Business Intelligence (HR Analytics) offers a great opportunity for the HR function to take a lead in developing indicators that demonstrate the value that people contribute. Over time, this will form a measurement tool which maps the impact of people management in the organisation as well as providing a way of tracking the success of various HR initiatives.

Business Intelligence: Are You HR Ready?

- Is your Business Intelligence Strategy clear?

- How long would it take you to analyse key measures such as turnover, absence, retention and training costs?

- What does your Business Intelligence tell you about the success of HR initiatives?

- Do manager's objectives align with the content of the reports they receive?

- Which level are you at on the Human Capital Measurement Model?

- Does the Senior Leadership Team set and demand specific data?

- Is there a demand for mobile analytics?

Focus on Competitive Advantage

Personnel was perceived......as a trashcan into which all unwanted tasks could be dumped, rather than a key element in the search for competitive advantage

David Guest, 1990

HR Ready organisations are not 'trashcans' into which unwanted tasks can be dumped, neither are they simply good administration factories, they keenly understand how they provide their organisations with unique capabilities that give the business a competitive edge. To achieve this, every strategy, policy, process and action should ultimately be directed towards creating competitive advantage. One of the defining features of HR Ready organisations is that they are outward looking – rather than being focused only on internal HR activities, they see the needs of the wider organisation, in particular their role in supporting the competitive strategy of the organisation, as well as monitoring the external environment. Effective HR functions build a reputation for action – if managers believe that HR is simply an administration factory, no amount of strategy documents, presentations and fancy job titles will make a difference. Action is what counts:

Strategy is what strategy does.

As Chapter 1 emphasised, effective HR service delivery is a highly important aspect of HR's role and indeed, many HR organisations are well regarded for their ability to deliver high quality administrative services. However, while providing good administration services is a key **role** of the HR function, it should never be considered as its **purpose**. A central theme of this book is that the HR function is (or should be) more than an administrative service delivery unit – its ultimate objective should be to help the business compete in its chosen market, to make the organisation better able to provide goods and services to its customers and ultimately to help the organisation be more successful than its rivals. A focus on Competitive Advantage is possibly the most important pillar of all the seven pillars of HR Ready, because it focuses the function on its primary purpose.

Competitive Advantage and HR Strategy

Received wisdom suggests that there should be clear alignment between business strategy and HR strategy; HR management textbooks generally point to a lack of alignment as a major cause of HR initiatives failing, relating to the failure to align HR to competitive strategy.

In the last thirty years, competitive advantage has become a central idea in business management theory as a way of defining how organisations approach their markets and the strategies available to them (see Breakout Box). In general, if the organisation has a competitive strategy that requires it to be a low cost operator (cost leadership) the role of HR is likely to be the provision of low cost basic services. As long as that approach matches the competitive strategy of the organisation, then 'no frills' HR should be the top priority.

The problem arises when HR is misaligned to what the business needs, either by doing too much or (mostly) not doing enough. For example, in a low cost operation, if the HR function focuses on highly strategic activities such as development programmes, succession planning and complex reward structures, there is likely to be a perception that HR is failing to reflect what the business needs and that it is obsessed with its own initiatives. It's at this point that HR departments gain a reputation for being too conceptual, ineffective and not 'gritty' enough. If all the business wants is good administration and to stay out of court, proposing an employee well-being programme will not go down well, despite its virtues.

At the opposite extreme, if the competitive strategy is based on differentiation or focus, the organisation typically needs to produce innovative goods and services that require a knowledge-based workforce, with an emphasis on good people management, higher levels of investment in employee development and career management. In this case, a low-cost HR function risks being too basic and will not provide enough of the value-adding activities managers expect. An HR function that spends it time looking at the design of its application forms will not make a positive impact in the board room.

> ### Competitive advantage: The Theory
>
> Traditional resource-based models of economics consider resources that are rare, valuable, non-substitutable and imperfectly imitable to be the basis of a firms' sustained competitive advantage.
>
> In his now classic work on competitive advantage, **Michael Porter (1980)** argued that to gain competitive advantage over its rivals, an organisation must undertake one of three competitive strategies. The first of these is *cost leadership*, in which an organisation attempts to be the lowest cost producer in its industry, based on a low-cost advantage gained through efficient operations, economies of scale, technological innovation, low-cost labour or access to cheaper raw materials. This strategy is often found in commodity markets where price is the main driver.
>
> Alternatively, it might pursue a *differentiation strategy*, where the organisation distinguishes itself from its industry competitors by obtaining a unique position in the marketplace, emphasising high quality, extraordinary service, innovative product design, technological capability, or an unusually positive brand image. This position typically justifies a price premium that exceeds the cost of differentiation (think Apple). Finally, it can follow a *'focus'* strategy by establishing an advantage in a narrow specialist market segment, achieved by either a cost advantage or differentiation approach aimed at a narrow market segment.
>
> According to **Barney (1991)**, a firm has competitive advantage when it implements a value-creating strategy which is not simultaneously being implemented by a current or future competitor.

Are People Our Greatest Asset?

Organisations possess many forms of capital. The most common use of 'capital' is in the sense of financial capital, i.e. money and credit, but it can also take the form of **'intellectual capital'**, which is far more powerful and includes structural capital (processes, methodologies, systems) that are unique to the organisation and **customer capital**, which is the value of the relationships and potential contracts organisations have with its customers. However, **Human capital** is believed to be the most long-term, enduring form of intellectual capital, to the extent that some would argue that the only significant differentiator between organisations is their unique capability to create value through people, potentially the only true source of competitive advantage. The term 'Human Capital Management' (HCM) has been around since the early 1960s, when it was first used as a term in economic theory to emphasise that people are a factor of production capable of producing wealth. Figure 11 sets out the various forms of capital available to organisations.

Human Capital is important because financial capital and some forms of intellectual capital are equally available to almost everyone in the market or are relatively easy to reproduce – for example, organisations tend to use similar machinery, raw materials, computer systems, processes and methods. In general, they have the same access to markets and distribution channels, and experience similar economic conditions.

How do People Create Value?

Unlike machines or money, organisations cannot actually own human capital, so at best people are 'on-hire' - they have a choice as to whether to stay or leave. They may decide to take their skills and experience with them, with no compensation due to their employer for the investment made in training and development or to cover their replacement costs. Unlike other forms of capital, people get ill, encounter joy, suffer tragedy, feel motivated, get bored, perform well, have bad days and so on. Moreover, people are not commodities, because each person works differently and brings their unique blend of capabilities, aptitudes and contribution to the business (that is, their talent).

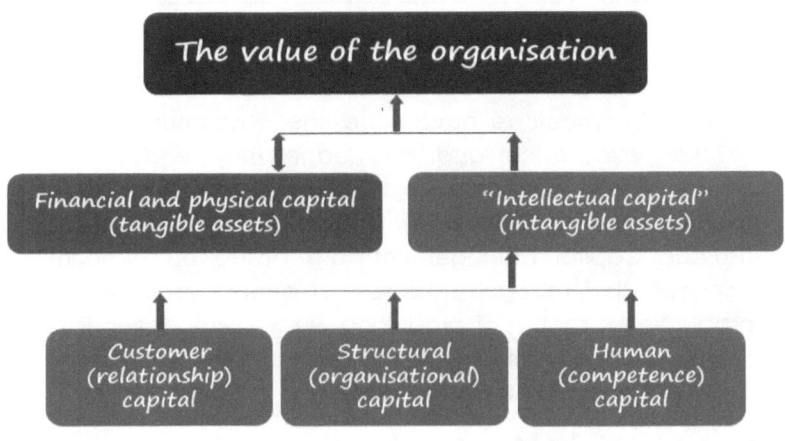

FIGURE 11: FORMS OF ORGANISATIONAL CAPITAL

Source: Mayo, 2006

The basic premise of Human Capital Management is that deriving value from people requires a strategic approach to people management, emphasising tangible business outcomes. In essence, it's about seeing people as assets that create value, rather than simply costs to be minimised. Relationships between co-workers, managers, subordinates, customers and suppliers are inherently complex and the value created by any individual is a function of all these factors working together. It's these individual variations that make managing people one of the most difficult tasks in organisational life.

Human capital management enables an organisation to be innovative and produce quality products; it allows an organisation to work in ways its competitors cannot and ultimately ensures the business can deliver a return on financial capital. However, unless organisations are able to create value through people and focus their performance on bottom-line business results, even the best-formed business plans will amount to nothing.

> **Human Capital Management: The Theory**
>
> Human capital theory sees people as a unique source of sustained competitive advantage, the *"Accumulated stock of skills, experience and knowledge that resides in an organisation's workforce and drives productive labour"* **(Nalbantian et al., 2003, p.75).** Contemporary approaches to 'Human Capital Management' are based on economic concepts that recognise the role of people as a factor of production capable of producing wealth, emphasising that people are the most long-term, enduring form of intellectual capital **(Barney, 1991; Pfeffer, 1994).**
>
> In economic terms, successful firms will strive to possess superior sources of human capital through recruitment, selection and development programmes and will seek to support this with better business processes **(Boxall, 1996)** that create a powerful form of competitive advantage **(Huselid, 1995).** Competitive advantage can be measured through business value (profitability, market share, market size), operational efficiency/cost reduction, management productivity and other strategic thrusts **(Strassman, 1988).**
>
> Early usage of the term 'Human Capital Management' stems from research by Nobel prize winning writers such as **Becker (1964)**, while accountants such as **Lev & Schwartz (1974)** and **Flamholz (1985)** later sought to explain how the contribution of employees added to the asset value of the firm, attempting to establish valid and reliable techniques for measuring the contribution of employees in organisations.

People management is clearly important to the achievement of competitive advantage and there is now mounting research evidence that good people management leads to higher profitability and more sustainable business results – as much as 80% of a company's worth is thought to be tied to how well people are managed. Poor people management can have expensive results - a PwC Saratoga report (2008) identified that people and cultural issues are now one of the biggest barriers to successful mergers and acquisitions and achieving the value these large deals anticipate.

At least, that's the theory. Despite all the economic theory that describes the importance of Human Capital, American management author Michael Hammer suggested that the phrase 'people are our greatest asset' is 'The biggest lie in contemporary American business' (In Stiles & Kulvisaechana, 2004, p.4), because few organisations behave in a way that demonstrates they believe it. One reason for this is a lack of understanding about how people actually create value – in a Foreword to The HR Scorecard (Becker, Huselid & Ulrich, 2001, p.ix), David Norton, co-inventor of the balanced scorecard, states that most organisations have a poor understanding of strategies for developing human capital, because few organisations behave in a way that demonstrates they believe it. Perhaps one reason for this attitude is a lack of understanding about how people actually create value – Norton believes that *"There is little consensus, little creativity and no real framework for thinking about human capital"* while others note that *"There is little consensus on what value creation is or how it can be achieved"* (Lepak, Smith & Yatlor (2007, p.180).

Indeed, the phrase has become so clichéd and parodied that any business referring to *'People are our greatest asset'* in company reports, newsletters and press releases is immediately greeted with suspicion. There's a great Dilbert cartoon that illustrates this point perfectly, in which the boss explains that although he's been saying for years that employees are the most important asset, it turns out that **money** is the most important asset after all. Employees are ninth - just after carbon paper. The cartoon is funny because it highlights how organisations often pay lip-service to the importance of people, yet still fail to recognise their value. Dilbert's manager just happens to say it out loud rather than pretend, adding further humiliation to employees. Of course, Dilbert's manager is partly right, in that not **everyone** in an organisation is an asset - some of them may even be liabilities! For copyright reasons, I'm not able to reproduce it here but if want to see the cartoon, just go to www.dilbert.com and search on 'carbon paper'. Younger readers may need to do a search on what exactly carbon paper was for.

Human Capital Management v Human Resource Management

Perhaps the most important difference between Human Capital Management and traditional Human Resource Management approaches is that Human Capital Management emphasises the role of people in creating competitive advantage, seeing people as a form of capital that is connected to the bottom line. However, because the contribution of people is difficult to measure and quantify, organisations have tended to take a predominantly Human Resource *Management* approach to people management, focusing on regulation and cost containment, potentially at the expense of the higher returns that may arise from a focused Human Capital approach.

The HR Value Model

The HR function shares a common problem with other business functions such as IT and Marketing – how to define and demonstrate the value that it creates and present it in a way that can be understood by organisational stakeholders. The HR Value Model (Foster, 2009) is a way of defining how HR functions create value and how they contribute to the creation of competitive advantage. It states that the HR function can contribute to competitive advantage in one of only three ways, as shown in Figure 12:

1. ***HR Operational Cost Reduction***

Cost reduction is a key lever in any competitive strategy and even an organisation that is pursuing a differentiation or innovation strategy will also seek to control and manage its costs. Operational cost reduction appears as a direct financial contribution and in HR terms is mostly concerned with the internal workings of the HR function – its impact is primarily on the HR function. Costs are reduced either through direct HR headcount reduction or indirect cost reduction (or cost avoidance) such as lower reliance on third party suppliers and reduced technology costs. It is the most tangible type of benefit because it refers to actual 'cashable' cost savings (or cost avoidance) that flow directly to the 'bottom-line'. Cost reduction is a major element in the development of a business case and HR needs to get a clear understanding of the factors that make up its operating costs.

However, HR operational costs typically account for only around 1% of total operating costs[9], so even a substantial percentage reduction in HR costs will make only a small contribution to a cost-focused competitive strategy. Indeed, line managers may prefer to pay more for a professional HR service that directly supports their people management activity rather than have a 'bargain basement' HR service. Moreover, under a competitive strategy based on product differentiation or innovation, low-cost human resource management may not be the highest priority, especially where people management issues are significant barriers and opportunities to business growth.

2. *People Management / Productivity*

Arguably, even if an HR function were the most efficient, cost-effective, lowest cost provider in its sector, it would still have little impact on the ability of managers to improve employee and business performance. The second area of HR contribution to competitive advantage is therefore to support managers in managing their people, as a way of improving productivity and performance. It's through this channel that the organisation is most likely to be innovative and develop new products, especially in support of a differentiation approach.

This area is particularly relevant to knowledge-based organisations such as professional services, technology and creative businesses, where the management of individuals becomes highly important and product cost is less of a differentiator than product quality or innovation. Unlike HR Operational costs, which are limited to the HR function, this form of value impacts on the whole organisation.

---

[9] This refers to the cost of running the HR function, not to be confused with the overall cost of employing the workforce

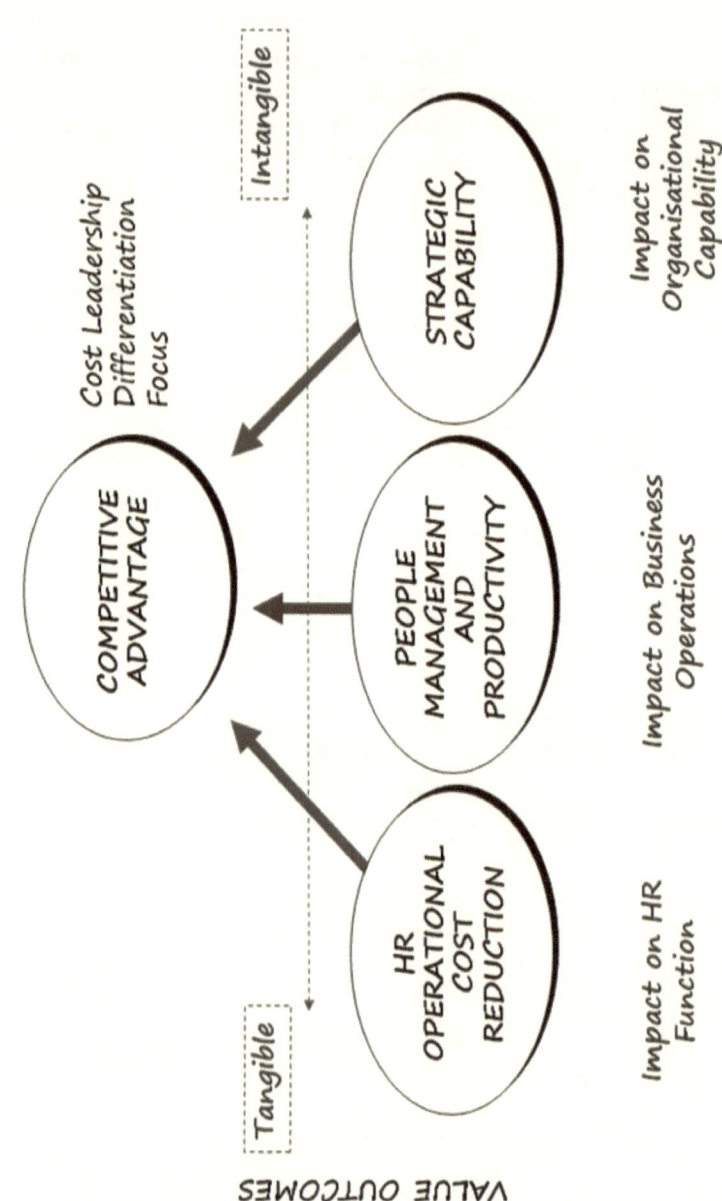

Figure 12: The HR Value Model

3. **Strategic Capability**

The final Value Outcome in the HRM Value Model has potentially the most significant impact on an organisation. Although it is the most elusive and difficult to explain and defend, it potentially allows the HR function to make its most powerful contribution to competitive advantage. This category includes capabilities such as being able to provide deep insight into the skills and competencies of the workforce, the development of senior leadership and ensuring the long term viability of the organisation. However, the intangible nature of this category can be a challenge and most accounting practices struggle to allocate a value to these long-term capabilities, perhaps explaining why they are absent from many business cases.

The HR value model will be revisited in Chapter 12 as the basis for creating an e-HRM business case.

Summary: Focus on Competitive Advantage

This chapter argues that the primary purpose of an HR function should be to support the achievement of competitive advantage. HR Ready organisations understand how their actions support the business in achieving this; indeed, without understanding their contribution to competitive advantage, an HR function will lack a focus for its actions (other than basic compliance). Human Capital Management, with its focus on building strategic capability through human capital is the key to competitive advantage, requiring the close alignment of business strategy, competitive strategy and HR strategy. At this level, HR becomes a true differentiator, providing the organisation with capabilities that others cannot match.

Competitive Advantage: Are you HR Ready?

- [?] Does HR see its role as supporting competitive advantage?

- [?] Is it clear how HR supports the achievement of competitive advantage?

- [?] Are HR strategy and business strategy aligned to achieve competitive advantage?

- [?] Does the business understand what HR is doing to support competitive advantage?

7 Business Engagement

Previous chapters have set out the key pillars that define HR Ready organisations. The seventh and final pillar of HR Ready – Business Engagement – is about translating the first six into practical action on the front line. It's important not to confuse this with engagement in the sense of **employee** engagement, discussed as an HR Practice in Chapter 2, which concerns the sense of connection employees have with the organisation and their motivation to perform at higher levels.[10] Although employee engagement is increasingly important as one of the practices available to an organisation to improve performance, **Business** Engagement relates to how the HR function engages with the business it supports and its primary customers, that is, line managers. It's one of the most important components of HR Ready, because Business Engagement defines how HR organises itself, the role it has in the business and the channels it uses to deliver its services. Without an effective engagement model, other pillars of HR Ready will fail to make an impact.

We Need to Talk About HR...

Let's face it, HR does not have a good reputation. The media loves to portray HR managers as either incompetent, remote pen-pushing bureaucrats or fluffy, tree-hugging, new-age

---

[10] Employee engagement is defined as "the harnessing of organization members' selves to their work roles; in engagement, people employ and express themselves physically, cognitively, and emotionally during role performances" (Kahn, 1990, p.694)

faddists. Journalists delight in relaying bad news stories about HR failures – it seems that every few weeks, there are headlines such as '*Fire the HR function*' and "*We don't need HR*", both of which have appeared recently in the British press. My personal hard drive is full of damning statements and articles about HR, collected over several years; frankly, it makes depressing reading.

I once thought that anti-HR feeling this was a very British thing, but evidence suggests that HR functions around the world struggle with their reputation, as if other business functions had made a collective decision to pick on HR (they probably voted to hate lawyers at the same meeting). Even television situation comedies tend to present HR people as joyless, ineffective, politically correct idiots. In the words of Michael Scott, Office Manager in the US version of TV show 'The Office', "*My job is to make working here fun; HR's job is to make it lame*".[11]

It's not just journalists and sitcoms that attack HR; consultancy firms love to join in the hunt. For example, one report concludes that "*At a time when human capital is being recognised as key to an organisation's sustainability, the reputation of the function is at low ebb. Its future is in doubt*" (PwC 2008, p.39). Another observed that "*HR is at a turning point... we believe HR is faced with a stark choice. It can either evolve and make a significant contribution, or be diminished and be dispersed into the business*" (Deloitte, 2009, p.1). Of course, consultancy firms have a vested interest in criticising the HR function (because it helps to

---

[11] The Office, US, Series 6

generate work for themselves to fix the problem), but academics also love to have a go – Richard Beatty, a Professor at Rutgers University claimed that typical HR activities have no relevance to an organisation's success *"They don't think like business people - many of them entered human resources because they wanted to help people, which I'm all for.... but I'm also for building winning organizations"* (McCann, 2009, in CFO Magazine). Ouch.

The history of the HR profession may shed some light on why HR is often at the wrong end of management criticism. What follows is based on the UK, but readers elsewhere will recognise historical similarities. The function initially evolved from a welfare role at the turn of the twentieth century, which possibly laid the foundations for its "soft" image. In the post-war economic climate of the 1950s and 1960s, the newly formed Personnel function evolved to establish an Industrial Relations role to counteract the perceived growing power of trade unions. The 1970s then provided the profession with a new role to protect the organisation against equal pay, employment protection and diversity legislation and ensure compliance. As a result, the HR function became steeped in law, policy and red tape, compounding a view that the function was staffed with bureaucrats with little understanding of business. Understandably, Personnel began to get a bad reputation, perhaps because of the shadow of the welfare role, with the popular media describing Personnel as a 'Cinderella' profession (because they never go to the ball). At the same time, some argue that the retreat from a welfare work was more apparent than real and that in fact the welfare role never actually disappeared, as many practitioners desperately clung to it (Beaumont, 1984). More power was eroded during the 1980s and the role of the function quickly shifted as HR appeared bloated, expensive and inefficient. One academic, in an article entitled 'Big hat, (but) no cattle' (Skinner, 1981) lamented HR/Personnel's appearance of being important but lacking any real power or influence.

The transformation agenda of the 1990s led to a raft of new initiatives including the introduction of service centres, Centres of Expertise and the Business Partner role, which introduced new language to the HR profession primarily based on the work of David Ulrich. Ironically, this rush to self-improvement may have fed a growing suspicion that HR was in trouble, adding to the confusion as to what actually HR does and creating uncertainty about the direction and role of the function.

So there it is – a history of HR in three hundred words. It suggests a bloated, dysfunctional profession that's been misunderstood for almost a hundred years. But is HR broken and badly in need of repair? Does it lack a single defining paradigm and lack clarity of purpose to such an extent that there is no such thing as 'Human Resources'? Or, in reality, is HR actually doing a great job but it simply suffers from poor Public Relations? It's an important question to answer, because without it, there can be no engagement with the business and no support for HR's actions. It would be ambitious and arrogant of me to claim there is a definitive answer, but it's a question worthy of exploration.

What Does the Business Really Want?

Although the popular media is cynical about HR, it's just as important (probably more so) to listen to what line management customers say about the function, especially regarding what they really want. Unfortunately, research suggests that managers frequently rate HR functions poorly, perceiving that HR lacks an understanding of business reality, places too many constraints on line manager's ability to act and that customers are generally frustrated at HR's slow response in understanding and dealing with business priorities. A recent study, cited in People Management (2013, p10) found that:

- Only 38% of executives say that their Head of HR is a 'key player'.

- Almost one third believe that the Head of HR is not of the same calibre as other business leaders.

- More than 40% thought the HR function was too focused on processes and rules.

- Over one third thought that HR did not understand the business well enough.

This suggests that HR has a long way to go to meet its aspiration to be 'strategic'. At the same time, organisations are demanding more from their HR functions, asking them to demonstrate the value HR brings to the business, with constant pressure to become a 'strategic business partner', an 'internal consultant', to become 'aligned to the business strategy', to provide 'added value' and latterly to become involved in 'Human Capital Management'. There's been an ongoing debate in HR for at least the last thirty years, based on an idealised HR strategic Utopia where HR finally achieves its ambition to be taken seriously. The general sense of unfairness experienced by HR functions is stoked by endless conferences, seminars and articles bemoaning HR's lack of influence, statistics about how few HR Directors have a seat at the top table and horror stories of HR being marginalised at every opportunity.

While HR's defence is often that the function is so pre-occupied with administration that it has no time to be strategic, of course, this may be a cosy excuse for not actually doing anything about it. It also raises questions as to whether HR is actually a proper profession, an idea that has long featured in accounts of the 'struggles' of HR practitioners (Guest & King, 2004). Of course, HR has sought to establish a professional identity, especially through the foundation of professional bodies (such as the CIPD in the UK, SHRM in the US, CHRP in Canada and the Australian AHRI) which have developed formal qualifications and professional development routes, including various constructs and profiles. However, there has been little academic research to define the components of the HR identity (Pritchard, 2010) and there is an opportunity at some point to develop a global model of HR based on a single unified theory. One might, of course, conclude that it doesn't really matter whether HR is a profession or not, but that what matters is whether and how HR achieves results, which is surely more important.

What's often missing from most analysis (both pro and anti HR) is the other side of the equation – defining what the business really needs from HR, rather than defining the role HR wants for itself. Research by IES (Hirsch et al, 2008) concludes that line managers want their HR function to undertake the following:

- Customers want an HR function that is strategically minded, focused on solving problems that are strategically important, but not creating separate HR strategies.

- Customers want a proactive HR function that identifies problems early and works closely with managers to address them.

- Customers want professional help from an HR function that understands the business and gets to know them and how they work.

- Managers want an independent-minded HR function which understands the workforce and is able to help management balance workplace and employee needs.

- HR needs to be responsive, clear about what it is there for, what services it offers and able to respond efficiently and effectively. Line managers are often unclear as to what the HR function offers and who they should contact over specific matters.

What's on the CEO's mind?

Although the HR function is often heavily criticised by line managers, there is some evidence that CEOs are relatively happy with the contribution of HR. Around 69% of CEOs believe that they have a good relationship with the Head of HR and 63% finds them of high value (Wells and Ghuari 2012) - in fact, CEOs rate the HR function more highly than any other business leader, seeing the function more positively in its role of identifying and recruiting key talent. This may be reassuring, given that it's always good to have the person at the top on your side when nobody else is. It may also be that many HR Directors offer their Chief Executives a form of executive coaching, becoming a sounding board for the more complex, emotional aspects of corporate life. A study by the Economist Intelligence Unit (cited in People Management, 2013) showed that CEOs and HRDs share common goals when it comes to 'surviving and thriving', both placing great emphasis on a strong HR agenda based on getting the best people, at the lowest cost, with the lowest attrition and the best performance. Close to the top of the CEO priority list is ensuring that the organisation has the right talent, whether people are able to do their jobs, and what skills will be needed in the next five years. This is potentially good news for the HR function.

The Golden Triangle

Many HR leaders find that one of the hardest internal groups to engage with is the Finance team. HRDs frequently find themselves under the microscope of the Chief Finance Officer (CFO), who is often cynical about the role and contribution of HR and evidence suggests that CFOs are much harder to please than even the CEO, frequently expressing cynicism about a lack of tangible returns and concerns over excessive HR spending. Chapter 5 discussed how modern accounting methods fail to ascribe a value to people, so it's likely these two issues are connected. After all, why should a CFO respect a function in the organisation that does not own any assets, can't define its value or contribution in hard money terms and struggles to create a business case for its initiatives?

There has been growing interest in the so-called 'Golden Triangle' that sometimes exists between the HR Director, Finance

Director and the CEO. Golden triangles represent the informal and intangible relationships between top executives (usually the CEO, CFO and one significant other) that often drive the strategy and direction of the companies they are leading. Being part of this triangle means that HR directors have access to key conversations and greater engagement with critical business issues. However, they are rare, with just one in eight HR directors believing they are capable of meeting the golden triangle entry requirements - it appears to be a role that is available to only a few exceptional HR directors.

Business Partners

In recent years, there has been a major expansion in the role of the HR Business Partner, as a technique for directly engaging with the business. The Business Partner role typically sits between the general service delivery function and the policy making Centre of Expertise, acting as the front line for the delivery of HR services. In theory, the Business Partner model only works if it is combined with a shared services structure (or separate administrative delivery team) and a Centre of Expertise to provide policy making and specialist services. If these other groups are not in place, there is a risk that the Business Partner simply ends up as a localised administrator. Business Partnering has often been characterised as one leg of the 'three-legged stool' model, because it relies on each of the other legs being robust and performing its role appropriately (see Figure 13). In general, where organisations have had mixed success with the Business Partner model, in part it's because of a failure to implement fully the full three-legged model. The Business Partner model therefore has important implications for the structure of the HR function and how it engages with organisation. For example, rather than reporting to an HR director, many organisations are now 'embedding' the Business Partner role into the client organisation, with a direct report to the head of the operational unit and only a matrix / dotted relationship back to HR. This allows for alignment to the specific business and HR strategies of the business unit being served, rather than being a monolithic, one size fits all structure.

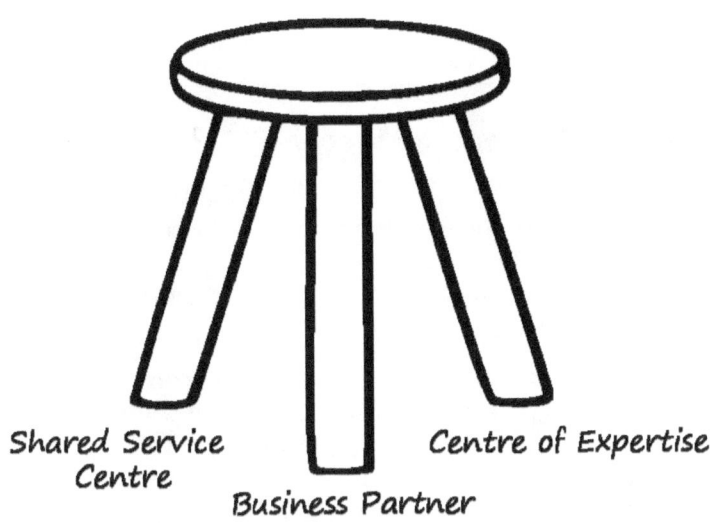

FIGURE 13: THREE LEGGED STOOL MODEL

What Exactly is a 'Business Partner'?

As the Breakout Box explains, it can be quite difficult to define the precise nature of the term 'Business Partner'. While many definitions are available, most focus on where Business Partners fit into the overall structure and their relationships with line managers, rather than providing any useful insight into what the Business Partner actually does. This may explain why so many organisations have failed to deliver the Business Partner model successfully.

Definitions of the Business Partner role typically focus on separating 'thinking from doing', although this can be a little unhelpful given that Business Partners generally need to 'do' as well as think and inevitably there is some degree of overlap between the various aspects of Business Partner roles.

Business Partners: The Theory

The work of Dave Ulrich in the 1990's established the Business Partner role in the HR landscape, although contrary to popular belief, he did not invent the term, with Ulrich simply noting its growth. Nevertheless, his work inspired a generation to adopt this model.

The UK CIPD (2012) defines Business Partnering as *"A process whereby HR professionals work closely with business leaders and/or line managers to achieve shared organisational objectives...this process may involve the formal designation of 'HR business partners', that is HR professionals who are embedded within the business, sometimes as part of a wider process of restructuring of the HR function"*. **Reilly et al (2007)** suggest that some organisations have over-simplified the Ulrich model by trying to separate 'thinking from doing', leaving the Business Partner role loosely defined and precariously positioned with respect to relationships.

Pritchard (2010) suggests that the central premise of the Business Partner role is that line managers are flawed as good people managers, justifying the need for the partner model to fill the gap. HR then places the blame for the failure of the Business Partner model at the door of business leaders for their lack of support for the model.

Research indicates that HR practitioners identify with a wide variety of roles and operate very differently in relation to HR issues **(Caldwell, 2003)**. In practice, the strategic partner role is a flexible and fluid and potentially, one might conclude that the Business Partner role is whatever the organisation chooses to make it, possibly to the point where as a concept it is rendered meaningless.

Research suggests that the Business Partner role is still maturing in many organisations, with many holders of the position finding themselves frustrated by the constant problem of never being able to get beyond 'fire fighting', often becoming overly caught up in legal issues and pseudo-administrative trivia, while struggling to perform the most valuable part of their role – developing people and supporting managers.

Nevertheless, research provides some clues as to what makes a good Business Partner, much of it aimed at being a good internal consultant. Some of the key activities that define a Business Partner are:

- HR planning
- Organisational development
- Organisational design
- Strategic planning
- Management and executive development
- Competency/talent assessment

(Hunter, Saunders, Boroughs, & Constance, 2006)

Research also suggests that a good Business Partner should possess the skills to build relationships, know when to intervene and how to create a contract with their clients. When work has been agreed, they should have the skills to deliver against this contract and follow up with appropriate evaluation. Likewise, the Bath Consultancy Group (2011) found that managers valued Business Partners who were challenging, gave open and honest feedback, were a good sounding board, became a trusted advisor, provided coaching support and perhaps most important of all, were actually available when needed.

Harrison (2008) believes that Business Partners will know that they are a true business partner when:

- They are brought in early to help resolve issues before they become solution.
- They are entrusted with confidential information.

- Clients share their plans.
- They become a 'confidant'.
- Clients ask for personal advice.
- They can challenge their client without losing trust.

Anecdotal and academic research generally finds HR functions to be enthusiastic about taking on a more strategic role. However, for all its proposed virtues, successfully introducing the Business Partner role is riddled with problems. For example, no other function in the business feels a need to describe itself a 'partner'. As far as I am aware, there are no internal Finance Partners, Procurement Partners, Manufacturing Partners or even IT Partners; they are so embedded in the business that there is no need for them to carry the 'partner' suffix. Being a 'Partner' implies that somehow HR is separate from the organisation and is only linked through a partnership arrangement. At worst, it could appear to be a desperate act to remind the business that HR is there – "*Look! We're your partner, let's work together!.*" What's more, there is little clarity on exactly what it means to perform 'strategic' work and the activities it may involve.

Likewise, being strategic is not about having more time – many HR professionals fool themselves into believing that the distraction of administrative work is the main barrier to making a strategic contribution. "*If only we had more time*", they argue, "*We could really make a difference around here*". Being a Business Partner involves more than a change in title – simply dumping the administration and changing the title on your business card does not make you a Business Partner. The Business Partner role is more about a way of thinking than it is about time-management; strategic people tend to think and act strategically in any situation and are usually not constrained by paperwork. Indeed, the paperwork is often the first thing to be neglected!

> **HR? What is it Good For? The Theory**
>
> One of the key questions at the heart of HR Ready is "What is HR for?" For several decades, academics have sought to define the role of the HR function **(Legge, 1978; Tyson & Fell, 1986; Storey,1992)**. Some have argued that the true value of the HR function is in helping the organisation develop the necessary capabilities needed to compete effectively, that is, to deliver competitive advantage through people **(Lawler & Mohrman, 2003)** and that the HR function should ensure *"The development of human capital that enables the enterprise to become more competitive, to operate for maximum effectiveness and to execute its business strategies successfully."* **(Alvares, 1997, p.9).**
>
> The 1980s and 1990s saw the profession pre-occupied by a debate as to whether 'Human Resource Management' (HRM) was substantively different from 'Personnel Management' and whether HRM was simply 'old wine in new bottles' **(Storey, 1989; Guest, 1997)**, re-labelled to give the illusion that it had evolved into something more substantive. Some have argued that modern concepts of strategic HRM effectively constitute a paradigm shift away from the old Personnel model - **John Storey (1989)** concludes that HRM marks a departure from the prevailing orthodoxy, implying something different from the collective bargaining, procedurally-centred model typically found in Personnel Management. Meanwhile, Karen Legge has argued that what differentiates 'Personnel' from 'HRM' is that HRM focuses on what is done to managers, rather than Personnel's focus on what managers do to employees **(Legge, 1989b).**

Perhaps the biggest barrier in moving to a Business Partner model is the difficulty encountered in stepping away from the previous generalist activity and making a full transition to Business Partner, together with the acquisition of new skills needed (Pritchard, 2010). The transition can be very difficult and frequently, continued involvement in administration is justified by claiming that new ways of working are still 'bedding down'.

Research suggests that Business Partners typically find ways of weaving their old generalist work into their strategic role sometimes leading to tension with the service delivery areas.

A Rose by any Other Name…..

The function currently known as 'Human Resources' has held many titles over the years; Welfare, Personnel, Employee Relations, Industrial Relations, Staff Relations, Employee Services and so on. Ultimately, it shouldn't really matter what it's called - after all, the Finance function has similar variations (Accounting, Comptroller, etc.) but I don't see much anxiety from them about their name. Yet, from time to time, the HR function works itself into a virtual frenzy about what to call itself. It was even raised at a conference recently where I was a panel member, although it was roundly rejected as an unnecessary distraction. Nevertheless, the question continues to lurk in the background.

Many Government HR functions in the United States (such as NASA and the CIA) are already renaming themselves as the 'Department of Human Capital Management', raising a concern that functions will simply change their name to be fashionable, without changing either their approach to people management or their service delivery model. There is a sense of déjà vu to this – you may recall that many organisations renamed themselves from 'Personnel' to 'Human Resources' in the 1990s without doing much more than changing the name above the door.

One reason the question has arisen again is the growth in recent years of 'Human Capital Management', which many people dislike because it suggests a hard, ruthless approach to business that does not deal with emotions or individuals. To some extent, the same is true of 'Human Resource Management'; so, why is it that being referred to as 'human' in this context somehow seems to de-humanise us? By describing ourselves as human, it's as if we strip away our individuality and reduce ourselves to pure biology. As 'humans' we seem to be no more individual than an insect in a nest. In contrast, the word 'Personnel' at least makes it clear that we're dealing with people - a quick examination of the Latin and French etymology confirms that we're referring to persons. But 'Personnel' now has a bad name, hence the rush in the 1990's to re-badge the profession away from 'Personnel' towards 'Human Resource Management'

('Personnel' had welfare connotations and that just wasn't cool enough). Business needed a term that made people management sound like a scientific activity and Human Capital Management takes Human Resource Management to the extreme.

Likewise, when we talk about people as 'capital', we think of money, credit and financial investment, or perhaps even its Marxist connotations, suggesting exploitation of the masses. Somehow, HR people simply do not like to think of people as 'capital'. Once again, etymology comes to the rescue and we find that 'capita' is a Latin word for head, referring to the individual. We should remember that rather than being exploitative, the word 'capital' is simply about what each person brings to the organisation, whether it is social, intellectual, emotional or otherwise. It's what allows us to be productive.

So we're caught between being too soft and cuddly as 'Personnel' and lacking in emotion as 'Human Resources' or 'Human Capital Managers'. My theory is that it's not the word 'capital' in Human Capital Management that causes the trouble but the 'human' bit. Would 'People Management' or 'People Capital Management' be just as meaningful? Or perhaps we should just look beyond the words used and concentrate on what's important, which is that people (humans, bipods etc.), individually and collectively create value and that managing them better than competitors makes organisations successful. More to the point, perhaps it doesn't matter whether it's Personnel, Human Resources, Employee Relations, Department of HCM etc. as long as the focus is on getting the best out of people.

Summary: Business Engagement

It's not enough just to deliver good administration services, nor is it sufficient to develop good HR practice - HR functions must engage with their customers more to find out what they really want; HR Ready organisations have thought through how they will engage with the rest of the organisation. Although this seems obvious, too many HR functions are insular and fail to engage with the business, seeing the world from their narrow functional perspective, rather than reaching out to solve business problems. Sadly, they implement an 'HR strategy' in the narrowest sense – a strategy that only meets the strategic needs of the HR function!

The important message from this chapter is that engagement needs to happen through a variety of channels, whether as Business Partners, through golden triangles or an individualised approach that meets the needs of the business.

Business Engagement: Are You HR Ready?

- [?] How engaged is the HR function with the business?
- [?] Do line customers understand what HR is designed to deliver (and is this the same as what the HR function believes it is intended to deliver)?
- [?] Do you demonstrate the characteristics needed to engage with the business?
- [?] Is HR part of the Golden Triangle?
- [?] Is the Business Partner model perceived to be effective by line customers?
- [?] Are the activities of being a 'strategic' HR function clear?
- [?] What is strategically important to the business?

Part II: The Six Tools of HR Ready

8 HR Technology (e-HRM)

> *In the future, HR professionals will be at the intersection of three sets of skills: Business strategy, HR mastery and technology.*
>
> **David Ulrich, From e-business to e-HR** (2000)

Although the HR function was one of the first business areas to take advantage of computers (through early payroll systems in the 1950s), it has been relatively late to implement and exploit the internet and other technology solutions, despite tools such as employee and manager self-services being widely available for over 10 years.

In the mid-1990s, the internet 'changed everything'. Now, almost twenty years later, most people have widespread access to high-speed broadband and portable technologies such as laptops, tablets and smartphones. Online shopping is displacing conventional retailing and many people now rely on the internet to manage their personal and work lives, for everything from booking holidays and ordering pizza to managing their bank accounts. As a result, people now expect immediacy in their dealings with service providers, rapid information flow and virtual around-the-clock access. This expectation is easily translated into the workplace, where employees also expect high levels of service with full access to online HR services.

> **The Expanding Internet**
>
> Internet use across the world has expanded enormously in the past ten years; in Europe, 63% of people use the internet, ranging from 15% in the Ukraine to 68% in Germany. Elsewhere, 78% of Americans have accessed the internet, as have 40% of Chinese people and 80% of Japanese. Only the poorest African countries have internet use rates below 10% of the population (*Source: Internet World Stats, 2012*).

What is eHRM?

E-HRM (electronic Human Resource Management) is a simple idea that constitutes a fundamental change in the way that employees relate to their organisation. In the same way that cash machines (ATMs) changed people's relationships with banks, e-HRM has the potential to transform how employees and managers conduct HR administration at work. For this reason, some employers see e-HRM as a means to create a more 'grown up' relationship with staff, where people are allowed to take direct responsibility for their affairs without any 'hand-holding' from the HR department.

When successfully implemented, e-HRM reduces operational costs, increases the productivity of staff and managers, supports the provision of better access to information and gives an opportunity to provide 'value-added' HR. It represents a significant step in moving an organisation towards improved HR services; when combined with shared services, outsourcing or other delivery models, e-HRM has a transformational impact and in most cases, these new service models simply could not work without e-HRM. Developing a capability in the use of technology is an important aspect of HR Ready and is fundamental to the operation of a modern HR function; as Boroughs, Palmer & Hunter (2008) observe, *"The development of human resources is bound inextricably to the technology that serves it."* Once an e-HRM network is in place – along with a culture where employees turn naturally to the system for information and interaction – it can be the basis for further initiatives that will change the way people work.

The Basics of e-HRM

An 'HR system' is rarely just a single layer of technology; it's likely to be a true **system** in its formal, dictionary sense, with multiple, related components. These can consist of:

- A **Foundation** layer consisting of the basic database and operating system, on which the basic HR Management System (HRMS) sits. This layer stores employee data including biographical, pay and organisational information.

- **Functional Modules** then work with the foundation layer to provide specific functionality, supporting processes such as recruitment, training, expenses and payroll.

- **Support Technologies** drive the administration of business processes, including the provision of management information through business intelligence, workflow, organisation charting and case management.

- The final **Presentation Layer**, often called employee or manager self-service, is delivered through an intranet or portal and provides access to the data beneath, with only minimal functionality of its own. Its main role is to present data in a visually pleasing, simplified format for end users. This final layer is the critical 'game-changer' for HR technology, because it enables HR and Payroll processes to be deployed outside the HR function to internal and external users. For many years, the only way to provide access to an HR system was to give access to the Foundation and Functional layers, which involved loading software onto every computer, then setting up complex network connections and security profiles, all of which were prohibitively expensive.

Figure 14 sets out these layers in diagram form, stripped down to basics to explain the structure as simply as possible. Technical people will no doubt argue that this is an over-simplification of a highly complex subject, but this way of conceptualising the structure of HR technology has proved to be a useful way of explaining how the technology involved works. From a design and change point of view, it's critical that non-technical end-users are able to understand technology in simple terms and in a language that makes sense to them; if not, they will be disadvantaged when it comes to exploiting what the technology can offer and in particular, in discussions with technical people.

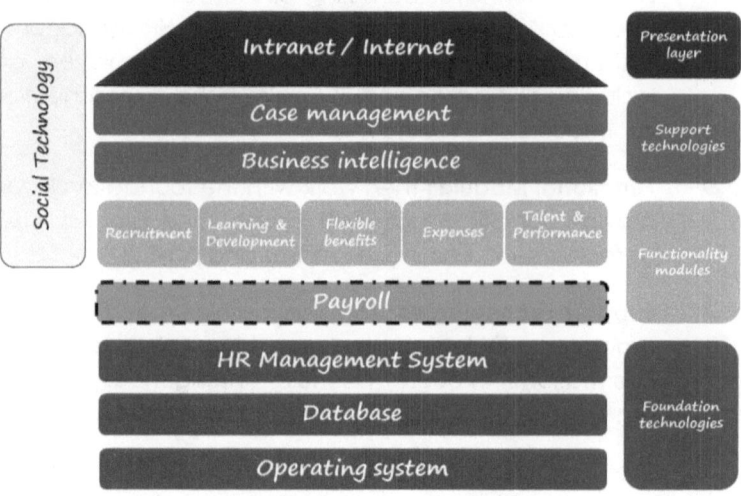

FIGURE 14: HR SYSTEM STRUCTURE

While it's Important to understand how technology works, how various parts of the system 'talk' to each other, how data moves around and how the various modules are configured, it's all too easy to be drawn into a techno-centric view of the world and ignore the ultimate purpose of the technology - to help HR create value. One way to think of this is to define technology in terms of business **outcomes** rather than technical **inputs**, and to take the view that organisations implement **processes**, not technology. Thinking about technology in this way may not be natural for technical IT teams following a strict project plan based on a 'go-live' imperative, but it's essential that HR sponsors ensure their needs are fully met in the system design.

To understand the business outcomes of technology, it's useful to divide technology into two distinct types – **Process Technology** and **Human Capital Technology**. Figure 15 sets out this distinction in diagram form, where the lower half focuses on operational process technologies that lead to efficiency and lower costs and the upper half impacts on strategic people management.

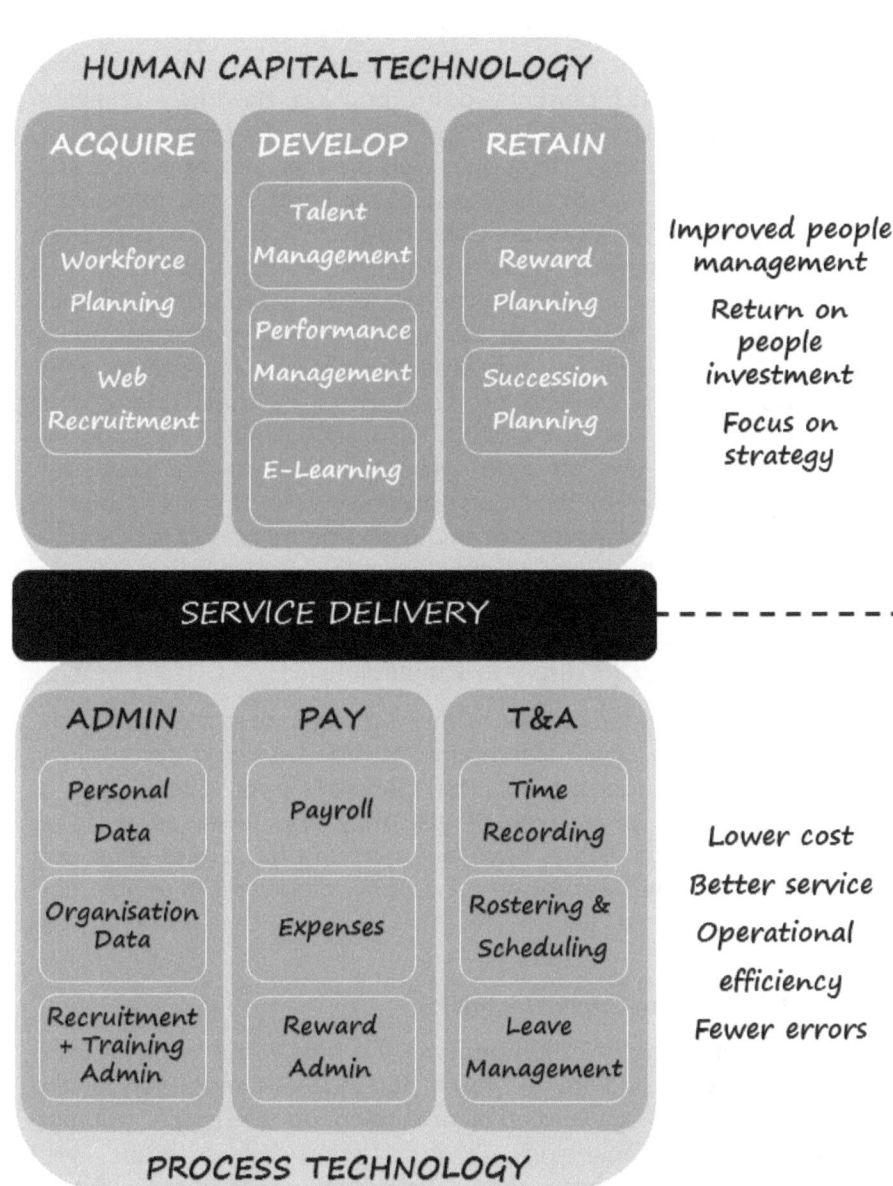

FIGURE 15: HUMAN CAPITAL V. PROCESS TECHNOLOGY

1. ***Process Technology***

Process technology describes a range of functions that support the delivery of HR administrative processes, including viewing and updating personal data, booking holidays, submitting expense claims and recording absence. These processes are typically managed through a web browser, including tasks such as initiating requests and approvals. Because the technology automatically populates basic data fields and validates data entered, it speeds up data entry and leads to higher levels of data accuracy. In theory, line managers could post vacancies, make offers, hire new employees, changing salaries and move people around the organisation, although in practice these activities are likely to be constrained by audit and control policies, as well as the ability of organisations to manage the education and change aspects of devolving processes. Likewise, external applicants can view vacancies and supporting documents, apply for jobs online and be managed through the process to the point of offer using the workflow built into the system. By removing paper from processes and pushing data capture to its source, data re-entry is reduced, accuracy improves and the response is immediate.

Process technology means that software does the hard work, through the basic automation of processes and calculations. The use of process technology generally leads to lower cost of operation, higher levels of efficiency and fewer errors. These process technologies have been around for several years and are now well established in many organisations – for most readers, there will be few problems in understanding the concept.

2. ***Human Capital Technology***

Even if an organisation became the best in the world at using Process Technology, it would not make its managers or the organisation any better at managing people issues. 'Human Capital Technology' is less concerned with administrative/transactional processes and more directly focused on supporting value-adding processes; applications are about getting the right people, with the right skills, in the right place and time, at an optimal cost. They typically consists of software that supports complex HR processes such as on-line performance and talent management, workforce analytics, reward management and skills profiling, with the objective of improving people management and supporting strategic activity. Research by CedarCrestone suggests that organisations adopting a full range of Human Capital technologies will be able to translate this into an 11% improvement in operating income growth, as opposed to a 4% growth experienced by those implementing fewer applications (Cedar Crestone, 2011, p.13). Human Capital technologies include Business Intelligence technologies and the deployment of workforce analytics, along with workforce planning tools to give organisations the power to measure workforce performance.

Human Capital Technology is strongly related to the HR practices described in Chapter 2, together with talent management and performance management; if used correctly, these forms of technology may become sources of competitive advantage, especially if they are able to support unique processes that competitors cannot replicate.

3.   *Service Delivery Technology*

Both process technology and Human Capital technology are typically supported by a layer of self-service, which presents process and human capital technologies to end users. This is effectively the presentation layer described in the previous section. It uses intuitive, web-based screens that allow users to perform tasks on their own, at any time, from wherever they can access the internet or intranet, whether they are inside or outside the organisation, such as managers, employees and applicants. It may also include facilities for social (media) technology, running alongside more traditional web browsers.

The division of Process and Human Capital Technology as set out above is not absolute – clearly, some technologies cross the boundary between process and human capital technologies. For example, e-recruiting systems typically have both an administrative and a strategic role, for the purposes of improving processes and reducing manual administration, as well as promoting the employer brand and supporting the selection and management of potential talent into the organisation.

eHRM: The Theory (1)

Academic and professional HR literature employs a wide range of terms to describe the use of technology in Human Resources Management. Many of these are interchangeable, the most common being e-HR, e-HRM, HR intranet, HR portals, HRIT and self-service. Older terms such as 'HRIS' (Human Resources Information System) and 'HRMS' (Human Resource Management System) tend to refer to the basic HR Database which is primarily accessed by HR staff, but these terms are still used by many organisations and some software vendors.

Other terms in use are 'web-based HR(M)' **(Ruel et al. 2004)** and 'Business-to-Employee (B2E) systems' **(Huang et al., 2004),** virtual HR.(M) and HR portals, although these are less common.

Some have even argued that e-HRM describes an overall approach or philosophy to the delivery of HR and that e-HRM potentially consists of *any* form of technology that supports the delivery of HR services **(Lengnick-Hall & Moritz, 2003)**. This broad definition suggests that eHRM includes not just the HR database and administrative elements of HR, but any form of technology that supports the HR function including social media, employee applications, Business Intelligence and potentially even email systems. The focus is on value creation, expressing outcomes as well as its inputs.

Bondarouk & Ruel (2009) conclude that researchers have not standardized a definition of e-HRM and there remains no common terminology set in which to create and test ideas, constructs, or concepts. Their proposed definition is *"An umbrella term covering all possible integration mechanisms and contents between HRM and information technologies, aiming at creating value within and across organisations for targeted employees and management."* (p507). This focuses on four key aspects of eHRM: its content, implementation approach, target audience and consequences.

eHRM: The Theory (2)

Academic literature has been exploring the development of HR technology for almost thirty years although to some extent research lags technology development. A general view in academic literature is that the subject remains under-theorized. As technology has developed, definitions have been based on a number of different perspectives:

Functionality view: This literature defines systems based on their ability to manage data at a technical level, a tool for processing data. **Walker (1986)** defines a Human Resources Information System (HRIS) as *"A systematic procedure for collecting, storing, maintaining, retrieving and validating data needed by an organisation about its human resources, personnel activities and organisation unit characteristics"*.

Role based View: **Voermans & Van Veldhoven (2007, p.887)** define e-HRM in terms of the role it has in the organisation: *"The administrative support of the HR function in organisations by using internet technology"*, again, focusing more on what technology is, rather than what it enables.

Technology as Enabler view: These definitions refer to what technology makes possible (enables) in terms of the broader impact on organisational capability and service provision, making a distinction between traditional processing capabilities and new ways of delivering HR services. Research by **Gardner, Lepak, & Bartol, 2003; Hempel, 2004; Marler, 2009 and Ruta, 2009** discusses how technology enables a move to a more strategic role and the mechanisms by which it does so. **Ruël et al (2004a)** and **Reddington & Martin (2006)** argue that while HRIS is directed inwardly at the HR department, e-HRM is focused outwards to the wider organisation and that it represents the *"Technical unlocking of HRIS for all employees of an organisation."* **Kavanagh, Guetal & Tannenbaum (1990)** refer to supporting strategic, tactical and operational decision making, evaluating programmes, policies and practices, supporting operations and providing management information.

Competitive Advantage View: Porter & Millar (1985) argued that the purpose of information technology was is transform the way that value activities are performed and the linkages between them, stating that *"Information technology has a powerful effect on competitive advantage in either cost or differentiation"* (p.156).

Evolutionary View: Others see e-HRM as a process of maturity and development **(Lengnick-Hall & Moritz, 2003)**, where the first stage is enabling the publication of HR information, a one way communication including policies, newsletters etc., developing into the automation of transactions including workflow and finally maturing into the full transformation of the HR function.

Symbolic View: **Tansley, Newell & Williams (2001)** see e-HRM partly as being symbolic, where technology is an organisational statement about new ways of working and delivering HR, using the concept of an 'e-greenfield' site to denote the symbolic effect of e-HRM, representing a break with existing employee relations practices, or a philosophical break with the past. Likewise, (Kovach and Cathcart 1999) saw that the use of e-HRM was a symbolic indicator of the desire to transform. At its most bold, technology provides opportunities for virtual and networked organisations, linking e-learning to knowledge management and the potential for new HR business models **(West & Berman, 2001; Martin et al., 2005).**

Reddington, Williamson & Withers (2005) claim that the greatest benefits of e-HRM arise when transformational outcomes are pursued to support and enable a more strategic approach.

e-HRM and the HR Delivery Model

HR service centres are increasingly being enabled by technology and the use of intranets, self-service (e-HRM) and call-centre technology (such as case management tools) provide the basis for many shared services and outsourcing arrangements. The business case for process technology can be very good, with savings typically indicating a 25% reduction in operational costs, or even higher in cases where processes are initially very poor (see Chapter 12). Following the introduction of technology, organisations generally see immediate improvements in service quality, because response is quicker and employee queries can be more readily answered. However, only technologically advanced HR Service Centres are likely to realise the full benefits of HR Business Transformation.

One of the implications of introducing self-service technology is that it requires the organisation to re-think how work flows through the service centre operation. In a non-technology based environment, where most HR transactions are based on paper, telephone/e-mail and personal contact, work is random and unstructured and must be allocated as it arrives. This often means that whoever makes initial contact with the employee deals with the enquiry, with the result that highly paid HR specialists can find themselves dealing with low level transactional enquiries or (perhaps worse) low level administrators find themselves totally lost in complex policy issues.

However, technology allows (or more strictly, **forces**) a new form of service delivery model to be put in place, based on a structured approach to the management of work. For example, within a Shared Services operation, a typical approach involves a multi-tier delivery structure, where specific activities are allocated to staff with defined skillsets (Reilly & Williams, 2003). This model ensures that the right problems are channeled to the right people and escalated appropriately. The Service Delivery Model shown in Figure 16 is often used in service centres, especially by professional managed service providers.

- **Self-service (Tier 0):** Technology such as employee and manager self-service, interactive telephone systems, web and e-mail forms deals with the majority of transactions and employees are encouraged to use technology rather than make personal contact. The target is that around 2 out of 3 requests (66%) are solved through automated technology, without human intervention or assistance. This reduces costs and speeds up transactions.

- **Human Interactions with Service Agents (Tier 1):** Should staff be unable to complete their transactions through Tier 0, service centre staff are available to handle unresolved queries and issues. Service agents are typically HR generalists who have a good knowledge of all processes provided by the contact centre. Fewer than 30% of queries should be escalated to this level.

- **Subject Matter Experts (SMEs) & Case Workers (Tier 2):** Tier 2 consists of subject matter experts and case workers that handle more complex requests passed to them through an escalation process. Industry standard data suggest that only about 5% of queries should reach Tier 2.

- **Policy Experts & Process Owners (Tier 3):** At Tier 3, only questions that potentially require new policy decisions or potentially policy changes should be managed. Industry standard data suggest that only about 1% should be dealt with at Tier 3.

For many organisations, implementing this model is a significant change from previous approaches. A tiered approach to service delivery ensures that the right skills are involved at the right time and routine transactions are dealt with by technology, reducing costs and improving service quality. Of course, this model is aspirational for many organisations and a transition to this way of working will not be immediate, with investment needed in process and job redesign, together with consideration of change and transition issues. Nevertheless, it forms the basis for service design and takes maximum advantage of technology.

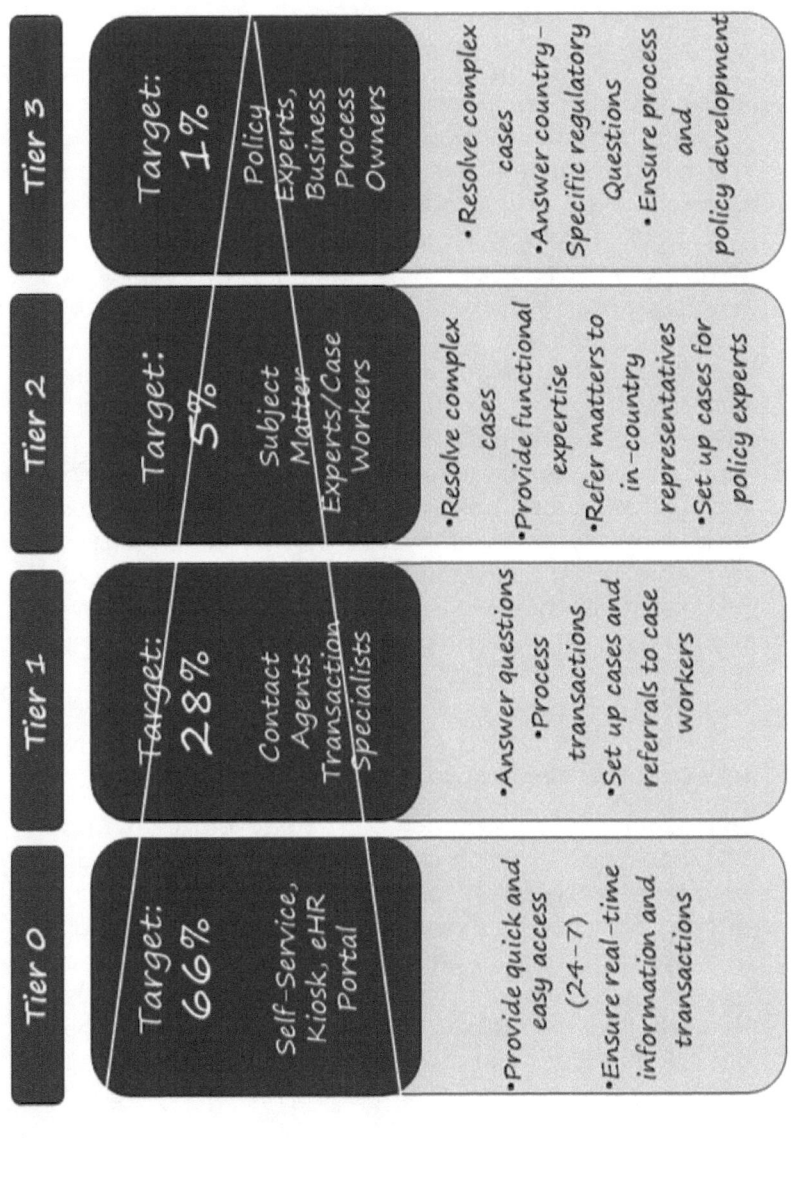

Figure 16: Target Service Delivery Model

e-HRM Strategies

Experience suggests that there is no 'one size fits all' for introducing e-HRM. Organisations typically follow one of three strategies (see Figure 17):

- **Replication:** This approach involves simply recreating the content and functions of the existing system(s). It is typically an IT 'refresh' activity, a strategy often followed because older technology becomes non-viable or is simply out of date. There is usually no desire to improve HR/Payroll processes or service quality – its intention is simply to reduce costs or avoid system obsolescence. Projects are relatively unambitious, with little vision and a focus only on technology, simplifying IT support and lower maintenance costs, rather than creating long-term business value. The main advantage of this approach is that it can be undertaken relatively quickly using technical resources. However, because there is no focus on business processes, it may result in missed opportunities to create business benefits and there is a risk that old processes will not work effectively under the new technology - end-users may have the same frustrations they had with the old system. It should only be undertaken in circumstances where old technology will absolutely fail if nothing is done and there is no time to take a more strategic approach.

- **Enhancement:** This approach can take several forms and it is shaped by intention and ambition - even when an entirely new system is purchased, organisations may decide that there should be only an incremental, *evolutionary* impact on HR service delivery and operations. There is often little appetite to use technology to drive through major changes; it may be that the organisation does not believe that radical change is possible, perhaps because it expects resistance, lack of resource or cost issues that prevent a full transformation. It may be that a strategy of 'change by stealth' is more appropriate, where the technology platform is developed over a period of time. However, by playing safe, organisations may not achieve the Return on Investment needed and the lack of a technology champion or adequate resource means that projects may not get beyond the initial implementation phase; it may have the same impact as if a pure Replication strategy had been pursued.

- A **Transformational** approach: Technology is part of a wider strategy, enabling highly devolved HR services, making managers more accountable, where the HR function takes on a more substantial role. It involves a *revolutionary* restructuring of HR service delivery, including the use of service centres, outsourcing and the Business Partnering model. For an organisation under cost pressure to transform HR services, this is a better strategy. The vision often includes giving on-line access to processes, policies and procedures and extensive self-service. Technology has a truly transformational role under this approach, with a major impact on the organisation, changing the roles of HR, managers and perhaps even employees. It is not an easy option and requires a large investment in infrastructure and resources to make it work, with an emphasis on managing the changes. However, the business case typically offers a good payback.

Organisations have a choice as to which technology strategy to pursue and the approach typically depends on factors such as culture, expectation, previous experience, an awareness of what is possible and the strength of the business case. These ideas are explored in greater depth in the 'Barriers to eHRM Adoption' section in this chapter.

The Technology Adoption Lifecycle

Research data from CedarCrestone (2012b) reveals that many HR functions are slow to adopt HR technologies. As Figure 18 illustrates, although almost 95% of all organisations are now using basic e-HRM administrative applications, the adoption of tools such as employee and manager self-service is substantially lower, being used by just over half of organisations surveyed. The use of strategic HCM applications such as talent management, performance management, learning, compensation and succession planning software is also relatively low, with substantially less than half of all organisations using these applications. This data may be surprising given the potential benefits of technology, raising important questions about HR's apparent reluctance to adopt technology.

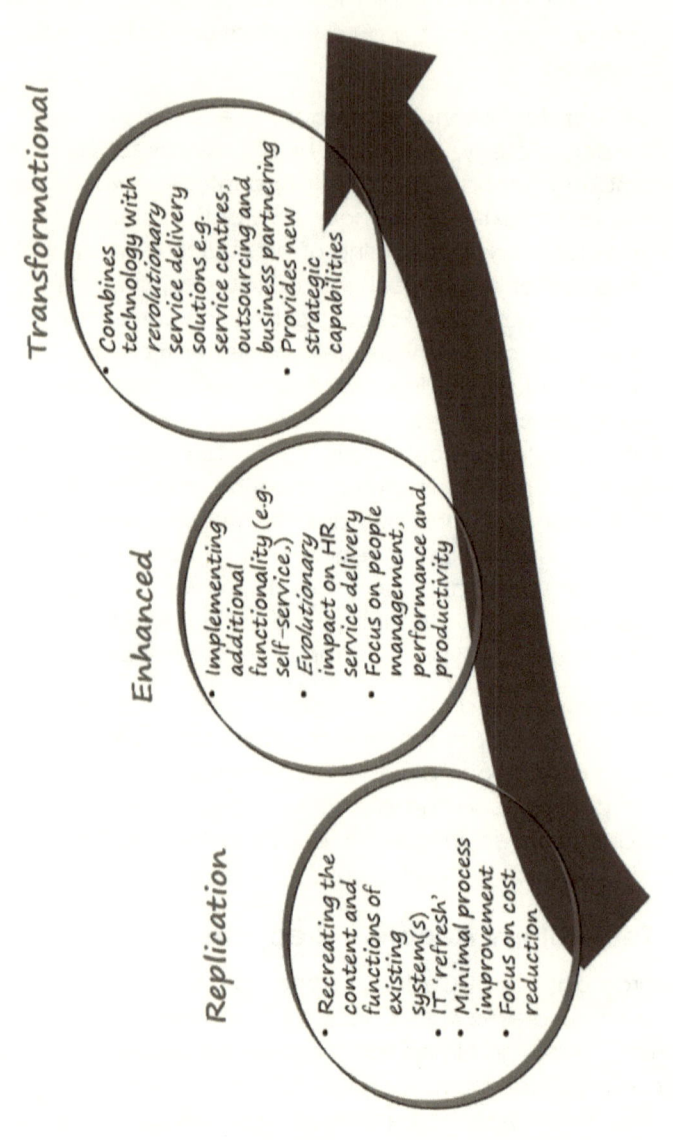

FIGURE 17: E-HRM STRATEGIES

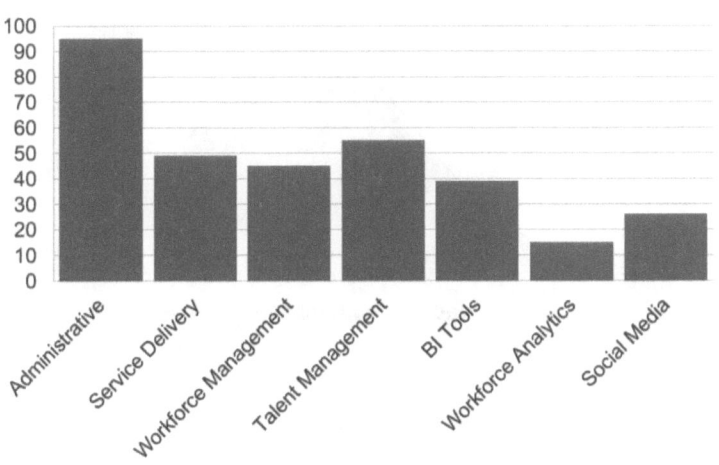

FIGURE 18: HR TECHNOLOGY ADOPTION RATES

SOURCE: CEDARCRESTONE HR TECHNOLOGY SURVEY 2012-2013

The technology adoption lifecycle was devised by Geoffrey Moore (1991) to explain why different groups adopt technology at different rates (see Figure 19). Firstly, there are the 'Innovators' who aggressively pursue technological developments, often making a technology purchase for the pure pleasure of possessing the latest gadget. Even though new technologies contain software bugs and may occasionally fail, innovators are happy to take the risk simply for the experience of being one of the first to use it. Others are naturally 'Early Adopters', a group of less extreme, lower-order 'geeks', who appreciate the benefits of technology, want it early (but not urgently) and will only wait a relatively short time before they are itching to experiment. Consider when Apple releases a new version of the i-phone or i-pad, creating a buzz of excitement – fans will camp out overnight outside Apple stores just to be the first to get hold of the latest technology.

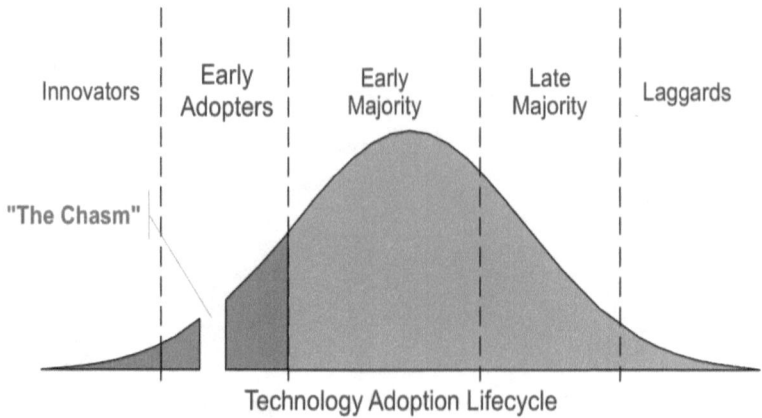

FIGURE 19: TECHNOLOGY ADOPTION LIFECYCLE

(Adapted from Moore, 1991)

Between the Innovators and Early Adopters groups, there is a gap, which Moore referred to as 'The Chasm'. It's a problem faced by any hot new technology, especially if it's not readily seen as a strategic leap forward for the non-technologist. For a technology to cross this gap, it must do more than simply appeal to a desire to own technology - it must demonstrate its value and a firm return on investment.

Behind Early Adopters come the large 'Early Majority' group, who expect a fully established product and some evidence that it is stable. It's only when technology starts to become fully mainstream that the Early Majority is prepared to make the investment; while Early Adopters are willing to invest time to become technologically competent and understand the implementation issues, the Early Majority is not willing to make much effort. Early Adopters do not make compelling reference customers for potential members of the Early Majority.

The 'Late Majority', is a group that is not only cynical about the benefits of technology, but also doubts its own ability to handle and make effective use of it. For the Late Majority, the technology must be so easy to understand and the business case so obvious that its use is beyond doubt. This group is looking for absolute guarantees and needs lots of help and support.

Technology Adoption: The Theory

Theoretical approaches to technology adoption are typically founded on the principle that a set of beliefs is formed about technology and actions are taken as a result of those beliefs, either positively or negatively. For example, the Technology Acceptance Model (TAM) **(Davis, Bagozzi, & Warshaw, 1989)**, the Theory of Reasoned Action (TRA) **(Ajzen & Fishbein, 1980)** and the Theory of Planned Behaviour (TPB) **(Ajzen, 1991; Venkatesh et al, 2003)** are based on the core concept that if individuals perceive that technology will help them to achieve job related outcomes, they are more likely to use such systems.

Rogers' (1995) Diffusion of Innovation Theory (DIT) model proposed that any new technology should have relative advantage over previous methods, be compatible with existing values and needs, be easily understood, have the potential for experimentation and be capable of observable results.

Martin, Massy, & Clarke (2003) believe the idea of 'absorptive capacity' to be important, both for understanding and realising the potential of technology. **Zahra & George (2002)** identify absorptive capacity as the acquisition, assimilation, transformation and exploitation of new knowledge to produce a new organisational capability. Those with higher absorptive capacity (i.e. those better able to make sense of its potential) will be better able to exploit technology and will adopt it more quickly. Other approaches to adoption suggest that managerial involvement in the design **(Preece, 1988)** and learning processes **(Bondarouk, 2006)** are important to successful adoption. Likewise, **Tansley, Newell & Williams (2001)** identified that a lack of awareness and understanding of HR systems, combined with a 'silo' mentality towards implementation and the independent mapping of HR processes by technologists tends to limit e-HRM development.

The Late Majority group expect case studies, defined service levels, product roadmaps and penalty clauses before they will invest in any new technology and even then, it's with a high degree of caution. Finally, the 'Laggards' are those that will only switch to new technologies when it is completely unavoidable and there is no longer a choice. For example, when cassette tapes were no longer available, the laggards finally upgraded to CDs or possibly MP3 players, but complained incessantly about how unfair it was that they were being forced to change. They will be the last to switch to electric cars, solar panels and hover boots.[12]

Although no research has been conducted into HR's position along this curve, my own non-empirical observations suggest that few HR people are in either the 'Innovators' or 'Early Adopters' group; cynically, I suspect few would be classed as Early Majority.

Barriers to e-HRM Adoption

Although e-HRM offers enormous potential, in practice organisation often implement only a small proportion of the functionality available. In many cases, organisations have bought the functionality but failed to switch it on or use it its full extent – this is like having a powerful car parked in the garage that is used for only short, low speed journeys. Yet, if the technology to implement e-HRM is available and provides significant benefits, it raises the obvious question, *"Why isn't doesn't every organisation deploy the maximum amount of HR technology"?* Several crucial factors influence the adoption of eHRM:

> **Competitive Strategy:** HR technology strategy should be directly related to the HR and competitive business strategy of the organisation. Where the overall strategy is solely based on lowering the cost of production, a simple e-HRM replication strategy is more likely. However, if the

---

[12] Hover boots are the benchmark for technical progress, together with the personal hovercraft and a teleportation machine, all of which have been promised by scientists. All I ask for is a phone that works everywhere.

competitive strategy is based on innovation or differentiation, the organisation is more likely to focus on good people management, leading to an enhancement or (ideally) transformational approach to technology (Wright, Gardner, & Moynihan, 2003). Highly cost-focused, low-margin organisations (for example, those in the distribution, basic manufacturing, catering and facilities management sectors) will find it harder to justify an investment in sophisticated people management technologies, whereas knowledge-based organisations such as those in the technology, pharmaceutical and professional services sectors are likely to view people as unique differentiators where 'talent management' is critical.

- **Size of the Business:** Larger organisations may be more willing to invest in complex e-HRM systems because they have access to larger budgets and other resources, as well as having a larger employee population to manage, reducing the per-employee cost. Larger organisations are also more likely to deploy a large ERP system, of which the HR module forms part of the infrastructure.

- **Management Perceptions of the HR Role:** If managers want HR to take a more strategic approach to HR, they will tend to be more supportive of e-HRM and favour a transformational approach; however, where employees and managers see HR as passive and transactional, they will tend to have a more negative attitude towards e-HRM. In some cases, line managers may see employee and manager self-service as a potential barrier to their relationship with HR (Voermans & Van Veldhoven, 2007).

- **HR Perception of Technology:** If HR teams perceive technology to be too technical, it will be difficult to make the transition. In some cases, e-HRM leaves HR professionals cold or at best, disinterested, especially where its use is perceived as a transactional, administrative activity that does not enhance HR's strategic reputation. For many HR professionals, e-HRM remains merely an administrative tool and its role in the development of strategic HR practice is often discounted; there is an underlying sense that somehow 'people'

people do not need to understand or use technology. This may partly explain why the majority of HR technology investments remain at the basic administrative/operational level; only obvious cost reduction is seen as a viable outcome of the use of technology, limiting its use to the most basic processing functions.

- **Lack of Technical Infrastructure:** It's easy for those who regularly have access to a computer at work to access e-HRM technology – a simple web link will take them to a wide range of services – but what of those that work outside, on factory floors or in remote environments? The answer so far has been to provide employee kiosks in cafeterias or other common areas, but there are issues of privacy and lack of time in the working day that mean this is a limited solution. However, the next few years are likely to see a reduction in the cost of tablet and smartphone technologies that will solve this problem and enable people to access HR services anywhere, anytime.

- **The 'Burning Platform' just isn't Hot Enough:** Things only get done when there is a strong, compelling reason for change. In e-HRM terms, the trigger for change can include organisational pressure to reduce costs, a new business strategy or even a change of leader. If everyone accepts that the current situation is good enough, then nothing will get done, whatever the reality.

- **Lack of a Technology Champion:** E-HRM projects are often led by IT specialists who tend to focus on the underlying technology rather than the opportunities for improvements in people management. Transformational strategies in particular require a persuasive leader to create a vision and help others to understand how technology will contribute to HR and management capability. Often, when a significant thought leader leaves a project, the project stagnates and little further development takes place.

- **Inability to Translate Business Requirements into Technology Requirements:** Many HR functions fail to connect the business problem to a technology solution. This is often based on a low level of technical HR Systems knowledge and lack of a clear understanding about 'the art of the possible' with regard to e-HRM and the opportunities for improving HR service. Many organisations are 'Late Majority' adopters, tending to wait to see what their competitors do before they commit, rather than leading the way. There may also be concerns that technology will somehow de-humanise the workplace and there is a view that technology isn't **real** HR work. While many customers of HR technology have become very sophisticated in their awareness of what's possible, multi-disciplinary teams are more likely to understand the relationship between what the business requires and what technology offers.

- **The Project Team Went Home:** Projects have a natural life cycle and by definition are temporary. Most organisations are able to complete the first phase of their project successfully, usually involving the implementation of Payroll and/or basic HR functions. At this point, project teams often breathe a sigh of relief and return to their day jobs, proud of their achievements. The period immediately after the go-live stage is so caught up with fine-tuning the system and fixing teething problems that no attention is given to the next phase, resulting in inertia. In the rush to deliver against milestones, no time is given to developing the next phase and there is no resource left to think about it (or the original project team has the wrong mix of skills to work on the next phase). A common result is that no further progress is made and any plans to implement or develop functionality such as self-service evaporate. Successful organisations avoid this to some extent by backfilling key roles to allow Subject Matter Experts to get closely involved with projects.

- **Inability to Translate Requirements into a Viable Business Case:** Making any kind of technology investment requires a strong business case, to quantify the benefits of technology and the impact on the organisation. If the project has been very technology-centred or has focused mainly on administrative processes, there may not be a good understanding of what might be possible at the next level. As Chapter 12 points out, HR functions often lack the skills to prepare and present a business case for making the change and may struggle to place a value on the contribution of technology.

It's All in the Cloud

Recent years have seen much discussion about 'The Cloud'. Cloud computing is seen as the next stage in the Internet's evolution, providing the means through which everything — from software applications, processing, storage, infrastructure and even entire business processes - can be delivered as a service to end-users. Of course, the 'cloud' is simply a metaphor and in reality, the technology is not actually in the sky, but in traditional data centres. However, the term suggests open, accessible technologies, alluding to its ethereal nature.

Organisations currently spend around 80% of their IT budget on maintaining their existing infrastructure, including everything from desktop office systems to complex business systems (Gartner, 2011). Suppliers of Cloud technologies can generate huge economies of scale that create lower costs for end users, needing a lower initial investment and offering predictable ongoing costs. It's often more cost-effective than traditional 'on-premise' solutions, where the organisation runs its own infrastructure and applications. The services can be easily scaled up or down and the end-user doesn't need to be concerned about managing the underlying technology – that's the job of the supplier. However, cloud computing demands that both provider and consumer accept certain obligations, for example, consumers must take responsibility for the governance of data and services in the cloud and providers must ensure a predictable and guaranteed service level, together with strong security to consumers

The HR sector is now starting to take notice of The Cloud, for example, where it increasingly forms part of an outsourcing contract. New projects often include the provision of cloud technologies to deliver end services through a 'Software as a Service' (SaaS) arrangement. The real power of HR-focused SaaS is in the potential to rethink and redesign HR delivery at a fundamental level; according to consultancy Deloitte (2012), SaaS-enabled HR transformations can help HR to accelerate talent strategies (workforce planning, performance, succession management, etc.), revenue growth (M&A, business transformation, globalisation) and operational excellence (workforce intelligence, HR policy, culture, and communications).

Another emerging trend is Business Process as a Service (BPaaS), an extension to SaaS where a customer buys not only access to cloud based software, but a fully configured set of business processes supported by a service delivery model.

Planning and Selecting e-HRM

Planning is an important aspect of an e-HRM project. However, as Sir John Harvey Jones, ex-Chairman of ICI said, "*People don't like to plan - it's more fun just to do*". Although time spent planning improves project outcomes, senior managers usually push for things to happen quickly, creating a risk that a project will be rushed, shortcuts will be taken and compromises made. Its polar opposite is that organisations spend all their time planning without actually doing anything, to the point where the business, people and technology move on and assumptions become worthless.

One of the key success factors in both selecting and implementing technology is the creation of a robust vision. In eHRM projects, planning is everything – the initial vision is important, based on an analysis of what the business needs and an understanding of the implications of the vision. A vision is more than a list of requirements or a project plan – it's about painting a picture of the future HR landscape and how people might behave and act differently as a result. Successful projects have a good vision, grounded in clear business terms and are fully understood by all stakeholders for the project. The vision addresses basic questions such as: "*Which processes will be supported*"? "*How will it enable HR to deliver services differently*"? "*How will it help managers to be more productive?*" "*What management information will it provide*"? The vision provides the basis for design of new business process, a sound functional and technical specification and finally a configuration/build that follows the model defined. Without a vision, an e-HRM project is likely to lack focus and the resulting implementation may disappoint those involved.

Creating a vision is a little like searching for a new house – you don't go to a (real) estate agent with a list of building materials and wiring diagrams, instead you develop a broad set of requirements about where the house will be located, how many rooms it will have and how you might use each of them. House searches rarely specify details such as what colour the walls are and what furniture it should contain – these can be 'configured' later. The decision is in part about meeting your basic needs, but it's also a statement about how the house will make you **feel** - an emotional reaction about how well it fits your lifestyle, the size of your family, your household budget and the way you live. Although it's unusual to talk about feelings and emotions when discussing technology, when organisations make poor technology decisions, the sense of disappointment and frustration is entirely emotional and the planning process should be structured to avoid this. Despite the analytical logic of selection processes, technology selection decisions usually have a strong emotional component to them that sometimes outweighs rational decision making (just don't tell those nice people in Procurement!).

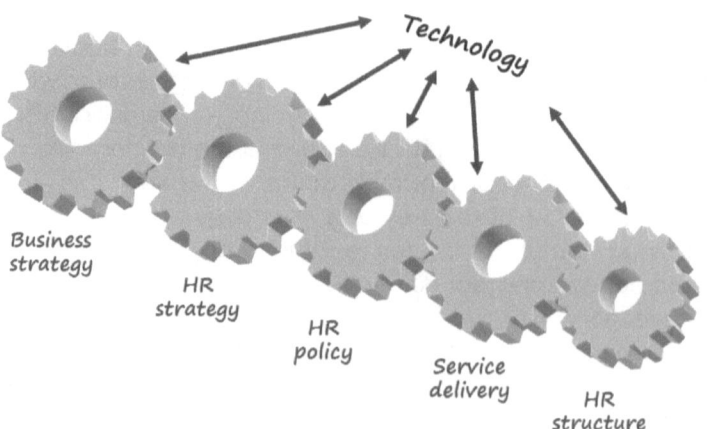

FIGURE 20: E-HRM STRATEGY LINKAGES

As Figure 20 illustrates, the technology strategy must be strongly linked to the business and HR strategies of the organisation, the policies in place to deliver the HR strategy, how HR services are to be provided and how HR will in turn be structured to deliver those services (for example, shared services, Centres of Expertise and so on). Each component acts like a cog in a machine - technology is both a driver of and is driven by each of the cogs. Selection decisions should be based on ensuring that technology supports what the organisation wants at each of these points.

It's important to remember that e-HRM is ultimately a *business system*, intended for the benefit of the business (not just the HR function) and a good HR system should define its success in terms of its overall contribution to the business rather than just the internal benefits to the HR function. It's essential to define the problem that's being addressed by technology and regularly asking the question '*What is the fire we're trying to put out*'? will help to frame the vision and technology selection decision. A key first step is to understand the business drivers for investing in HR technology and set out clearly what it needs to achieve, a stage that demands some 'big picture' thinking before the business case is developed. Consider how business processes will change and what functionality will be required to support these new processes. For example:

- Is the business simply seeking cost reduction or is there a specific service quality problem?
- Will it help to engage line managers more in HR activities and make them more accountable?
- Is it a problem only the HR function perceives or is it shared by line managers?
- Would line managers see the technology as adding any value, or is it just about HR experimenting with some new technology?

A good starting point is to ask line managers directly for their opinions, perhaps by creating a vision that shows how their time might be spent differently with e-HRM tools and the benefits it could create. Workshops, interviews, focus groups and visioning sessions are all good ways to shape expectations and build support for the project.

When searching for new technology, organisations often make mistakes that leas them to make the wrong choices. One involves the initial definition of requirements during preparation of the Invitation to Tender (ITT) document. In this stage, prospective software buyers often set out a long (sometimes **very** long!) list of system functions they want, leading to a check list that can include every possible item of data that might be handled. However, a modern HR system is more than just a collection of data fields – what really counts is how the system handles the data, makes it all work together and how it is ultimately presented to end users. During the procurement process, it's much more important to understand how the technology will support the overall process rather than to think in terms of data fields or the functionality of specific modules. Excessively robust procurement processes can sometimes be counter-productive, by focusing on technology 'inputs' rather than business 'outputs'. The same principle applies even if you're just trying to get more from your existing system – asking the question *"Is there any functionality we're not using?"* will probably limit your thinking. Ask instead *"We have a problem with this process – what can the technology do to improve it?"*

A further flaw in the selection decision occurs when technical issues overshadow HR business needs. While it's natural that there will be some technical input into the process to ensure that whatever is implemented will work with the rest of the corporate technology infrastructure, it's easy to get caught up in technology and end up with something that meets the requirements of the IT function but fails to give HR what it really needs. If HR has to compromise its requirements to fit in with corporate technology demands, or the technology choice results in HR plugging gaps in processes in other ways (messy workarounds or 'clunky' interfaces), then it's essential that business outcomes take priority.

I will return to this topic in Chapter 12 when building a business case is discussed.

Guidelines for System Design: Go Configure

Even when a packaged HR system is bought (sometimes known as a 'Commercial Off-The Shelf or COTS solution), there is a need to configure it to the specific requirements of the business. Configuration involves building or adapting entirely new functionality, whereas configuration is about set up, alignment and adjustment of what already exists. A useful comparison is when you buy a new car, you 'configure' the mirror, driving position and radio settings to suit your personal preferences; however, if you replaced the engine or changed the colour, you would be 'customising'. However, the configuration stage should not be under-estimated – getting this right can make the difference between an effective system and one that is hard to use and fails to meet business needs. A design is needed and the following principles should be taken into account:

○ **Focus on Business Processes:** Business process design should be the starting point for any system design. Even if technology acquisition is based on a simple replication strategy (see the section on eHRM strategies) some form of change to business processes is inevitable - because software packages are based on an underlying process / workflow model, it's simply not possible to introduce new technology without making changes to business processes. Chapter 11 discusses the importance of business process improvement, including a review of potential approaches.

○ **Focus on Business Outcomes:** As discussed in the previous section, developing a clear vision for what the system needs to do is critical. Rather than looking at technology inputs, the vision should focus on what impact technology will have on the business, based on either a good business case or a series of principles that demonstrate the types of changes the business will experience.

○ **Don't 'Design Out' Future Options:** The worst design error is to create a system with built-in obsolescence. For example, failing to design a robust position hierarchy can mean it's more difficult to introduce self-service in a later phase. Even if your initial approach is based on a 'replication' strategy, the decisions made in the first phase will have consequences for later development. If business processes are likely to change in the future, this requirement should be included in the initial planning rather than have to undo the work at a later time. It really comes back to the visioning phase – how much will business processes change and what will be different? Is self-service important to the organisation and when will it be implemented? Is this a major transformation in the way HR works or only a slight change in tactics? Once again, it's important to understand what problem is being solved – choose the wrong tools or solve the wrong problem and you'll make an expensive mistake.

- **Make HR the 'Master' Source of Data:** There's a critical decision to be made early on in the planning phase – will the HR system be the ultimate source of people data? This is sometimes known as the *'single source of the truth'* argument – which system are you going to trust when data in the finance system is different from what's in HR? There is a strong argument for making the HR system the master source of people data, even though people data may reside in several other technologies, for example, a time and attendance system, a billing system or a separate resource management system. Other core systems such as those operated by the Finance Department may hold salary data for budgetary purposes, but it may not change in real time or even reflect the actual employee salary; for example, it may be held as the average for a grade or include additional elements such as the labour burden.

- **Focus on Business Change and Transition**: This topic is addressed more fully in Chapter 13 but it's worth making the point here also. Unless the new system is actually capable of being implemented and the organisation can manage the changes, no amount of technology will make a difference!

At design workshops, I often ask clients to brainstorm their key design principles for a project. It's a good way to get project teams to establish guidelines that will help them make process based decisions throughout the project and to ask important questions. Some responses may seem as obvious, but they nevertheless force the team to find common ground and ensure everyone is thinking in the same direction.

There is a remarkably high level of consistency across organisations when it comes to this activity, with the most typical responses being shown in the following pages as a list of 'Top Ten Design Principles':

1. Business processes will be automated as far as possible (if transaction volumes are sufficient).

2. Any processes that do not add value or are not required for compliance will be eliminated.

3. Business processes will be standardised across the business.

4. Local variations will only be allowed if there are policies and procedures that cannot easily be changed in the short term and there is a clear business case for allowing variation.

5. Processes will be shaped by the functionality the HR system can provide; processes will be adapted to work with what the system offers, rather than the other way around

6. Standard system configuration will be used as far as possible and system customisation will be avoided (although interfaces to other systems may be required).

7. Data will be entered into the system once only and as close to the source of the data as possible (ideally, applicants, employees and managers should enter their own data).

8. Approval processes through self-service will be simple (within audit requirements), done by people who understand what is being asked for and have authority to approve.

9. Adequate controls will be put in place to ensure compliance, consistent with internal audit requirements.

10. Change management and transition issues will be considered as part of process design.

FIGURE 21: TOP 10 DESIGN PRINCIPLES

Integrated Solutions or Best of Breed?

The HR function often has to make a choice between selecting an Enterprise Resource Planning (ERP) based solution or buying 'Best of Breed' software.[13] Since their development in the 1970s, ERP systems have emerged as a solution to the problem of managing large volumes of data and overcoming the need for multiple software applications. IT Directors have been attracted to the idea that software from a single supplier can meet all their business needs, improve processes and reduce the cost of operation. The major suppliers – SAP, Oracle, Microsoft, Lawson, Sage and around 15 others – operate in a global market worth around $24billion, covering all areas of business from finance, logistics, manufacturing and of course, Human Resources (now often called Human Capital Management in ERP systems). One definition of ERP systems is *"A form of integrated computer system architecture that spans multiple business functions in an organisation, to facilitate the flow of information inside the business and manage connections to outside stakeholders"*. This effectively means that there is one single, integrated software program in place, covering all business functions in real-time, with a common look and feel and all data potentially available to all users throughout the system.

The alternative to ERP is the 'Best of Breed' approach, where the organisation evaluates all the suppliers in a market and selects what it considers to be the best within each functional area. For example, it may select a financial management system because it can comply with certain accounting procedures, but choose a customer management system from another supplier because it fits their particular business model better. The ERP v Best of Breed debate attempts to balance the seeming technical efficiency of large scale unified systems against the advantages of specialised systems that are designed for a specific business function. Both

---

[13] The original use of this phrase is of course in the context of competitive dog shows, with the winner of Best of Breed (BoB) going on to compete in Best in Show.

strategies are equally viable and the decision depends on some fundamental strategic and operational decisions.

ERP: The Pros & Cons

For many large organisations, the ERP decision is based on the fundamental premise that business processes should be managed through the use of software provided by the same software supplier.

1. **Advantages of ERP**

The advantages of ERP systems are:

- ✓ ERP contains an overall business model that provides organisations with an inherent set of business processes, linking together different organisational functions and ensuring the most efficient flow of data.

- ✓ ERP links physically separate business processes such as order tracking, finance and Human Capital Management, based on common data sets. ERP eliminates the time delay that can prevent accurate forecasting, for example, allowing inventory and resourcing estimates to be kept at an optimum level.

- ✓ Because ERP Systems centralise data in one place, they eliminate the problem of synchronising changes between multiple systems and the consolidation, for example, of different finance, payroll and manufacturing applications.

- ✓ ERP links revenue, cost and profit data at a high level of detail, enabling real-time financial modelling.

2. **Disadvantages of ERP**

The disadvantages of ERP systems are:

- ✗ ERPs are often seen as too rigid and too difficult to adapt to the specific workflow and business process of some companies.

- The re-engineering of business processes to fit the "industry standard" prescribed by the ERP system may lead to a loss of competitive advantage. Some organisations operate unique, value-adding processes that provide a competitive edge but these often do not fit within the limits of highly structured ERP systems.

- Implementing ERP is expensive and buyers often report substantial cost and time overruns against their original budget. Once an ERP system is established, switching costs are very high, leading to dependence on a single supplier and lack of organisational flexibility. In some cases, project costs spiral out of control – in November 2012, the US Air Force abandoned its plans to implement an ERP system after spending the first $1 billion, concluding that finishing it would cost far too much more money for too little gain.[14]

- In theory, ERP systems should allow organisations to consolidate support around a common set of skills. However, in practice, ERP systems require different specialist skills across each application – so the Finance module needs different skills from Logistics and different skills again for Human Capital Management. Organisations may therefore have to hire in additional consultants to get the range of skills needed.

- Research has found an inherent paradox in ERP - organisations with the scale needed to justify an ERP system may be the least equipped to derive benefits from the technology (Botta-Genoulez, Miller & Grabot (in Lengnick-Hall & Lengnick-Hall, 2006); Dery & Wailes, 2005). Organisations that are mechanistic, dominated by routine, highly programmed technologies and tightly regulated operations present the best initial fit with ERP requirements but are the least able to capitalise on the information potential these systems provide. However

---

[14] Reported by Computer World, November 13, 2012, *"Air Force scraps massive ERP project after racking up $1 billion in costs"*

those that are flexible and adaptable are the best placed to create value from the knowledge but are often a poor fit with the requirements (and budget) of ERP systems.

Best of Breed: The Pros and Cons

Best of Breed (BoB) refers to the use of the best product of its type for performing a particular function. In the case of HR and Payroll, it relates to software that has been specifically designed to meet the needs of the HR function rather than being a module in a larger ERP system. Specialist vendors in this market have one single objective - to produce the best possible HR and Payroll software. To be successful, these vendors must stay close to their markets and continuously improve and develop functionality that reflects not only legislative change but the changing needs of its customers. This specialisation means that software designers build up expertise and are able to focus on developing functionality and tools for their market, in some cases for a specific industry vertical or specialised function (for example, an online recruitment tool).

1. Advantages of BoB

The advantages of Best of Breed HR applications are:

- ✓ Best of breed software providers are typically quicker to respond to market trends and the requirements of particular sectors.

- ✓ Each Best of Breed component can be implemented as a stand-alone application. This incremental approach subjects the organisation to smaller amounts of change, reducing organisational trauma.

- ✓ Best of Breed HR software contains an inherent best practice business model that is specific to the function rather than the overall flow of organisational data. As such, HR functions have greater freedom to review business processes and change their approach and organisation structure.

- ✓ Although integration is often cited as a reason for selecting ERP, the reality is that integration need not be complicated or expensive. In an HR context, most organisations need only 10-12 key integration points to link the HR / Payroll system to Finance (for example transferring transactions to the General Ledger and providing basic data to populate headcount tables).

2. **Disadvantages of BoB**

The disadvantages of Best of Breed HR applications are:

- ✗ The potential cost of evaluating all options within a given market to identify the most appropriate software may be prohibitive. In the HR market, there are many potential providers with very different offerings, which can confuse or delay selection decisions.

- ✗ Perhaps the strongest argument against Best of Breed applications is that they are often produced by small, start-up organisations that initially get a good foothold in the market, become popular but cannot then sustain the growth needed. This has been particularly true of highly specialised providers that operate in niche markets – for example, when flexible benefits initially became popular, several small providers launched web-based systems to support flex and many subsequently went out of business, leaving customers with unsupported systems. The solution is to thoroughly check the financial status of any software vendor.

- ✗ The need for the organisation to acquire a different set of skills to support specialised software. Increasingly, support contracts are available to minimise the burden of maintaining these skills; organisations are also turning to cloud-based solutions to transfer the organisational system management overhead outside the business.

Is the use of HR Technology an HR Practice?

Technology can have a major impact on the way that HR works – for example, US research suggests that greater use of technology is associated with taking on a more strategic HR role (Lawler & Mohrman, 2003). HR is most likely to be a full strategic HR partner when effective HR technology is in place - not just because it allows access to better strategic data, but also because it increases the reach of HR, making line managers more self-sufficient and improving communications across the organisation. Although simply having technology won't automatically make HR more strategic, one study (Cedar Crestone study, 2012) suggested that top performing companies appear to use HR technology in different ways from lower performing companies. Performance was judged by a number of factors, including revenue and profit per employee, operating income growth and return on equity. The study found that top performers had a number of technology related characteristics, including:

- Top performers have more HR technologies in place and spend less on technology per employee. Top performers have higher rates of technology adoption and typically spend less on it (around 12% lower cost per employee).

- They avoid extensive customisation of their HR Technology – top performers tend to adopt systems as packages, choosing to configure rather than customise their technology.

- Higher adoption of employee and manager self-service – self-service functionality is used in 81% of organisations whereas poorer performers have adoption rates around 62%.

- Processes are standardised and tend to be delivered through service centres. Eighty four per cent of top performing organisations use a service centre approach to deliver HR and Payroll services.

- Top performers have an integrated talent management system on the same platform as the core HRMS solution. Seventy per cent of top performers use a common talent platform.

- Top performers have more sophisticated business intelligence solutions and are more likely to put them in the hands of their managers.

Summary: HR Technology

Technology is possibly the biggest investment that any HR function will make and it's important to get it right. HR Ready functions are built on effective technology which underpins it processes, policy and strategy. As HR technology becomes increasingly sophisticated, its use will shape perceptions internally and externally; getting the best from the system involves more than simply a technical implementation. Selecting and implementing technology will be a critical HR Practice for HR Ready organisations - good system design, based on well-designed business processes, innovative service delivery and relevant Business Intelligence, together with a focus on change and transition will make the difference between failure and success. Future HR leaders will need to have a good grasp of what technology can achieve and how to derive benefits from it and in particular, manage the changes associated with its introduction.

HR Technology: Are you HR Ready?

- [?] Is there a long-term vision for the development of e-HRM?
- [?] Is there a business case for the extended use of technology?
- [?] How often is technology reviewed to ensure it meets business needs?
- [?] Are the main barriers to eHRM cultural or technical?
- [?] Is there a champion who will drive forward future development?
- [?] Does your system design address the most important business requirements?
- [?] Are you (personally and organisationally) an early adopter, later majority or a laggard?

HR Strategy

Without competitors there would be no need for strategy, for the sole purpose of strategic planning is to enable the company to gain, as effectively as possible, a sustainable edge over its competitors

Keniche Ohmae (1982)

From Business Strategy to HR Strategy

HR strategies vary immensely across organisations. They may consist of a few bullet points on a single page, or amount to thick volumes containing a detailed analysis of every aspect of Human Resources Management. Some strategies are well thought through, dealing with important issues about the 'how' as well as the 'what', 'why' and 'when; others merely pretend to be strategies, based on generic, meaningless statements that lack real substance, referring to being 'an employer of choice', 'supporting line managers' and 'contributing to cost reduction'. A good HR strategy helps business leaders move from the uncertainty of complex goals and performance measures to clarifying its priorities and is is critical for any organisation wishing to become HR Ready because it addresses the fundamental question of *'Ready for what?'* and *'What do we need to do to become HR Ready?'*

What is 'Strategy'?

The word 'strategy' is generally abused, misinterpreted and often misappropriated in modern business. An entire chapter could be filled with the difference between a plan, a tactic, an approach, a scheme, a methodology and a strategy. Interesting though that might be, it would be counter-productive to this book, since what matters is where strategy fits into the development of an HR Ready organisation. So, in simple terms, strategy includes an assessment of the present, speculation about what might happen in the future, a view of what needs to happen, together with a vision, a series of actions and a defined outcome. It's a giant 'what if' assessment that might change at any time depending on the variables that were taken first into account.

The word 'strategy' derives from a Greek word 'strategia', meaning "office of general, command, generalship", rather than the planning process we now understand in modern business. In fact, the term 'strategy' did not come into general use in Britain until the late 18th century – it's interesting to think that the strategies behind the Roman and Greek empires that lasted for centuries were built without a proper term for them. Just think – no strategy meetings, no strategic planning managers, no need to spend months working on strategic documents only to store them on the top shelf at the basilica (although the Romans and Greeks probably had some clear, simple well-defined mission statements about ruling the known world!). The roots of strategy are mostly military in nature and can be traced back to classic works such as Sun Tzu's *The Art of War* and Machiavelli's *'The Prince'*, although these works tend to present strategy in a somewhat sinister context. When used in a business sense, strategic management typically provides overall direction to the enterprise and deals with initiatives that shape its long-term performance, usually with some reference to the organisation's mission, vision, objectives, policies and plans. Strategies also allocate the resources (people, equipment and funding) needed to implement the plans. The following are generally thought to be the benefits of having a strategy:

- It defines strengths, weaknesses, opportunities and barriers in achieving business objectives.

- It prompts new thinking about people issues - focusing and educating participants and providing a wider perspective.

- It tests management commitment to actions, creating a process for allocating resources to specific programs and activities.

- It develops a sense of urgency and commitment to action.

- It focuses on selected long-term courses of action that are considered to be a high in priority over the next X to Y years.

- It provides a strategic focus for managing the HR function and developing HR staff talents.

As the Breakout Boxes show, many definitions of strategy are available, but a simple one that gets straight to the point comes from Paul Kearns. It's *'The art of joining all the separate elements into one coherent whole'* (Kearns, 2003, p7). In short, "*What are we going to do next?*"

Developing Strategy

Strategic Human Resource Management grew to prominence in the early 1990's, in what was a decade of great change for the function. As its name suggests, it emphasises the need to establish a close, two-way relationship between business strategy and HR strategy. Strategic Human Resource Management also stressed the need for a shift in the role of management to enable, empower and facilitate workplace relationships. These new models emphasised a shift from the previous Management / Trade Union relations model which had existed since the 1950s based on conflict management, to a Management / Employee Relations model, which saw building relationships as important, where staff are managed in order to maximise their commitment to the organisation. Ulrich et al (2009) believe that an HR strategy should answer three basic questions:

- **Who are You:** What is the vision for the HR function, how will to be perceived, what does the HR brand represent?

- **What do you Deliver:** How will HR create value, including defining the capabilities the organisation needs to build to be successful?

- **Why it is Done:** What are the results that will be delivered?

Classic Strategy: The Theory

Academics tend to see strategic management as the highest form of management activity, giving direction to corporate values, culture, goals and missions. Under the broad corporate strategy, there are typically business-level competitive strategies and functional unit strategies.

According to **Michael Porter (1980)**, a firm must formulate a business strategy based on either cost leadership, differentiation, or focus to achieve a sustainable competitive advantage and long-term success. The right strategy is the one that best allows it to achieve competitive advantage over its rivals.

Alfred Chandler (1962) argued that a long-term coordinated strategy was necessary to give a company structure, direction, and focus. Chandler set out a view of management that recognised the importance of coordinating the various aspects of management under one all-encompassing strategy. Before this, business functions were separate, with little overall coordination or strategy.

Igor Ansoff (1968) developed the concept of the 'gap analysis', still widely used today as a tool for understanding the gap between where organisations are currently and where they would like to be, in order to produce actions based on reducing the gap.

Gary Hamel and Coimbatore (C.K.) Prahalad (1994) proposed that strategy should be more active and interactive, with less "arm-chair planning". They developed the idea of core competency, that each organisation has functional area(s) in which it excels and that the business should focus on opportunities in that area, letting others go. Most theories of outsourcing are based on the idea that an organisation should focus on core competence and outsource everything else. This idea is closely related to **Peters & Waterman's** book *In Search of Excellence* **(1982)** that identified eight common themes which were responsible for the success of the chosen corporations, including 'stick to the knitting' (staying with the business you know) and productivity through people (treating employees as a source of quality).

> ## Contemporary Strategy: The Theory
>
> **Kenichi Ohmae (1982)** claimed that strategy is a creative art, requiring intuition and intellectual flexibility. The Western approach to strategy is generally seen in terms of analytical techniques, rote formula, step-by-step processes and fast decision making. However, Japanese culture saw vagueness, ambiguity, and tentative decisions as acceptable, partly explaining the success of Japanese business.
>
> **Henry Mintzberg (1989)** views strategy formulation as ad-hoc, piecemeal incomplete and negotiated where managers attempt to manage their external environment. This can sometimes be an irrational process whereby strategies simply 'emerge' rather than result from detailed planning.
>
> **Ralph Stacey (1993)** believes that strategy is a way of creating order from chaos, through a variety of techniques to stabilise the environment (short term plans, budgets, timelines etc.) and monitor them through formal 'feedback loops'. However, people respond to changes gradually and often under and over react to them. This pulls people in several directions (disintegration and fragmentation), or ossification (rigidity). The result is that organisations constantly swing between centralisation and decentralisation.

One area of interest to researchers is defining the relationship between business strategy and HR strategy. The idea is important because it opens up the chicken/egg question of whether organisations first develop a strategy then organise around it, or whether strategy is derived from a more realistic assessment of the opportunities, resources and constraints already in place. In everyday terms, what comes first – the strategy or the capability? Academics like to take a more formal approach to this question and two main approaches define this relationship: the structure follows strategy model and the resource-based view.

1. **Structure Follows Strategy**

This view asserts that HR strategy will always vary with business strategy and the HR function should therefore organise itself based on the strategic requirements of the business, hence 'Structure Follows Strategy' (Chandler, 1962). If, for example, an organisation planned to move to a more customer focused approach, this would drive an HR strategy that brought about changes in the attitudes, skills and behaviour of staff, which in turn would drive structural changes in the way that certain HR practices are conducted, the skills needed in HR and possibly changes to business processes, workflow and management information. The components of the strategy might include training, culture change and a focus on change management, with potential changes to job descriptions, reward strategy and organisational design.

To further complicate matters, there are two variations of this model - (i) the open / contingent approach and (ii) the closed approach. The open approach holds that strategy must be dynamic and flexible to meet organisational and individual needs and be adaptive to a changing environment. The closed view is more dogmatic in its approach, proposing that for any specific business strategy there is a single appropriate HR strategy (or at least a limited range of HR strategy options). However, the closed view tends to be more mechanistic and idealistic about approaches to strategy, and assumes much about manager's willingness to deploy HR strategies and adapt to changed roles.

2. **Resource Based View**

The Resource Based View (Barney, 1991) turns the 'Structure Follows Strategy' approach on its head, arguing that strategy should follow structure, rather than being led by it. The Resource Based Approach argues that in the real world, organisations cannot create new strategies in isolation from the realities of its human and other capital – it must work broadly within the limits of what it has or can acquire. In practice, organisations should develop their strategies based on the distinctive capabilities and strengths the organisation possesses, including the available resources and even the culture of the organisation. While the 'Structure Follows Strategy' approach treats staff as a resource to be exploited and controlled in response to business strategy, the Resource Based View takes into account what resources are available and seeks to make the best use of them in generating new strategies. An excellent example of this is in consumer electronics and technology companies which are highly skilled at creating or quickly entering emerging markets. Sony was the first organisation to create the Walkman (for which there was no previous market); Apple created a new market for portable MP3 players, then went on to create new markets for tablet technology, while Google used its skills to develop a range of innovative applications by investing time in creating new products. In each case, the business did not first develop a strategy then hired people who could fulfill the strategy, they first hired the people and asked them to develop products and strategies. The logic of the Resource Based View is clear – strategy develops from structure. it would be irrational for a low-cost manufacturing company (where most employees have only basic skills) to devise a strategy that assumed access to a large group of highly skilled knowledge workers (irrational or at least highly ambitious).

In practice, the development of HR strategy must be responsive enough to adapt to both the 'Structure Follows Strategy' and the Resource Based View. Indeed, this adaptability is the essence of HR Ready – being flexible, responsive and adaptable for whatever the business does.

Strategic management techniques can be viewed as top-down, bottom-up or collaborative processes. The top-down approach is by far the most common, whereby the CEO decides on the overall direction the company should take. In the 'bottom-up' approach, employees submit proposals to their managers who, in turn, transmit the best ideas further up the organisation. In both cases, strategy development is often accomplished by a capital budgeting process and proposals are assessed using financial criteria such as return on investment or cost-benefit analysis. Some organisations are starting to experiment with collaborative strategic planning techniques that recognise the emergent nature of strategic decisions. The proposals that are approved form the substance of a new strategy, all of which is done without a grand strategic design or a strategic architect.

> ### Strategic HRM: The Theory (1)
>
> The concept of strategic HRM is diverse and ambiguous as well as contradictory, often relying on inconsistent assumptions **(Mabey, Salaman & Storey, 1998, p.16)**.
>
> **Martell & Carroll (1995)** point out that there is little consensual definition of strategic HRM. However, certain common themes exist that differentiate it from 'operational' HR, such as its long-term focus and an expectation that HRM should have an impact on bottom-line organisational performance.
>
> **Huselid et al (1997)** observed that strategic HRM involves the development and implementation of policies, supporting the 'new mandate' HR models proposed by Ulrich that define the role of a Centre of Expertise in developing and deploying policy **(Ulrich, 1997b; Ulrich, 1998; Ulrich & Brockbank, 2005)**. **Karen Legge (2005)** dismisses the classical, rationalistic, top-down model of HR strategy, arguing that integrating HRM and business strategy is a highly complex and iterative process, dependent on many stakeholders, such that it cannot be owned by a central HR function. Even the term 'HR strategy' is ambiguous as to whether it refers to a general people management strategy or the internal strategy for the HR function.

Global HR strategy

Economic activity is becoming increasingly global and many employees find themselves working for an employer that is based in another country. Over 200 UK businesses are bought by foreign owners each year, increasingly from outside the EU. More than half of Canadian oil, gas and manufacturing sectors have foreign ownership and around one quarter of US business are owned by non-US based owners. In recent years, more than 300,000 foreign companies have invested in China, with major corporations such as Coca-Cola, Nike, Citibank, Unilever and General Motors setting up operations; it is a similar story in all large emerging economies. As a result, the way in which large corporations operate across international boundaries has important implications for people management and employment, especially given that organisational structures typically transcend national and regional boundaries. What happens in one part of an organisation is often highly dependent on decisions taken in another part of the world; other than the constraints of legislation and national government intervention, global organisations are free to operate processes that cut across national boundaries and are highly interconnected. These features have crucial implications for HR decisions.

Understanding the importance of global HR strategy requires a short lesson in global economics to define the significant changes that have taken place in recent years. Perhaps the biggest change in this time has been the development of flexible production technologies that have enabled the de-centralisation of manufacturing. As a result, multinational companies have moved major aspects of their production processes outside their home countries, especially to developing areas in the Asia-Pacific region, giving them a low cost competitive advantage.

This new international division of labour throws up opportunities, together with a range of ethical issues such as low pay and working conditions that cannot be dealt with here, other than to acknowledge that they are real and a source of concern for many. At the same time, markets have also become global and products manufactured in one region are often sold in other markets. Even service industries, which are harder to globalise because they often rely on local delivery, are becoming multi-national in their approach.

Other than the constraints of national legislation, global talent management is one of the key issues facing international organisations – a major challenge is the growing number of individuals that have little loyalty to a country or region and are comfortable crossing cultural and geographical boundaries to find work opportunities. Organisations must compete to hire and develop the best talent in a global pool; despite the recession, there is still a scarcity of high-knowledge talent. Typical issues for international HR strategy include:

- How will talent be developed across international boundaries?
- How to identify and select cross-border managers?

- Will the organisation adopt a single set of HR practices, or will practices remain diverse?
- Will common practices be in place with regard to assumptions about reward, motivation and performance, given the need to recognise diversity issues?
- Will business systems (in particular HR technologies) use a common language or be adapted for local language and customs?

> ### Strategic HRM: The Theory (2)
>
> A key message from HRM literature is the need to establish a close two-way relationship between business strategy and HR strategy **(Beaumont, 1992). Fombrun et al (1983)** and **Schuler & Jackson (1987)** believe that for a particular business strategy, there is a single HR strategy, or at best a narrow range of possible strategies. Others believe that the role of HR strategy is to ensure that certain key elements are present in the strategy (the closed approach). Another school believes that the only test of HR strategy is the appropriateness of fit (the open or contingent approach).
>
> There are a number of problems with relating business strategy to HR strategy **(Mabey et al., 1998)**. One important hurdle is that there is no obvious way to translate business strategy into HR strategy – the links between HR structures, systems and business strategy are complex and multi-faceted and it's not easy to identify the ingredients of HR that will lead to the strategy being delivered. For example, if the business wants to develop into new markets, there are some obvious implications for people management such as acquiring new skills, but how this is achieved cannot be reduced to a simple formula. Much depends on what skills currently exist, whether they are available on the market, what should be bought in, developed internally and so on.

Problems of HR Strategy

Until recent times, the classic approach to strategic planning meant it was possible to develop a five or even ten year plan with some degree of certainty that the business environment would be very similar in the future. Historically, the past has been a guide to the future, but in a changing world, business planning is more tentative, short-term and issue-focused. Ten years ago, few organisations would have factored the impact of the cloud and tablet technology into their strategic planning.

Schuler and Walker (1990) suggest the following structure for the development of strategy (see Figure 22):

- **Human Resource Issue**: What is the HR problem? Issues can potentially be identified as a result of changes in the business environment, business strategy or organisational circumstances.

- **Analysis:** What evidence is there of the issue, what is the scope of the issue, what is the potential business impact of the issue and what alternative solutions are available?

- **Management Actions**: What course of action will be implemented over the next 1-2 years and beyond? What specific action programmes are proposed, who will be responsible and accountable for them, when will they be complete, what financial and staff resource will be needed?

- **Measures/Targets:** How will the results be measured in terms of outcomes, measures and targets?

However, models like this tend to represent HR strategy in a highly idealised form, where HR strategy neatly fits into corporate business strategy, as well as being measured and rational. Textbooks and formal strategy methodologies tend to assume a linear, rational, consensual, explicit and clear approach to strategy, but this is not reality; in practice, every stage of strategy development is complex and subject to economic, social and political pressures that constantly challenge the development of strategy. Formulating and implementing HR strategy is complex and evidence suggest that most organisations do not do this well.

Some researchers (Storey and Sisson 1993) note that one of the limiting factors in aligning business strategy to HR strategy is line management reluctance and inability to execute centrally developed strategies.

FIGURE 22: OUTLINE HR STRATEGY FRAMEWORK

Summary: HR Strategy

Much has been said and written about the importance of HR strategy; yet, many organisations still lack a formal strategy and many are little more than a vague set of statements about the role of HR and at best, a strategy *for* the HR function, rather than the HR component of an overall business strategy. HR Ready organisations understand their role in creating competitive advantage and are aware of the need to develop a robust but flexible strategy with suitable measures to track implementation success.

HR Strategy: Are you HR Ready?

- [?] Should structure follow strategy or does the organisation develop strategy based on the resources they have available?

- [?] Is the strategy formulation process effective?

- [?] Is the HR strategy a strategy for the HR function or does it link to the overall business strategy?

- [?] Does the HR strategy provide enough detail about 'how' or does it simply a mission statement? Is there enough detail to take meaningful actions?

10 HR Transformation

What is HR Transformation?

HR transformation has been a key component of HR strategy over the past 10 to 15 years. Textbooks and management consultants usually explain transformation in terms of the urgent need for HR to make a fundamental change in the way the function organises itself, its relationship with line management, the services it delivers and how they are delivered. According to the transformation mantra, unless the HR function makes these changes to the way it operates, it will lack the credibility and support needed to make an effective contribution to the business.

If only it were that simple. 'HR Transformation' has now become a fully-fledged HR buzzword, idly tossed into strategic discussions to the point where it has become so distorted that it is meaningless. For some, HR transformation is about improving basic business processes, perhaps something as fundamental as improving payroll accuracy. For others, it's about making a dramatic change in the way the HR function operates – literally changing *(trans)* the nature and structure *(form)* of the function. I was in two minds whether to include a chapter called 'HR Transformation' and perpetuate the abuse, but decided to retain it because it has become such an important part of the HR lexicon that it offers a starting point for joining the debate.

The first task is to define terms; although there are many definitions available, one which best seems to summarise the objectives of HR transformation is:

"The process of recreating or reinventing the HR function – such as re-engineering, restructuring, implementing new systems or a new HR service delivery model, outsourcing or co-sourcing – with the specific intent of enhancing HR's contribution to the business" (Mercer, 2007).

One of the biggest influences on the HR function has been the work of American academic David Ulrich[15]; who, together with various consultancy firms, put 'transformation' firmly on the HR agenda. His evangelistic approach to reinventing the HR service delivery model has been instrumental in bringing about some major structural changes in the HR function in the past 15 years, through a series of books[16] and influential academic papers. *'The New Mandate'* demands dramatic changes in the way HR professionals think and behave.

Such is the popularity of his ideas that some HR Directors talk of 'applying the Ulrich model' and the Breakout Box (*Ulrich in a Nutshell: The Theory*) explains the essentials of his approach. However, many HR professionals have gained their knowledge of the Ulrich model second-hand, through a variety of sources - consultancy firms, magazine articles, conferences or professional networks, so that knowledge of its theoretical origins is often limited, diluted and misunderstood. Indeed, research has found that few HR professionals and consultants have actually read his original books or articles (Boglind, Hallsten, & Thilander, 2011) and in some cases, only the basics of the idea remain. One consequence of this is that organisations tend to 'cherry pick' elements of the transformation model to suit their needs, often ignoring those parts of the concept that seem either too difficult or are not well understood, casting doubt on whether they were ever properly understood and possibly explaining why many attempts fail.

---

[15] This is already the 22nd mention of him in this book....

[16] See the References section for a good list of his works

Ulrich in a Nutshell: The Theory

The basic idea behind the **Ulrich** model **(see Ulrich, 1997; Becker, Huselid, & Ulrich, 2001; Ulrich & Brockbank, 2005a; Ulrich, Younger, & Brockbank, 2008;)** is that HR must fulfil a series of key roles, including those of (a) becoming a Business Partner with line managers (b) becoming an advocate for employees and representing their concerns to senior managers (c) becoming an agent of change and transformation and finally (d) what Ulrich terms the 'administrative expert' role, delivering process efficiency in a cost effective manner. Importantly, Ulrich stresses that unless HR fulfils the administrative role, it cannot progress to the other roles; administrative excellence is effectively the 'price of admission' to the strategy table (see Figure 23).

Ulrich never intended these roles to be a blueprint for organising the HR function and he did not directly translate them into specific jobs, although his work has generally been interpreted as if he did. Nevertheless, the majority of organisations making transformative changes have adopted the basic philosophy set out by Ulrich, based on the separation of the HR policy making, administration and Business Partner roles. He concluded that HR professionals should focus less on getting work done and more on deliverables and creating value, measuring their effectiveness in terms of increasing competiveness and lead transformation rather than simply do what it has always done. Ulrich was also clear that responsibility for transforming HR did not lie with the HR function, but with the CEO and that line managers had ultimate responsibility for the processes in a company, being answerable to shareholders for creating value and customers for creating product or service value.

Ulrich's concepts about HR transformation and the shared services organisation have been criticised as overly normative **(Caldwell, 2003)** and lacking in empirical evidence that supports successful implementation **(Truss et al., 2002; Hope-Hailey et al., 2005; Maatman et al., 2010).** However, there are few academic studies on the Implementation of the shared services model **(Cooke 2006)**. Basing her conclusion on a case study, she argues there is a significant gap between the model's intentions and its results.

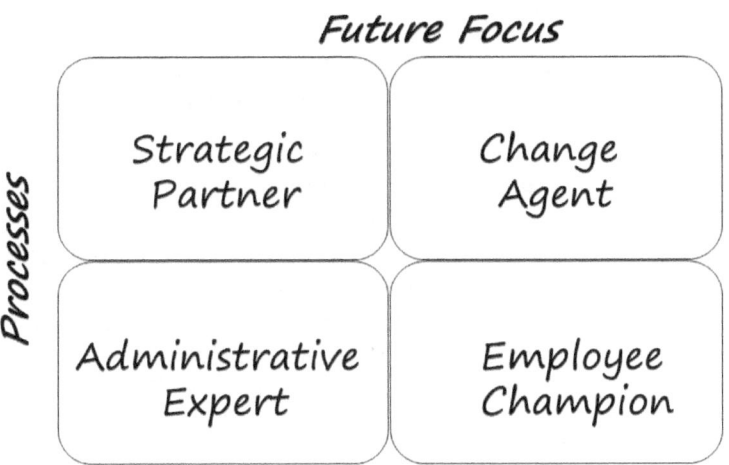

FIGURE 23: ORIGINAL ULRICH HR ROLES MODEL

HR Transformation: The Basics

Although Ulrich's proposed structure has been refined and amended over the past 15 years, the basic argument remains that successful HR Transformation increases the value that Human Resources adds to the business. As Chapter 6 (*Focus on Competitive Advantage*) reinforces, the biggest challenge for HR professionals is to help their organisation compete in its chosen market. One of the ways it can do this is by changing the way the HR function operates, although it's important to remember that transformation is only a means to help the company achieve its business objectives, not an end in itself.

Ulrich et al (2008) more recently developed the original model into a more complex arrangement, with one key change being the addition of an 'Operational Executor' role, introduced as an intermediary between the embedded Business Partner role (discussed in Chapter 7) and the service centre. The Operational Executor role is designed to deliver mainly operational, tactical work to support service delivery and can either be project based, case based or as a support role, but its main aim is to make sure that HR delivers what the business needs. While this new role has an unfortunate name (line managers will no doubt have endless fun with it), these HR professionals link the delivery of state-of-the-art HR practices from the Centre of Expertise to Operational Support provided through the embedded Business Partner role. This new role requires project management, business and strategic skills.

One purpose of transformation is to move the organisation to a new level of maturity in its development. The model shown in Figure 24[17] sets out the different stages in the development of HR, running from 'No formal HR' at one extreme through to 'Fully integrated HR' at the other. There is a critical point 'tipping point' between Stage 3 and Stage 4, where people become regarded as a source of competitive advantage rather than a resource to be managed. The five stages of HR maturity are:

Stage 1: No Formal HR

Some organisations have no obvious HR function, often because the business is too small (one hundred employees seems to be the tipping point at which an HR function first appears). Even then, HR is often an administrative support function with no professional HR leadership. Labour intensive, low skill operations such as those often found in the manufacturing sector typically fall into this category. In smaller organisations, HR administration tends to be the responsibility of one of the management team (often the Finance Director), with payroll typically being run by an external provider. HR questions are handled directly by line managers, with support from external bodies such as recruitment agencies and legal advisers. Concepts such as talent management and performance management may be in place but they are ad hoc and unstructured.

Stage 2: Chaotic HR

This is the worst kind of HR – an HR organisation is in place but there is little structure. HR staff do the best they can with what they have and fight their way through each business day with no expectations or promises. This type of HR structure tends to exist in small to medium sized organisations (SMEs) or where the organisation has gone through rapid growth but HR has not kept pace. These organisations can be characterised as:

---

[17] Adapted from a model by Paul Kearns (2003)

- No identifiable business processes. Even where processes have been written down, they are ignored or performed differently by each individual.

- Dysfunctional – the HR team consists of enthusiastic generalists who help out when they can, with only one or two experts who carry all the knowledge. Whoever answers the phone picks up the problem and deals with it, with no documentation or audit trail.

- Poor use of HR technology, often based on an eclectic mixture of systems with no integration and no strategy for improvement.

- No formal HR strategy is in place and where it does exist, it is mostly focused inwardly on the HR function rather than aligning to the overall business strategy.

- A general failure to deliver anything on time or to a good standard. Occasionally, major compliance problems arise that are damaging to the business, such as financial penalties or missed opportunities.

Internal customers are often surprisingly tolerant of these HR organisations because the organisation itself has a highly chaotic culture - HR simply echoes what goes on elsewhere in the business. In highly stable firms, where people tend not to move either in or out of the organisation and staff turnover is low, nobody knows any better because they have never experienced anything else. Expectations are low and poor quality is usually forgiven, despite frequent (often costly) errors. *"We're doing our best with limited resources"* is the typical plea. The trajectory of these HR organisations is usually downward, because there is little motivation to change and little desire to make any contribution other than keeping on top of the most basic legal compliance issues. It usually takes a major incident to highlight the problem – an expensive court case or catastrophic process failure, or more likely, new managers enter the business that have experience of better HR departments and are not prepared to tolerate such chaos. Size need not be the main factor - some larger organisations allow chaotic HR structures to survive unchallenged. However, knowledge-based organisations such as software houses, biotechnology firms and professional services organisations need a highly skilled workforce, so place greater emphasis on people management processes such as recruitment, learning & development and career development. This type of organisation tends to introduce an HR function at an earlier stage in their growth.

Stage 3: Good Practice

At this stage, HR is about ensuring good practice and compliance, with an emphasis on being a good employer. It's likely that a number of sophisticated HR practices are in place, for example, competency driven recruitment programmes, a well-developed performance management scheme and formal Learning & Development needs analysis. HR actions are focused on the outputs of appraisal schemes but with a relatively short term emphasis. Much of the role of HR is concerned with encouraging line managers to comply with policy requirements, although the line management population does not necessarily respect HR or its contribution. HR tends to pick up issues after the event and spends a lot of time 'fire-fighting' line problems.

Stage 4: Effective HR Management

This is the first stage in the maturity of the HR function where the Board starts to value the contribution of HR – in previous stages, HR is frequently regarded as a back-office function. At this stage, there is some attempt to undertake succession planning, with a 3-5 year focus and an outline talent management strategy. HR works with line management to develop joint approaches to recruitment, with a focus on increased accountability for line managers, who are actively involved in the career development of staff.

At Stage 4, business processes have been streamlined and standardised, aligned to HR business strategy and are flexible and efficient. Contact with HR is via a service delivery structure and service quality is seen as important, although few formal measures yet exist. Technology is in place to support the HR function in managing core processes and line managers have access to employee information and can conduct certain transactions online. Recruitment plans are in place for the short and medium term and skills development is aimed at meeting future requirements. The function is well enough developed to focus on continuous improvement, although often it is payroll centred rather than focused on HR practices.

Stage 5: Strategic Focus

The overall strategy process is supported by a strategic planning role or function; however, the plans of the HR function remain an appendix to the main business strategy and at times can be isolated from the overall business. HR has its own objectives which are not necessarily aligned to the performance objectives of the business. The HR strategy is written by the HR function but it is likely that senior managers pay only 'lip service' to the plans, with often no systematic review process in place. There is some monitoring of achievement, but it is mostly in general terms and as a result it is often diluted. HR drives processes and programmes but they do not always have full line ownership, being seen as 'HR Programmes'.

At this stage, service delivery is highly effective and efficient, based on a service centre approach through shared services or an outsourced partner. Technology is deployed widely across the organisation, with managers being fully accountable for processes and able to manage many activities through their desktop. Management information is integrated with other systems and managers have access to real-time information, probably accessed remotely through analytics.

Stage 6: Fully Integrated HR

In this stage of the development of HR, people management plans and business strategy are inter-connected and seamless. HR strategy is owned by senior management and is critical to the development of business strategy, including organisational culture and structure. Line managers feel a strong ownership of people plans, which are monitored, measured and reviewed regularly. HR's role is to formulate strategy and manage change, as well as contribute to general business strategy. Technology is fully exploited including the use of HR analytics, social technology and service portals; managers and employees use mobile technologies such as smartphones and tablet technologies to support processes. The function is constantly looking for better ways to develop its use of technology with champions accountable for technology development.

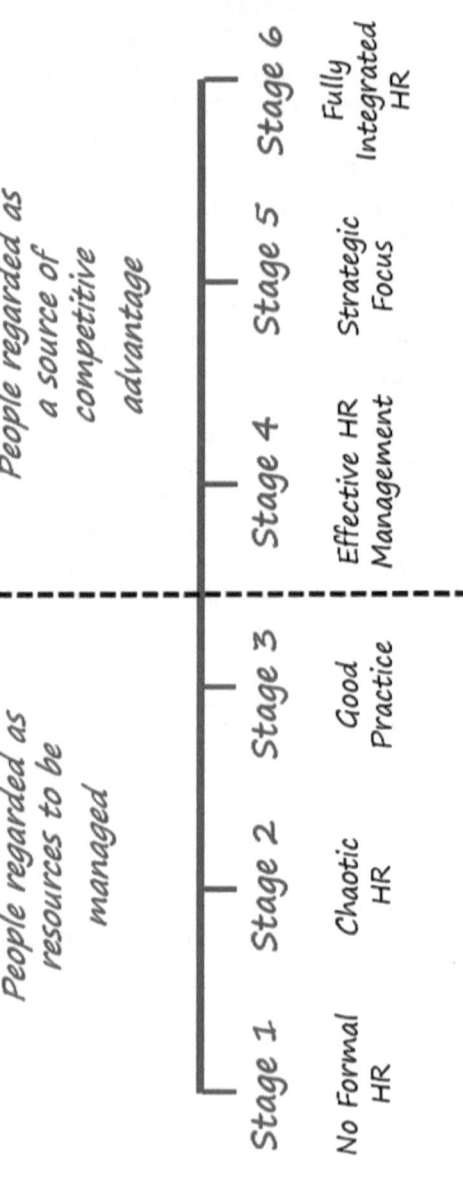

Figure 24: HR Maturity Levels

Transformation: The Trouble with Payroll

One of the starting points for any transformation strategy is the Payroll function. It's a critical business process, one where accuracy is paramount - improving Payroll may even be the primary focus of a transformation strategy. A review of Payroll usually throws up a number of big questions that are also addressed in this section.

Payroll has long been the 'twilight' function in organisations; often schizophrenic, not quite Human Resources, not quite Finance, it sits uncomfortably between the two and never hits the headlines until something goes wrong (especially if it relates to a Director's bonus payment). Good payroll[18] processes are also the foundation of good employee relations - anyone who has ever faced the prospect of a shop-floor walkout when overtime doesn't get paid will understand the central role it plays in maintaining workplace relationships. It's one of the few business processes that is thoroughly audited by every single employee every week or month and problems will be immediately brought to HR's attention, sometimes in a highly emotional manner. If Finance sends out an incorrect invoice, it will not upset few people and is easily put right, but get someone's pay wrong and they will tell everyone. Payroll has to get it right.

Fortunately, Payroll teams are generally highly dedicated people who work hard to make sure that people are paid accurately and on time. Several years ago, I worked on a pan-European payroll improvement project; what struck me was that payroll processes across Europe were quite homogeneous – although local legislation was, of course, very different in terms of what rules were applied, the business processes that supported them were very similar. More interesting to me was that the types of people who worked in the Payroll function had similar character traits, being highly dedicated individuals who were exceptionally devoted to getting things right. Because of these similarities, I did

---

[18] Opinion is mixed as to whether to capitalise 'Payroll' or not. Certainly, when it's the Payroll function or Payroll tea, it deserves a capital 'P' as a proper noun but in its general sense (as an activity or process) I've gone for the lower case. I believe it's the same principle as Sales v. selling.

wonder whether there was a special Payroll gene somewhere out there...

What is Payroll?

No, this is not a trick question. Although it sounds obvious, the word 'Payroll' can mean different things in different organisations. One of the first questions with any new client is working out where HR ends and Payroll begins and the dividing line is often arbitrary. In fact, the role of Payroll is slightly different in almost every organisation I have worked with – for some, payroll is simply about final processing and payment, applying tax rules and transferring funds to employees and third parties. For others, payroll goes deep into HR administration, including collecting data on new hires, changes and leavers.

Rather than focus on the activities Payroll undertakes, it's more useful to think of it as a series of processes and outcomes – this avoids the mistake of defining 'Payroll' in the terms of the organisational structure, rather than the processes delivered. This is the Christmas Party test – The Payroll Process is more than the people who get invited to the Payroll Christmas Party. Another way to look Payroll is to define it as a 'Pay People Process', defined as:

"The process which links HR policy, statutory processes, entitlement and payment"

In its purest form, payroll is simply the application of a series of rules to ensure that employee pay is managed in accordance with statutory rules and company policy, including ensuring employees are paid in accordance with their contracts, that tax is applied at the right rate and that proper financial processes are followed for statutory and internal reporting. Strictly, the reference should not be restricted only to employees because temporary staff, contractors and pensioners are often handled through Payroll. The appropriate term is 'Payees' but this can be equally misleading. There are three main drivers for payroll activity:

- **The Legal Environment:** Statutory and tax rules, social security, including compliance requirements for reporting etc. These matters are generally outside the organisation's control and must simply be 'right', with the risk of financial penalties for getting it wrong.

- **Company Policy:** Rules on payment of overtime, salary increases, terms and conditions, including internal rules on who has the authority to approve changes. These are all largely within the control of the organisation but outside the control of payroll, which is subject to audit controls.

- **Operational Methods:** How the payroll function checks and audits data changes, how data is initiated and approved, how rules are applied, how exceptions and corrections are managed. These are under the control of the organisation but Payroll is accountable.

While most payroll activity is the result of a chain of events that has its roots in HR policy and statutory entitlement, the biggest driver of Payroll workload is organisational complexity. Consider this - if all Payroll had to do was to run the same numbers every week or month with no change, everyone could go home and leave the computers to get on with it. But of course, it's not that easy - people join and leave the organisation, change their jobs, receive temporary allowances, are sick, go on maternity leave and work different hours and work patterns. People can leave (or start) without payroll being informed, have deductions attached by outside bodies, work unusual work patterns or even fall down dead at work. It's these variations to the standard that drive all the work, unpicking all the non-standard human activities that are part of organisational life. Payroll has no choice but to meet the challenge.

Improving Payroll

If an organisation is looking to make genuine improvements to payroll, it should look upstream and understand the flow of pay data from its source, often generated by line managers (or perhaps more realistically, by what line managers **fail** to generate). Many organisations are seeing their systems costs spiral as older systems reach the end of their useful lives and multiple patches and fixes become unwieldy to maintain. There are several causes of payroll inefficiency;

- Payroll often over-delivers its services. By trying to meet the needs of everyone, it sometimes ignores the basic cost of doing business - Payroll staff will often spend days ensuring the numbers add up to the last decimal place, regardless of the cost of achieving it.

- Too many checks and balances – in some cases, checking can account for 25% of payroll effort. Ironically, the more checking payroll does, the more it is needed - line managers and HR administrators submit input documents in the knowledge that Payroll will check them and find errors, their input will tend to be less accurate. The answer is to transfer accountability for data accuracy to the originator or ideally, use online systems that validate data entry at source.

- A further 25% of payroll time (related to the point above) can be accounted for in referring poor quality data back to line managers for verification. Data inaccuracy, lack of policy compliance or incompleteness such as the lack of signature reveals apathy towards pay processes. The challenge here is whether refusing to accommodate managerial incompetence is unfair to the employee.

- Organisations that have high levels of manual calculations often have poor systems that cannot cope with policy, or worse, mean that staff do not trust the output. Around 15% of payroll time is spent performing secondary checks either to validate systems output or make it compatible with data entry requirements.

- Organisations that have a high level of data transfer between systems tend to be less efficient. Even spreadsheet based loads can be time-consuming or worse, data can be lost in the process. In some cases, up to 20% of time can be spent moving data between systems, such as printing data out and re-keying.

- Payroll spends a lot of time answering queries, with administrators spending 10-15% of their time dealing with minor queries. Queries are ultimately a result of problems generated by all the previous points

The above suggest that if Payroll could do less checking, less referring back to managers, avoid the transfer of data between systems and reduce queries, a huge amount of time could be freed to work on *managing* the payroll rather than administering it.

Big Question 1: Integrated vs. Separate HR and Payroll?

Organisations often agonise over the best approach to running their HR and Payroll systems, with a common question being whether to have a fully integrated HR and Payroll system or to operate entirely separate systems. The arguments for and against each option are set out below:

1. Arguments for Integration

In an integrated system, the core HR Management System and payroll modules sit on top of a common database, so all data about an employee such as their pay, conditions, cost centre, organisation, position and personal information are simultaneously available in every module. This has several advantages in terms of processes and workflow. For example, a newly hired employee can be set up in the system by an HR administrator, the employee can add personal data through self-service and pay details can be added by a payroll administrator using the same core data. There is no need for cross-referencing or waiting for data to flow through the system.

The biggest risk with separate (non-integrated) HR and Payroll systems is that the same core data is frequently needed by both, relying on either an electronic interface or even manual re-keying, requiring additional work to manage and validate the transfer. Both these methods almost always cause delays and potentially problems in reconciliation. From a business process perspective, it's usually much easier to design a process based on a smooth flow of data between HR and payroll within the same system. Retaining all data within the same system also reinforces the idea that the HR module is the master source of data about people.

If the two systems are not synchronised, it could lead to problems in performing certain calculations, for example, where pay calculations are based on position-related data that needs to refer to Terms & Conditions (held at the HR level) in order to work out overtime pay or calculate a pay increase.

2. **Arguments for Separation**

In some cases, separate HR and Payroll systems may make good sense on cost grounds. For example, when implementing the payroll module of a large ERP module, it may not be economically viable to implement the payroll module to pay only a small part of the organisation, which may have its own pay rules. Paying a relatively small number of people (for example a country where only a few people are employed) involves many of the same set-up costs as those for a large population and it's not uncommon for global implementations to feed separate, stand-alone payrolls or to outsource to a local provider. The 'tipping point' for these calculations will vary according to several factors such as payroll complexity, the availability of local providers and scale.

In some organisations, the payroll system seems to be working well enough – people are paid the right amount every week or month and the view is that there is no point throwing something away that is fit for purpose - '*If it's not broken, don't fix it*'. When the same payroll system has been running for some time, it will probably have reached a point of maturity where the team responsible for it feels comfortable, knows it thoroughly and is reluctant to change. Staying with the same system means there is no need to set up new software and its operation will not require staff to be retrained. The current license period may not have expired, in which case the team may wish to let the contractual period naturally expire, saving cost. However, it's important to recognise that introducing an HR system will inevitably have an impact on payroll process (as outlined in the pro-integration argument) because of the fundamental need to reconcile the systems. This may actually introduce more cost as the data will need to be passed to payroll by some means, either through re-keying or via an interface.

Big Question 2: Should Payroll Be Part of HR or Finance?

Anecdotal evidence and personal experience suggests that there is roughly a 50:50 split between Payroll functions reporting through HR or Finance, a statistic that seems to apply generally around the world. The reasons are lost in history, being as much to do with organisational evolution rather than any formal design or logic. As there appears to be no formal research into the pros and cons of either approach, it seems reasonable to put forward some ideas in this book.

1. Arguments for Reporting to HR

Many business processes such as bringing in new hires, terminating employees and managing changes such as promotions and contract changes often start out as HR processes, then progress to the Payroll Section for processing. However, the handover to another section with different reporting lines means that accountability for the whole process might be diluted. It's rare for organisations to have internal service level agreements that specify accountabilities and process boundaries, putting internal effectiveness at risk. If there is an integrated HR and Payroll system in place, it's illogical to create a functional split to the administration. This continuity of process also affects query resolution; while the Payroll team may be able to answer questions about tax and data submission, the HR team has often been involved in the contractual aspects of promotions and allowance changes and is better placed to answer questions about why something has happened, not just what has gone wrong.

However, perhaps the key argument for both HR Administration and Payroll to report to the same place is ultimately more about employee relations than Accounting and Finance. Managing Payroll is not like managing an accounts payable section - get the payroll wrong and you may find that employees down tools and walk out. I'm aware of entire factories striking over the company's failure to pay overtime or bonus payments in line with a trade union agreement. The way that an employer responds to a pay problem is a key part of managing the employee relationship and HR will have a different perspective on a policy decision.

2. **Arguments for Reporting to Finance**

The main argument for Payroll to report into the Finance Department is a perception that it will ensure legal and policy compliance. As part of its governance role regarding the organisation's funds, Finance naturally want to ensure compliance with legislation and policy, either in the application of tax rules, formal reporting or when dealing with third parties. However, this argument doesn't really stack up – HR professionals work within a large range of constantly changing employment legislation and know well the consequences of failing to comply. Tax rules are hard-coded into software so it's unlikely that this will be a source of problems, and a well-trained HR administrator should be able to spot a tax calculation problem. The other argument is that it's more efficient to have both the Payroll and Accounts Payable Sections reporting to the same person. After all, it's argued, the work is similar - both manage cash (although this is now minimal in most organisations) and the same legal and audit requirements affect each.

HR functions are often reluctant to take on responsibility for paying people because it's seen as too transactional and HR is quite keen to distance itself from administration. One solution would be to manage Payroll as part of an overall shared services or outsourcing operation that is ultimately controlled by HR, but still subject to service level agreements and key performance indicators set by Finance. Of course, the right arrangement depends on your organisation, your department and the people in it.

Barriers to HR Transformation

According to one report, less than one in five HR organisations believe that their HR model delivers the right combination of efficiency, value and level of service demanded by their businesses (Mercer, 2013) HR organisations often make mistakes when undertaking HR transformation, some of which are set out below:

- **Lack of Strategic Focus:** Transformation efforts are directed at cost reduction or fixing service delivery issues rather than defining the requirements of the business. In many ways, the term 'HR transformation' is the worst possible starting point for making the changes required, because it focuses HR on itself. Chapter 1 explored alternatives to service delivery, which may include the introduction of service centres or outsourcing; however, these initiatives are not enough in themselves and must fit into a wider strategy that links structural changes to the organisation's needs. Unless HR transformation starts from the perspective of generating benefits for the entire business, HR will appear to be self-centred.

- **Flawed Implementation:** Many HR organisations fail to define new roles and accountabilities for service centre staff, or fail to describe how staff will operate in the newly transformed function – in many cases, transformation has involved no more than changing staff titles, with little evidence of true transformation. This is particularly evident where organisations have introduced the HR Business Partner role (as discussed in Chapter 7), originally intended to deepen the HR function's ability to play a strategic role in supporting line managers. Yet, evidence suggests that many Business Partners are still spending significant time providing administrative or generalist services.

- **Lack of HR Capability:** Transformation is not simply about taking the existing resource and infrastructure and re-arranging it. Transformation will involve (as a minimum) updating the skills of the current team and potentially moving some existing resource out of the business to make space for new skills and new levels of energy.

- **Incremental Changes:** Some organisations make only small changes yet claim they have been transformed. For example, they introduce new technology or a Business Partner model, but taken alone these are not sufficient. See Chapter 2 on the importance of developing a critical mass of HR Practices.

- **Efficiency Equals Transformation:** Efficiency improvements (cost reduction, cycle time and headcount reduction) are only measures of transformation, they do not necessarily equal transformation in themselves.

- **Lack of Satisfaction with Technology:** In organisations where managers receive a highly personalised service from HR ('High Touch') the transition to e-HRM can be difficult. If managers and employee do not embrace technology and continuously seek ways to avoid using it, transformation efforts are likely to fail. Change and transition management are essential items in the HR transformation toolkit.

- **Lack of Line Manager Support:** Line managers must play their part support the transformation of HR, whether it involves technology, shared services, Centres of Expertise outsourcing or some hybrid version of these. Transformation efforts should ultimately serve customers, not the HR function; without line support, they will fail.

Why Transformation Efforts Fail: The Theory

Although **John Kotter's** (1995) Harvard Business Review article is almost 20 years old, the message is still valid – transformation requires time, resource and leadership. Kotter believes transformation efforts fail for a number of reasons:

- Organisations move too quickly and fool themselves they are making good progress
- Critical mistakes early on are amplified later in the transformation project
- Lack of a sense of urgency
- Lack of vision or the vision is not communicated
- No guiding coalition
- People are not empowered to act
- Lack of planning for short term wins
- Improvements are not consolidated

Summary: HR Transformation

Transformation is one of the key tools of HR Ready, an umbrella term that is based on business process redesign, the use of technology, improved service delivery, new organisational structures and new ways of working. Although many organisations claim to have transformed themselves, many are still struggling with the basics of good service delivery and making technology work. Nevertheless, there are some basic transformation principles that promote success; in simple terms, it's about understanding what the business needs and what already exists, setting a strategic direction and designing a suitable infrastructure. Finally, it involves putting in place metrics and governance that allow the new structure to be measured and continuously improved.

HR Transformation: Are You HR Ready?

- [?] What is the appetite in the business for transformation?
- [?] Are business requirements clear?
- [?] How will HR transformation make the organisation more competitive?
- [?] Will HR need new skills and capabilities to deliver the vision?
- [?] What needs to be done to ensure that transformation efforts do not fail?

1. Business Process Improvement

"In many cases, technology is the easy part. The tough part is how you apply it to your business, how you optimise your processes, how you find new levels of collaboration, how you reduce risk, how you become more competitive, how you please your customers more and how you constantly seek innovation"

Information Week, June 2004

An organisation is only as good as its processes – even if it has access to all the right forms of capital (financial, human etc.) unless it can create processes that put various forms of capital to work, it will fail. For this reason, good business process design is a basic tool for organisations wishing to become HR Ready. A thorough review of business processes is especially important when implementing new HR technology, since in most cases, buying new technology is linked to a desire to transform the HR function, either through an external outsourcing provider or a new internal HR operating model.

Even if technology acquisition is based on a simple replication strategy (see Chapter 8) some form of change to business processes is inevitable - because software packages are based on an underlying process / workflow model, it's simply not possible to introduce new technology without making changes to business processes. Nevertheless, some organisations attempt to recreate their *current* business processes in their new system and do not build a process design stage into their implementation plans; this almost certainly leads to project failure. One reason for this flawed strategy is the desire to get a sense of progress after buying technology, often being driven by unrealistic project deadlines. The argument often runs along the lines of *"Let's just get the system up and running, then we can think about the processes later"'*. This is illogical and counter-intuitive, raising questions about how business benefits can be achieved by simply implementing what already exists. It's also a high risk strategy – it means that bad processes are designed into the new system, the only outcome being the creation of fully automated, but fundamentally bad processes! In the meantime, any operational problems are likely to be blamed on the technology rather than the real cause (a poor implementation strategy). If the organisation does eventually look at business processes (and this often gets forgotten), some aspects of the system may even need to be re-configured or possibly re-implemented to adapt to changed processes. Please take the following sentence and write it in large letters on the whiteboard in your project office:

> *No amount of automation will turn a bad process into a good process!*

Good process design leads to the identification of opportunities for automating business processes as well as significant cost reduction and quality improvements, making activities transparent, clarifying roles, accountabilities and responsibilities. It also has the effect of ensuring that processes meet business and customer requirements and ensuring better compliance with legal requirements.

Of course, process improvement need not be limited to the introduction of new technology or transformation of service delivery – in theory, they can be improved at any time but new technology usually provides an excellent reason for making and supporting the changes. Good processes have the following characteristics:

- Manual intervention is kept to a minimum.
- Duplication of effort and data is eliminated.
- Information is captured at source where possible.

- Processes are automated where it improves efficiency, through employee/manager self-service and workflow. Processes are NOT automated for their own sake, with a balance being struck between the need for face-to-face human interaction and automation.
- Accountabilities are clear – everyone understands who owns each process step, who should perform each part of the process, who needs to be informed and who needs to be consulted.
- Users should have the knowledge needed to deliver the process and be fully trained.
- Process design should take into account the management information that will be needed as an output and designed into the process.
- Performance measures for processes should be established and implemented, with a focus on continuous improvement.
- Processes are consistent with the culture of the organisation, aimed at meeting customer requirements.

Identifying Processes for Improvement

As the 'Process Framework' diagram (Figure 26) illustrates, HR and Payroll includes around 16 high level (Level 1) processes, plus four supporting technology processes. Processes fall into one of four process categories:

- **Strategic Processes:** These govern the overall direction and structure of the HR organisation. They include processes for the development of HR strategy, organisational development, workforce planning and labour/employee relations and are generally not transactional in nature. They are not strictly processes in the traditional sense, but are best seen as activities, often with no defined start and end point. However, the information needed to support these activities typically derives from data generated through transactional processes.
- **Value Processes:** By definition, these processes deliver high value to the business. They are sometimes referred to as talent management processes because they focus on

bringing people into the organisation, developing them, rewarding them, managing their performance and ultimately arranging their exit from the business. Although they often have an important transactional element to them, these processes are linked closely to people management processes and are usually tied to the culture and style of the business. Performing these processes well can provide competitive advantage - for example, good recruitment processes give the organisation access to the best talent.

- **Operational Processes**: These are highly transactional in nature and are an inevitable part of employing people. They include payroll, time & attendance, workforce administration and other lifecycle processes. The business objective should be to deliver these processes as efficiently as possible and at the lowest cost, as they rarely provide competitive advantage (other than reducing the overall cost of operations). However, in some cases (for example, where time & attendance is linked to rostering/scheduling tools), they contribute to improved productivity. Processes in this group can usually be improved and are often outsourced.

- **Support processes:** These processes are mostly internal to the operation of the HR function, for example, the management of third party vendors, processes for maintaining the HR system and HR reporting. In some cases, they include processes that ensure continuous development of the HR function and its processes.

Business processes can be defined to several levels of detail, typically as follows (see Figure 25):

- **Level 1** processes describe the process area (Recruitment & Selection, Learning & Development, Performance & Talent management).
- **Level 2** processes break down Level 1 processes into sub-processes - for example, in the case of Recruitment & Staffing, the relevant sub-processes would include Vacancy Management, Post Creation, Job Posting,

Advertising, Application management, Assessment, Selection and Offer Management.

- **Level 3** processes go down to swimlane level – a diagrammatic representation of the key steps and activities in each process, showing accountabilities for each step.
- **Level 4** consists of Standard Operating Procedures (SOPs), a detailed definition at each step as to how the process operates.
- **Level 5** is the Detailed Work Instructions (DWI) level, providing detail about how each step in the process works to Operator level, including screenshots of system use.

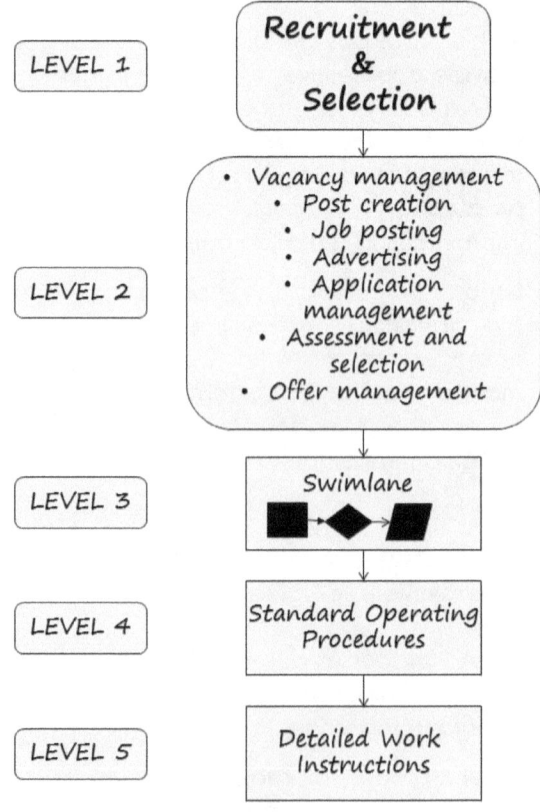

FIGURE 25: PROCESS LEVELS 1 TO 5

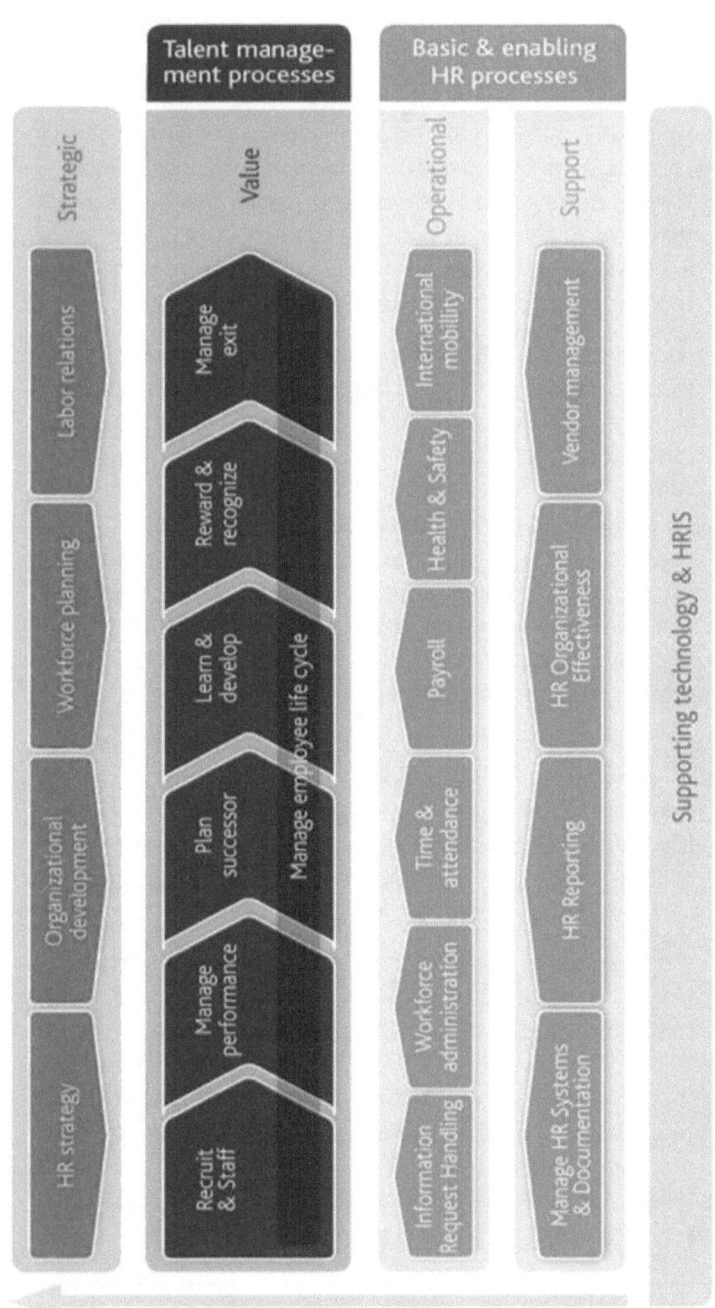

Figure 26: Process Framework
Reproduced with the permission of NorthgateArinso

Business Processes: The Theory

Business processes are actions that firms engage in to accomplish a business purpose or objective (Ray et al. 2004), that is, the routines or activities that a firm develops in order to get things done. Most academics acknowledge that resources can only be a source of competitive advantage if they are used to 'do something;' that is, if those resources are exploited through business processes.

Some have argued **(Behenchod, cited in Rummler, 1996)** that an organisation is only as good as its processes. Firms that fail to efficiently and effectively translate their resources and capabilities into business processes will fail to realise the competitive advantage potential of their resources. **Stalk, Evans, & Schulman (1992, p62)** argue that *'The building blocks of corporate strategy are not products and markets but business processes'*, while **Porter (1991, p108)** argued that *Resources are not valuable in and of themselves, but they are valuable because they allow firms to perform activities ... business processes are the source of competitive advantage.'*

Remus (2007) argues that in order to achieve the greatest benefits provided by technology, processes and activities must be aligned with the new system. In many cases, the underlying business processes have to be redesigned before the solution is deployed. Process integration should integrate tasks and sub processes at the operational level.

A firm may excel in some of its business processes, be only average in others, and be below average in others. However, the net effect of these business processes can affect a firm's position in the market place. Not all business processes will be a source of competitive advantage - the resource-based view suggests that business processes that exploit valuable but common resources will not provide competitive advantage but business processes that exploit valuable and rare resources are likely to be a source of advantage.

Best Practice Processes: Buzzword or Reality?

The breadth of activities HR and Payroll functions undertake can at first appear overwhelming – in total, it's possible to define around 150 x Level 2 processes across the entire range. This highlights the huge range of business processes that must be managed and partly explains why the HR function is often swamped by its administrative workload. But it doesn't stop there - within each process, there are potentially many variations. For example, the process of advertising a job in a local newspaper is quite different from posting it on an external job board or the internet; managing applications for a junior role needs to be handled differently from applicants for a senior management position. Some processes can be performed using the automating features of software, some will use elements of self-service technology, whereas others may need a manual paper-based approach for employees without access to technology. In each case, there is usually an opportunity to do things better.

A critical starting point for any review of business processes is to define which processes provide strategic capability and which simply need to be done as effectively and efficiently as possible to ensure compliance and contain costs. One recurring theme in recent years involves whether organisations should adopt industry standard processes, often referred to as 'Best Practice'. Although once popular for the purposes of ERP implementation, the term 'Best Practice' has fallen into disrepute in recent times, and it has now achieved 'buzzword' status (see Breakout Box). This is unfortunate, as the idea behind Best Practice was originally that it represented the most efficient, effective and legally compliant way to undertake a transaction, taking into account variables such as the software being used and any industry specific requirements. The main problem with the notion of 'Best Practice' seems to be the underlying assumption that a single process design can meet the needs of all organisations, across all sectors and that there is a single ideal way to perform each process. This is similar in nature to the arguments raised in Chapter 2 about 'Structure Follows Strategy' and the 'Resource Based Approach', as to whether there is a single best way of running a business. A more useful term may be 'standard practice' or 'good practice'.

'Best practice' also runs against the idea of competitive advantage - in some cases, an organisation may develop a new process that gives it an edge over its competitors, such as a unique approach to recruitment, Learning & Development or talent management. Where an organisation manages to create unique, high value processes, it's important that others cannot easily copy them, so that any advantage they provide can be maintained. Creating a unique process inevitably carries a cost, but if it provides competitive advantage, a **non-**Best Practice approach, it may be a good investment and these 'better than best practice' approaches become the source of true value. Paradoxically, the success of competitively advantageous processes probably lies in factors relating to organisational culture rather than the formal process flow; for example, many have tried to emulate the supply chain processes of Japanese car manufacturers without success, because the execution of the processes is embedded in the culture of the business, not just followed dogmatically.

Case Study: The Church of England

Prior to implementing a new People and Payroll system covering HR, Recruitment, Training, Self-Service and Payroll, The Church Commissioners undertook a detailed review of HR and Payroll Business Processes, with a clear objective of introducing best-practice (standardised) HR processes. Working with subject matter and policy experts, the process review highlighted opportunities to develop self-service, including new proactive alerts and improved Business Intelligence that would ensure more efficient operation of administration. The output from the business process design was then used by the implementation team to configure and build an 'out-of-the-box' solution.

Andrew Brown, Secretary to the Church Commissioners commented "*We are already seeing how an integrated solution, when built to a tailored solution design specification, can add value and reduce the time spent on day-to-day administration. This has enabled us to identify a number of business benefits derived from the new system..... we would recommend this approach.*'

Best Practice: The Theory

'Best Practices' have been defined as routine uses of knowledge that are judged to be superior to others **(Wagner et al. 2006)**, while **O'Leary (2000)** defines best practice as *"The better or best ways of performing a particular process"*. Likewise, a best practice may be seen as a successful way to treat a particular problem that may need to be adapted in skilful ways in response to prevailing conditions **(Mansar & Reijers, 2007)**. The notion of Best Practice was created during the development of ERP models - the popularity of ERP is in part due to its promise of transferring exemplary business practices embedded within the technology's design **(Timbrell et al., 2001)**. Some have declared that the introduction of best practices is a prerequisite for success in the 21st century **(Davenport, 2000)**.

As 'Best Practices' become available to all organisations in the software marketplace, best practices shift from a source of competitive advantage to a standard prerequisite for business efficiency. The adoption of a 'best practice' process carries the risk that the organisation potentially sacrifices a better, perhaps even more competitive, way of performing a key business process **(O'Leary, 2000)**. This may not be an issue for routine processes, but it may be of concern for value high value processes. There is also evidence that Best Practice options are not sufficient for creating a working information system, because the process templates limit configuration choices only to those practices that can be accommodated by the system **(Boudreau & Robey, 2005)**.

Gratton & Ghoshal (2005) argue that high performing companies not only use standard best practices, but they also embrace internally developed idiosyncratic "signature processes" that reflect the history and values of the organisation. Ultimately, it may be that 'Best Practice' is simply better than what most firms currently employ **(Davenport, 2000)**.

Approaches to Process Improvement

It's important that process improvement is driven by a robust methodology, using established techniques that are right for the organisation. Many techniques and tools are available for undertaking business process improvement, including Lean manufacturing and Six sigma, Capability Maturity Model Integration (CMMI), Process Improvement and Management (PI&M), Theory of Constraints, Total Quality Management and the Trillium Model. There are potentially many other approaches to process improvement, but this book is too short and the subject is too specialist to do justice to all these techniques; however, Lean Manufacturing and Six Sigma are explained in the Breakout Boxes.

Every technique available starts from a common desire to make businesses operate more efficiently and eliminate non-necessary or wasteful steps; there if of courses wide variation in the methodology, the philosophy and factors such as the level of variance and freedom to act each technique will allow. Some methodologies insist that current ways of working (the 'as-is') should be mapped out, to provide context and ensure important activities are not overlooked, especially where they provide unique competitive advantage. The alternative view is that spending time on how things currently operate is a waste of time and that old ways should be dismantled and ignored. Some would argue that looking too closely at current processes reinforces them in the minds of process owners and makes it even more difficult to change. Opinion is divided on this – my personal view is that for routine, standard processes, as-is mapping can be wasteful, whereas a simple SWOT analysis will flush out the key requirements; however, for strategic and value added processes (which tend to be non-standard) there are benefits to exploring current processes to capture the source of value.

However, too often, the rush to build technology or implement a new service structure means that business process design is not considered at any stage, resulting in compromises being made in the early part of a project that are hard to correct later.

Lean Process Design: The Theory

The 'Lean' technique has its roots in the auto manufacturing industry originally developed by Toyota. Lean manufacturing is often seen as a more refined version of earlier efficiency efforts, building upon the work of earlier leaders such as **Taylor** or **Ford**, learning from their mistakes. It is based on preserving value with less work. The primary goal of lean is to increase productivity, reduce lead times and costs, and improve quality. The main themes of lean are the elimination of zero value activities and continuous improvement, the introduction of multi-functional teams, Just in Time processes, integration of suppliers and flexible information systems **(Sanchez & Perez, 2001)**. It considers the expenditure of resources for any goal other than the creation end customer value to be wasteful, and a target for elimination. Its aim is to improve effectiveness by improving productivity, reducing lead times, costs and improving quality.

Lean design is concerned with creating a lean solution from the start, resulting in more value and less waste across the four value stream of design, supply, manufacturing, and customer. It involves concepts such as rapid learning cycles, managing the knowledge value stream, systematic problem solving and systematic innovation. It works from the perspective of the customer who consumes a product or service, "value" is defined as any action or process that a customer would be willing to pay for.

It is based around the idea of 'seven wastes':

- Transportation (reducing the cost of transporting goods)
- Inventory (reducing the amount of stock)
- Motion (minimised transfers where work takes place)
- Waiting (minimising waiting time)
- Over-processing (doing only what is required)
- Over-production (producing only what is required)
- Defects (reducing errors)

It can be difficult to justify the introduction of lean, as according to some research, in its initial use there can be productivity decreases **(Ahlstrom & Karlsonn, 1996)**.

Six Sigma: The Theory

Six Sigma seeks to improve the quality of process outputs by identifying and removing the causes of defects (errors) and minimising variability across processes. It has now grown to become a business strategy that focuses on improving understanding of customer requirements, business productivity and financial performance.

There are at least four definitions of Six Sigma, ranging from a set of statistical tools, an operational philosophy, a business culture and an analysis methodology. These are not mutually exclusive and overlap considerably **(Tjahjono et al., 2010)**. Most techniques are based on DMAIC (Define, Measure, Analyse, Improve, Control), a problem-solving method which aims at process improvement and the Design for Six Sigma (DFSS), mainly used for new product development.

Six Sigma is based on quality management and statistical methods and the name comes from the notion that if there are six standard deviations between the process mean and the nearest specification limit, virtually no items will fail to meet the specification. At Six Sigma, 99.99966% of the specification will be met. The practice of Six Sigma creates a special infrastructure of people within the organisation ("Champions", "Black Belts", "Green Belts", "Orange Belts", etc.) who are experts in these very complex methods. Six Sigma can be used to find and eliminate the root causes of a problem, reducing the variability in the process in order to prevent defects.

Six Sigma has been met with a mixture of enthusiasm and criticism. While many have actively embraced the technique into their cultures, a Fortune magazine article **(Morris, 2006)** criticised Six Sigma as "narrowly designed to fix an existing process" that fails to "come up with new products or disruptive technologies". It has also been seen as overly rigid and over-reliant on methods and tools, stifling creativity and not being focused on prevention. **Davenport (2008)** argues that it is elitist and enables only incremental improvements, not radical breakthroughs and should only be used in product manufacturing.

An analysis of business processes can be a great learning experience for a project team. It's always amazing to gather people together from different parts of a business to hear them discuss a process that they consider to be the same across the organisation, then to discover how wildly different it is being performed. Often, it will be the first time the organisation has stood back from its business processes and asked the question 'why?' and it can reveal the extent of change management needed. Ironically, the term 're-engineering' is often used to describe this activity, when in fact processes were never actually 'engineered' in the first place! The following sets some general principles for this activity:

- **Involve the right people**: Business process redesign is about looking at familiar ways of working and asking challenging questions about each step. Asking people who are very close to a process is unlikely to lead to an innovative or creative new solution, as they will be too 'locked in' to the way things have always worked and may only see the future in terms of the present. Henry Ford (allegedly) said that if he had asked people in the late 19th Century what they wanted from a transport system, they would have asked for a faster horse that ate less hay. Nothing in the mind-set of the people at that time would have led them to conceive of a motorised vehicle powered by gasoline.

- **Understand the Context:** Even if you do not undertake an 'as-is' process definition, it's important to understand the business strategy of the organisation to ensure that processes are set properly in context. It's also important to understand what currently works, perceptions of what could be improved and what needs to change. Defining the barriers to changing processes is part of this activity – many participants resist changes because *'We've always done it this way'* or worse, nobody actually knows why things are done in a certain way.

- **Review and challenge current processes**: This involves making a decision about each step in a process sequence and asking whether it can be automated, improved or potentially eliminated altogether. This is the basis of even the most sophisticated techniques - evaluating whether a step creates value.

- **Develop "Prototype" Processes**: This usually involves running workshops with key users and other interested parties, to identify process improvements and develop options. Managing this activity is a skilled task and striking the balance between allowing the team to air their views and making progress requires good facilitation. Arguably, it's impossible to design a good process without knowing how the functionality of the HR system will support it, since most HR systems are based on an underlying business model that makes assumptions about how processes will flow. Without access to those assumptions, processes will be designed in isolation and are likely to need revision - technology both supports and enables processes.

- **Define Performance Measures:** An important aspect of the process design workshops is the collection of data on current volumes (sometimes referred to as 'volumetrics'). Data about the number of applicants, new hires, training courses administered etc. provide a baseline for current performance levels and the basis for developing metrics for the newly designed processes. For example, a key performance measure might be a target for reducing the time and effort taken to produce an offer letter.

- **Define Reporting Requirements:** Design workshops are a good opportunity to discuss what management information is needed from each process. This also ensures that the base data needed for reporting is being captured at the right point; ideally, data should be gathered as a natural step in each process, rather than asking users to enter data specifically for reporting purposes.

- **Identify Short-Term Process Improvements:** Sometimes, workshop sessions identify high-value improvements (quick wins) that can be realised immediately, once they have been assessed for their impact. These help to promote the benefits of a business process review and are valuable in demonstrating its value to organisational stakeholders.

- **Validate & Refine "Prototype" Processes:** Once processes are defined, they can be used as the basis for discussion with end users about the changes that new processes will bring. This helps the project team to validate each process and test the reactions of key groups such as line managers and HR users.

- **Link Processes to System Design:** Although alignment with HR technology will have taken place during the initial design stage, business processes need to be designed into the HR system and specified at a level of technical detail, using a fit-gap approach.

A final consultation stage with a wider group is an important aspect of the change and transition activity, allowing the project team to consult a wider range of people than were involved in the workshops. The project team can then refine each of the process maps, workflow descriptions and performance targets to reflect the participants' ideas and suggestions.

Summary: Business Process Improvement

Business Process Improvement is an important tool in the HR Ready armoury – getting the right processes in place has a significant impact on HR services and ultimately, on competitive advantage. While many techniques are available to support business process design, there are some general principles that should be applied to this exercise to ensure that planned business benefits are delivered.

Whatever approach is taken to business process improvement, it's essential that workshop sessions are well facilitated in a way that will challenge current ways of working and not accept tradition ("we've always done it that way") as an excuse and will push the group to think of alternative approaches. It's also important to ensure there is good representation from across the organisation, attended by people who are keen to make change happen and have a mandate to make decisions. Process questions usually open up a wide range of policy and procedure issues, so it's important to have a channel back to key decision makers (such as a steering group) to resolve questions.

Business Process Improvement: Are you HR Ready?

- [?] Are your business processes as efficient and effective as possible?

- [?] Do your processes meet the needs of your customers?

- [?] Are your processes legally compliant and auditable?

- [?] Are there opportunities to use technology to automate your business processes?

- [?] Are processes properly documented and available to everyone?

- [?] Are new members of the team properly trained in using the processes?

- [?] How often do you review HR and Payroll processes to ensure they are keeping pace with developments in legislation, technology and people skills?

12 Building the HR Ready Business Case

Nowadays, people know the price of everything and the value of nothing.

Oscar Wilde, The Picture of Dorian Gray

Challenges of the Business Case

Perhaps one of the most complex and challenging aspects of any HR project is obtaining financial funding. This applies whether an organisation is seeking support for outsourcing, shared services, e-HRM or a leadership development programme. Creating a business case is usually unavoidable - all organisations have limited funds available to invest and there will always be competition for capital, so investments will be made where an organisation believes it will achieve the greatest return.

A basic requirement of any business case is to quantify the costs and benefits of a proposed investment in financial terms, enabling comparison to be made between projects competing for funds. Investments must be seen to make a positive contribution to organisational success, by bringing about a fundamental improvement in the way the business operates against a defined set of financial targets. By measuring the absolute amount of money created or saved by an investment, a business plan becomes a form of 'due diligence' to assure the organisation its money is being spent wisely. Conventional accounting techniques regard financial results as the 'proof' that a plan or strategy works.

However, as well as raising capital to fund a project, the business case serves other important purposes, including formally defining the objectives and scope of a project, understanding the potential barriers to implementation and anticipating the risks involved in delivering a successful project (although it's often difficult to assess accurately the variables that might affect achievement of the objective). In some cases, creating the business case also requires the development of options for the overall solution, not just a financial evaluation of pre-defined alternatives. Projects are generally much clearer and more likely to succeed if they are based on a well thought-out business case that has a clear link to the overall HR strategy and broader business goals.

The need for a business case is especially relevant for technology, which typically requires a substantial initial capital investment, although defining benefits consistently ranks as one of the top issues in the management of all forms of information technology (Ashford, Dyson, & Hodges, 1988; Powell, 1992; Sethi & King, 1994; Willcocks & Lester, 1997). Because of the challenges involved in technology-based business cases, the main focus of this chapter will be on creating a business case for technology investment, although the principles are the same for non-technology-related projects. This chapter mostly deals with the rational, 'science' part of building a business case – identifying benefits, understanding costs, creating value and the planning process. However, there is also an 'art' to writing a persuasive business case that will attract the backing of management and other stakeholders – a good business case is part economics, part politics and part creative writing and it should tap into the *'What's in it for me'* aspirations of its audience.

This chapter won't tell you how to 'fake' a business case where it doesn't exist or how to stretch the truth about what benefits might be available. Likewise, there is no guarantee that you will always find a successful Return on Investment (ROI) - sometimes it's just not economically viable to proceed. Likewise, this chapter cannot anticipate all the subtleties and vagaries of every organisation or industry sector and it can never replace a detailed study or professional advice. Hopefully, it will help avoid a situation where, as some researchers argue, the use of e-HRM is *"Often predicated on unproven claims about its functional consequence, potentially leading to the conclusion that in many cases, an eHRM investment is little more than a 'leap of faith'* (Stone, Stone-Romero, & Lukazweski (2006, p242).

Cost / Price vs. Value

Every one of us makes hundreds of decisions every day. We weigh up the pros and cons of every choice, gathering data, evaluating the options and selecting the best solution, based on a mix of hard data, past experience and the preferences we hold. Some of those decisions are about when to cross a road or what to eat, while others involve economic choices - for example, should you buy an expensive coffee from the coffee shop, or wait until you get to the office and use the less expensive coffee machine (here the decision is about cost versus the value created by the intangible benefit of taste). Do you stop to buy fuel now or wait until later (this involves factors such as cost, urgency and the risk of running out of fuel). These types of personal economic decisions are effectively 'mini' business cases - whether you are making a decision about where to go on holiday, buying a new house or car, or comparing prices as you walk around a supermarket involves the same decision processes as an investment in HR technology. The main difference is that most of our personal decisions are made unconsciously and informally, whereas a formal business case must justify the logic and provide analysis that supports the argument, usually for others to make a decision. The process by which people make decisions is also an important component in the development of a business case (see Breakout Box), so the starting point is a lesson in basic economics and psychology.

If a business case simply involved absolute, tangible financial measures, it would be a relatively straightforward exercise, a simple process of comparing costs against savings. However, 'cost', 'price' and 'value' are very different concepts that potentially complicate any evaluation (see the Breakout Box). For example, the economic value of something is not the same as its market price – cost relates to the amount of money that changes hands, whereas 'value' relates to the perceived ability of a good or service to satisfy a particular need. Cost is absolute, but value is relative and subjective. A person dying of thirst will pay more for drinking water than someone who has a full bottle in their hand because it will be valued differently, so the economics of supply and demand also have a role to play in any analysis.

Business cases must deal not only with hard financial facts (and there are fewer 'facts' than you might suppose)[19] but also with perceptions of value and how individuals perceive and evaluate what is important. This applies whether it involves the construction of a new airport or the replacement of an office printer - a good business case must recognise that some benefits cannot be defined as absolute financial outcomes (tangible outcomes). Although certain types of benefits at the operational level (such as headcount savings) can easily be reduced to financial metrics, many other types of benefits require a complex 'value judgment' to be made as to the worth of a particular outcome. For example, an investment may enable a new organisational capability, support an HR function becoming more focused on strategic work, or give line managers more time to manage their teams. The financial returns of these outcomes are much less direct than headcount savings and unless those evaluating the business case have a mechanism and structure for placing a value on intangible outcomes, they will not count towards a business case.

For this reason, value outcomes must at some point be converted into the common language of financial measures, making assumptions about their economic value. This inevitably creates conflict between those who seek absolute financial outcomes and those who recognise the intangible nature of value based outcomes. Perception, subjectivity and utility with regard to value all have important implications for the development of a business case and at this point, the art of writing a business case becomes as important as the science.

The HR Value model (first raised in Chapter 6) offers a framework for exploring these less tangible outcomes and allocating a

---

[19] The idea of 'facts' and 'truth' have occupied the minds of philosophers for centuries, going back to Socrates, Aristotle and Plato. Most major philosophers from Kant to Bertrand Russell have taken a position on this subject. Mark Twain got it right when he said "Get your facts first, and then you can distort them as much as you please".

value to them. In recognition of the importance of value, an adaptation of the HR Value Model, The e-HRM Value Model[20], states that technology-based business benefits fall into only one of three categories:

1. Operational benefits: The impact of headcount reduction and other direct operational cost savings
2. Productivity benefits: The impact of improvements in performance and productivity enablers
3. Strategic benefits: The creation of new organisational capabilities

Each of these is explored in detail below and shown diagrammatically in Figure 27.

> To illustrate the HR Value Model, examples are given based on a fictitious organisation with the following characteristics:
> - Total Business Sales = £100m
> - 3,000 employees,
> - Total salary bill = £82.5m, based on 500 managers, average salary = £40,000 and 2500 employees, average salary = £25,000
> - HR Function = 15 people, average salary £25,000

---

[20] The e-HRM Value actually came first and the HR Value Model was adapted from it.

Value: The Theory

In classical economic theory, the value of an object or service is its worth in an open and competitive market (that is, its *market value*). The '*value in use*' must be at least equal the amount consumers would be prepared to pay to buy a good or service. To add further complication, the original meaning of 'price' referred to the '*exchange value*' of something, rather than the amount of money that changes hands (what it could be traded for – that is, the 'prize'.

Economic value, a concept dating back to **Adam Smith (1776)**, expresses value from the perspective of its utility for the user, as distinct from the amount paid, where value is how much a desired object or condition is worth relative to other objects or conditions. This idea borrows from the *subjective theory of value* (a concept that has been around since the middle ages – see **van Mises (2010)**) which states that the value of a good is not determined by any inherent property of the good, nor by the amount of labour required to produce the good, but by the importance an individual places on that object or service for the achievement of their desired ends. However, traditional accounting regards 'value added' simply as the selling price less the cost of raw materials and production activities.

Two other concepts are important; firstly, *instrumental* value (something which acts as a means towards getting something else that is good) and secondly, *intrinsic* value (something that is worth having as an end for itself). This concept goes back to **Plato** in Ancient Greece. The original meanings of the words make a distinction between cost, price and value.

Ultimately, value (like beauty) is in the eye of the beholder, which can lead to the Paradox of value - the apparent contradiction that, although water is on the whole more useful (in terms of survival) than diamonds, diamonds command a higher price in the market because they are more rare. In compiling a business case, it's important that concepts of value, cost and price are taken into account, with an awareness of the role of *subjective value* and *instrumental value*.

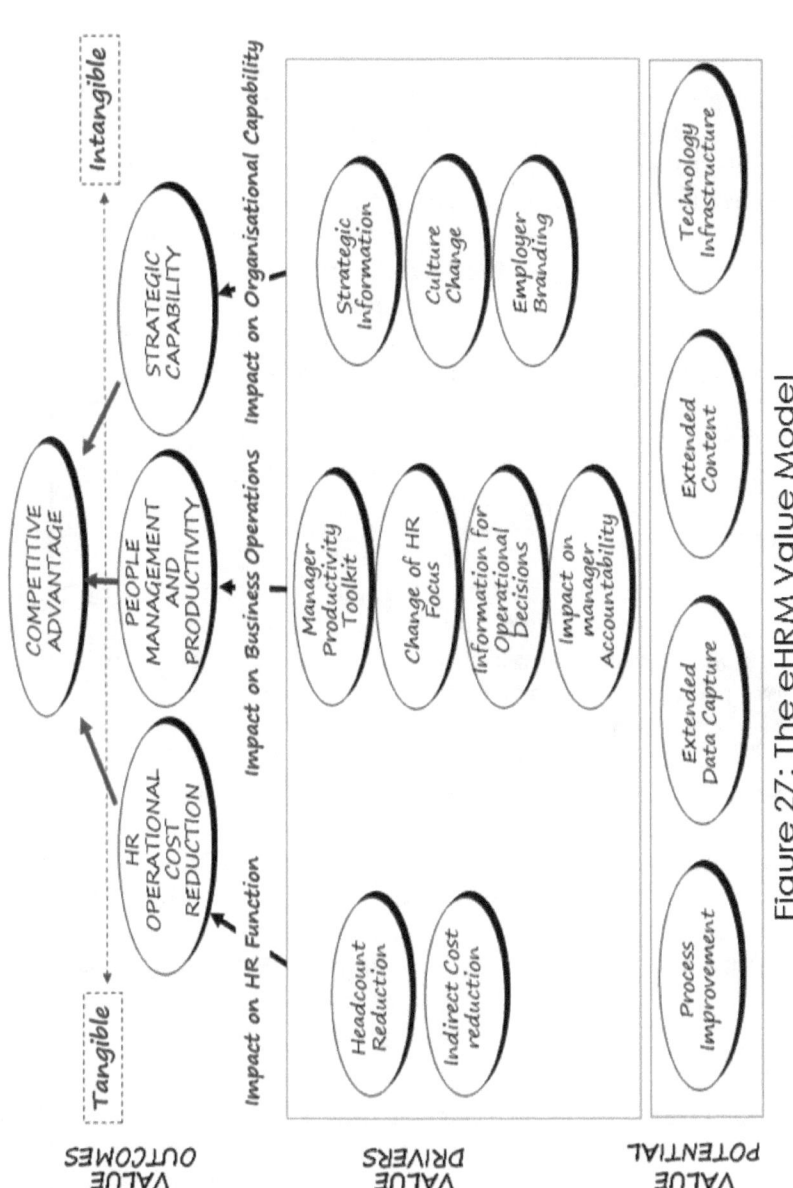

Figure 27: The eHRM Value Model

Decision Making: The Theory

Decision making is the mental process that results in the selection of a course of action among several alternative scenarios; every decision making process produces a final choice or action **(Reason, 1990)**. Decision making can be rational or irrational and may be based on explicit or tacit assumptions. The *"Rational Choice Theory"* proposes that we maximise benefits and minimise the costs to maximise personal advantage **(Friedman, 1953)**. However, these theories assume an individual has full or perfect information about the choice made, together with the cognitive ability and time to weigh every choice against every other choice. Later theories suggested the idea of *"Bounded rationality"* to express the idea that human decision making is limited by the available information, available time, and the information-processing ability of the mind **(Kahneman, 2000)**.

When making decisions, most people are constrained by lack of time, together with significant limitations to the amount of complexity they can cope with. To overcome this, people use cognitive 'rules of thumb' to speed up decision making (heuristics) but this can lead to errors such as bias. **Herbert Simon** coined the term 'satisficing' which denotes the situation where people seek solutions or accept choices or judgments that are "good enough" for their purposes, but could be optimised. Likewise, the way in which a problem is framed can have a significant effect on how decisions are made. For example, financial decisions can be affected by whether you see yourself in a position of loss or gain; in a position of gain, people tend to become risk averse; in a position of loss, people tend to take risks to avoid or recover losses.

Simon (1983) defined two decision making styles: maximisers try to make an optimal decision, whereas satisficers simply try to find a solution that is "good enough". Maximisers tend to take longer making decisions and make trade-offs carefully; they also tend to regret their decisions more often (perhaps because they are more able than satisficers to recognise that a decision turned out to be sub-optimal).

Type 1: Operational Benefits

Operational benefits are the most tangible type of benefit and refer to hard savings (or cost avoidance) that flow directly to the bottom-line. It's unlikely that there will be investment support without this fundamental type of return on investment, even though in real terms productivity or strategic benefits could deliver better long-term outcomes.

In the case of HR technology projects, value creation at the Operational Benefits level has two Value Drivers:

a.   Reduced HR headcount

Operational tasks such as the manual entry of data, maintaining employee records, performing calculations, filing and dealing with enquiries are expensive because they are heavily reliant on the people that operate them. Employing people involves the costs of their salaries and wages, plus certain overheads such as benefits, facilities and equipment. Adequate cover must be provided for sickness and holidays, as well as the need for regular re-training to maintain their skills.

Evidence suggests that the introduction of technology reduces the amount of time spent on operational (i.e. administrative) work through the automation of routine business processes. As a result, most business cases typically identify opportunities for cost reduction, based on a classic model that has existed since the industrial revolution - that is, the exchange of human work for machine work, leading to a reduction in the requirement for human effort and the removal of people related costs. Automation typically reduces transaction costs by 25%, cycle time by 66%, and service centre enquiries by 20% (CedarCrestone, 2011).

One important HR measure of administrative efficiency, apart from cost, is the number of HR people required to deliver the service or process relative to the number of employees supported – most large organisations strive for an overall ratio better than 1:100, that is, one HR person serving every 100 employees, although this can vary across industry sectors. The HR Ratio can be a useful benchmark for ensuring that efficiency targets are being met and it often becomes a Key Performance Indicator in service centre operations.

Converting these potential benefits into bottom-line results is more difficult than identifying them – 'realising' headcount related benefits (that is, actually achieving the planned benefit) often requires an employee redundancy programme to remove costs (which should be factored into the cost of realising the benefit) or through the redeployment of people to another area of HR or the wider business. Of course, the extent of benefits achieved depends on the initial level of inefficiency – the greater the current level of inefficiency, the higher the headcount needed to support it and the more likely it is that improvements will be made.

b.   Reduced Direct expenditure

Organisations often experience reductions in non-headcount related costs as a result of their investment in HR technology. These other forms of cost benefit arise as a result of displacing existing technologies, with resultant savings in IT licensing and support costs, or switching to electronic rather than conventional media. The introduction of technology may also mean that more documents (offer letters, interview invitations etc.) can be managed on-line, with a reduced need for stationery, postage, facilities and other day-to-day costs. In particular, recruitment processes are often heavily reliant on expensive physical mail, whereas e-recruitment eliminates this need by automating applicant contact. This category can also refer to savings that do not involve people, such as reducing recruitment agency budgets, reducing staff training costs, fewer facilities etc. While this is a secondary effect and less likely than direct headcount reduction to yield significant financial benefits, the structural changes that e-HRM enables create an environment for additional cost benefit.

Table 3 offers examples of a number of operational benefits, presented here simply as suggested areas for exploration – they will not apply to all organisations and may not be relevant or available to everyone. The benefit assumptions are based on experience across a wide range of organisations but are consistent with data provided by external analysts and experience of working with clients across various industry sectors.

Benefits can also be justified against the avoidance of costs, for example, an organisation which is growing but wishes to provide the same level of service without increasing its headcount or other costs in line with the growth may be able to accommodate growth with lower marginal costs. Avoided costs are valid in a business case if there is an incremental improvement in service or efficiency, requiring a disproportionately lower investment.

> **Operational Benefits: The Theory**
>
> The cost reduction capability of e-HRM is well documented in research and there is general consensus that HR technology lowers HR operating costs, although estimates as to the potential for savings vary. Some research has identified a reduction in administrative staff of up to 40% and reductions in transaction costs of 50% **(Wiscombe, 2001).** US evidence suggests a 20-25% reduction in HR costs is possible through e-HRM **(CedarCrestone, 2009). The Aberdeen Group (2009a)** found that Best in Class organisations decreased the number of manual HR transactions by 11% and shortened HR service delivery cycle times by 5%.

Key Questions

- Which paper-based processes could be conducted through e-HRM?
- Do you understand the current costs of your HR processes?
- How much money could be saved by investing in HR technology?
- What future costs could be avoided?

TYPE OF BENEFIT	BENEFIT ASSUMPTION	EXAMPLE
A. Headcount savings Automation of business processes results in the following: • Reduced process time • Reduced error correction time • Reduced form completion • Reduced data entry times • Reduced enquiries • Reduced cycle times	Assume 20-25% reduction in HR FTE cost per process for core process automation, 30-40% reduction when using self-service. Assume HR administration team of 15 people	**Reduction of 30% FTE in HR at an average salary of £25,000 = £112,500**
B. Reduced Direct Expenditure • Elimination of existing IT systems • Printing, documentation and communications • Facilities costs (buildings etc.) • Reduced travel costs • Avoidance of external fees	Actual costs for each item such as: • Elimination of software license costs, maintenance and support • Reduced facilities costs • Reduced external printing and support costs • Reduced professional fees	**Varies by organisation – assume savings on current system license costs for two systems at £50,000 for HR and £20,000 for standalone recruitment system**

TABLE 3: EXAMPLE OPERATIONAL BENEFITS

Type 2: Productivity Benefits

Chapter 6 highlighted the fact that HR operational costs typically account for only around 1% of total business operating costs, so even a 30% reduction in HR costs will make only a small contribution to a cost-focused competitive strategy. However, if the competitive strategy is based on product differentiation or innovation, low-cost human resource management may not be desirable, especially where people management issues are a significant barrier to business growth. In this case, the business will be better able to recognise the *instrumental value* of these benefits and more willing to make an investment in improved people management and higher performance outcomes.

Productivity benefits are 'enablers', meaning that they are part of a value chain which leads to different ways of working, new processes and new behaviours. It relates to how managers spend their time and how they work, how HR functions provide better support for managers in managing their people and the information that supports operational decisions. This category is potentially more powerful than Operational Benefits, because the benefits relate to the wider business, not just the HR function. However, they rely on certain assumptions about how this value will be created and an acknowledgement of their less tangible nature. The Value Drivers in this category are:

a.   **Manager Productivity Tools**

Organisations are increasingly devolving responsibility for HR actions to their line managers - one study found that more than 80% of organisations have pushed out transactions to managers, with substantial growth predicted in this area (cited in Williams, 2008, p.47). By making technology tools and information available to managers and supervisors (and employees) to perform their jobs, line managers become less reliant on the HR team, more self-sufficient and more productive. For example, online performance management systems, workforce planning tools, online time management systems and even simple team planners give managers greater control over staff and remove some of the administrative burden. As a result, managers are able to spend more time working on their job to increase organisational productivity.

Calculating the benefit that derives from this is more complicated than the relatively simple headcount reduction associated with Operational Benefits. While there is a time-saving element for managers, in general this represents only a small proportion of managerial work and generally it's not possible to remove whole management layers from the business (unless the supervisory structure allows this). It's more likely that managers will save twenty to thirty minutes per day on people administration (for example, by removing the need to complete manual timesheets), so the question arises as to what they can do with that time to become more productive. The business case challenge is to convert that additional time into a genuine productivity improvement.

b.   Change of HR Focus

A central theme in human resource management over the past 30 years has been the idea that HR needs to undertake a more strategic role. Even in organisations where the HR Business Partner model has been implemented, evidence suggests that Business Partners frequently find themselves pre-occupied by operational issues, leaving them little time to diagnose and develop strategic HR solutions (Deloitte, 2009). It's often the case that highly paid professional HR people become embroiled in routine administration at the expense of supporting line managers in achieving higher levels of employee productivity.

Changing the focus of HR refers to the opportunity that technology provides to enable HR to concentrate on other activities, such as supporting line managers, with an impact on employee productivity, employee morale, decision making and information. The introduction of technology means that repetitive, manual, paper-based work can more easily be separated from professional HR work and as a result, the HR team becomes more productive and can concentrate on value-adding people management tasks, rather than administration. This change of focus is most effective when it is linked to a shared service or outsourcing approach for service delivery (as discussed in Chapter 1) and the introduction of a Business Partner model (as discussed in Chapter 7).

c. Information for Operational Decisions

As described in Chapter 5, good Business Intelligence is critical to any organisation. e-HRM supports this benefit by providing improved access and better quality information to line managers and the HR function. The Productivity Benefits category makes a distinction between operational information (relating to short / medium term planning data) and strategic information (aimed at long-term decision making); strategic information is dealt with under the Strategic Benefits section. Operational information relates to providing managers with meaningful data such as employee headcount and staffing levels, cost and overtime data and sickness absence rates. Retention data can lead to reduced employee turnover, lower employee replacement costs and fewer vacancies. My own research (Foster, 2009) indicates that this is one of the most powerful benefit areas for the introduction of technology, one that is highly valued by line managers and therefore an important area to stress when compiling a business case.

d. Impact on Manager Accountability

Line managers have an important role to play in delivering HR programmes, but many organisations find that managers sometimes avoid the people management aspect of their role. Research shows that in some cases, line managers are either indifferent or reluctant to carry out team development activities (Harris, Doughty, & Kirk, 2002).

The introduction of HR Technology can be a major driver in encouraging managers to become more accountable for HR processes. Engaging line managers in implementing HR technology exposes line managers to HR issues and gives them better appreciation of HR practices, with significant positive outcomes for HR (Preece & Harrison, 1988). The introduction of e-HRM, linked to business process redesign, is an opportunity to highlight and transform managerial accountabilities, where technology acts as both a practical enabler as well as a 'symbolic' representation of new ways of working (Kossek, Young, Gash, & Nichol, 1994). New technology can act as a stimulus for a fresh approach to Human Resource practices and new employment relationships (Tansley, Newell, & Williams, 2001).

The Aberdeen Group (2009a, p.13) found that Best in Class organisations were two and a half times more likely to allow managers self-service access to HR and payroll data.

While the Productivity Benefits of the business case are less tangible than hard operational savings, they are potentially very powerful. However, because they are less direct and based on the 'enabler' argument (*the **instrumental value***), productivity improvement proposals may be accepted positively and greeted with enthusiastic support, or they may result in loud laughter from the office of the Finance Director. I have personally worked on business cases with organisations and had both reactions; knowing when to use these arguments is part of the 'art' of preparing a business case!

Table 4 provides examples of various forms of Productivity Benefit. The examples shown are representative only and are likely to need deeper analysis and negotiation to get agreement that they can be accepted and delivered.

Productivity Benefits: The Theory

Managers spend on average 20 per cent of their time working on HR duties **(Luthans et al, 1988 in Brandl, Toft Madsen & Madsen, 2009, p.196)** dealing with topics such as employee administration, performance, recruitment and development. Most HR policies rely on line manager action or support; line managers' skills at handling HRM also influence employee commitment to the employer and the job **(Purcell & Hutchinson, 2007)**. However, **(Nehles et al, 2006)** note that lack of training, lack of interest, work overload, conflicting priorities and self-serving behaviour mean that managers often neglect HR work.

Nevertheless, **Kochan & Dyer (1993)** and **Karakanian (2000)** point to an organisational trend for deploying HR responsibilities to line managers, making them more self-sufficient in dealing with day-to-day people management, in areas such as performance management, managing employee disciplinary meetings and organising learning and development. For HR specialists, high quality managerial involvement can liberate them from operative routine work **(Cunningham & Hyman, 1999)** and this is a prerequisite for focusing on strategic HR work.

The UK **CIPD (2007b)** found that 91% of survey respondents ranked improving the quality of information available more highly than reducing the administrative burden on the HR department (83%) when investing in technology. **Teo & Rodwell (2007)** found that the top reasons for implementation were to achieve more accurate HR information and better tracking of HR information.

e-HRM has the potential to eliminate the repetitive, manual, paper-based chores from HR work, allowing the HR team to focus on value-adding people management rather than administration, consistent with the findings of others **(Hope Hailey et al., 1997; McGovern et al., 1997; Cunningham & Hyman, 1999).**

TYPE OF BENEFIT	BENEFIT ASSUMPTION	EXAMPLE
A. Manager Productivity Tools Reduced administrative burden on managers allowing them to focus on managing performance, managing absence and employee development	Assume 30 minutes time saved per manager per week on HR administration following full manager self-service	**30 minutes saved per week = £285,714 or 1,253 hours available per year for more productive work**
B. Change of HR Focus By removing the administrative workload, HR can focus on important activities.	HR staff are able to switch to more value adding roles to support the delivery of the business strategy	**Potentially a 0.5% increase in business productivity (negotiable), potentially a £200k sales increase**
C. Information for Operational Decisions: Attendance management: Employee self-service tools for recording and reporting on absence give managers critical information to understand patterns and trends.	Potential absence reduction of 1%; assume current absence level of 5%	**A 1% absence reduction equates to a £750,000 cost reduction**

TYPE OF BENEFIT	BENEFIT ASSUMPTION	EXAMPLE
C. Information for Operational Decisions: Employee turnover: Better information about leavers supports the development of strategies for improving retention	Average replacement cost for a leaver is £4,300; assume that better data leads to a 1% reduction turnover. Current turnover rate is 8%	**For a 3,000 employee company with 8% employee turnover, a 1% reduction would equate to £129,000**
C/D. Improved operational budget management: Technology leads to better quality management information, helping organisations spend the HR budget more effectively.	Assume that for each area invested in, you 10-15% better spend of the budget can be achieved	**Annual spend on recruitment agencies = £250,000; annual external training cost = £1m, 10% reduction based on better supplier intelligence = £125,000**
C/D. Information for Operational Decisions: Improved compliance: Better management information improves internal compliance as well as better reporting	Take the cost of penalties for non-compliance, or the savings in time against manual methods of producing data	**Avoidance of an equal pay claim against the company, which has an unlimited penalty; assume average £75,000**

TABLE 4: EXAMPLE PRODUCTIVITY BENEFITS

Type 3: Strategic Capability Benefits

This third area offers the least tangible Value Outcome, yet potentially creates the most long term value and the strongest links to competitive advantage. Some studies have identified linkages between IT strategy and overall firm performance; for example, finding a correlation between companies with high IT capabilities and levels of profitability, although evidence remains inconclusive (Bharadwaj, 2000; Santhanam & Hartono, 2003). This category includes any outcomes that provide the organisation with new strategic capabilities - for example, it might reinforce the external brand of the organisation, improve employee engagement, provide long-term strategic information and in some cases, enable a shift in the relationship between the organisation and employees. These types of benefits are less direct than headcount savings and (like Productivity Benefits) are enablers, in that they bring about deeper changes in the organisation at the behavioural or perceptual level. Due to the intangible nature of strategic benefits, attaching a monetary value can be complex, but the scale of benefits can be substantial. The relevant Value Drivers related to technology are:

a. *Strategic Information*

You can be sure that a Production Manager on an assembly line knows the tolerance, speed and output of every machine in the factory and the Warehouse Manager knows exactly what is on every rack, how long it has been there and when it is due out. But managers often do not know the skills and capabilities of their team, where there are gaps in skills levels and even whether the business plans can be achieved given current employee skills.

The powerful information available from the data within an HR system supports strategic decision making and creates competitive advantage. As previously noted, strategic information is different from operational information, having a different focus and a greater role in long-term planning. At an operational level, knowing the total headcount and absence rate of the workforce is valuable, but strategic information has a more predictive role because it provides the business with deep insight, such as knowing what skills will be needed in five years to enable the success of the business plan. Failing to understand these issues and take the wrong actions could put the entire business plan at risk for the organisation or lead to expensive mistakes. For business case purposes, it is often acceptable to factor in a proportion of company revenues, as the impact of strategic information is at the total organisation level. This topic was explored more fully in Chapter 5.

b. *Culture Change*

The people-technology relationship provides the potential to alter drastically the pattern of organisational communication and development in an organisation and as a result, to reinforce or change organisational culture. E-HRM therefore becomes a vehicle for supporting corporate leadership, culture and relationships and acts as "*An indispensable enabler for developing corporate character through strategic HR intervention*" (Sadri & Chatterdee, 2003). Technology also provides opportunities for creating greater levels of satisfaction with internal processes – consider how employees and potential employees are becoming increasingly technology-literate, choosing to manage their personal lives through the Internet, using services such as on-line shopping for electrical goods and groceries, booking a holiday or arranging insurance and banking. As a result, the Internet has raised expectations generally about the quality and method of service delivery in the workplace and staff will find it increasingly unacceptable to work with old-fashioned, paper based processes at work. The use of technology in HR has an impact not only on employee communications, but also on perceptions of HR service delivery and these can lead to improved employee satisfaction and engagement.

Passing greater levels of accountability to line managers through e-HRM can be a powerful statement of a change to the culture in the business. Indeed, many employers see e-HRM as a means to create a more 'grown up' relationship with staff, where people are allowed to take direct responsibility for their personal data and HR administration without any 'hand-holding' from the HR department.

Strategic Capability: The Theory

To achieve competitive advantage, an organisation must identify, acquire, develop and apply distinctive strategic capabilities, which are most often derived from the unique relationships an organisation has with its suppliers, customer or employees. In broad HR terms, these capabilities might include a skilled, flexible workforce or a unique culture that enables the organisation to gain superiority over its competitors.

Porter & Millar (1985) argue that information technology creates competitive advantage through the value chain, where improved access and quality of information supports better strategic business planning and the development of future initiatives. **Beckers & Bsat (2002)** support the use of an HRIS for producing competitive advantage, through its role as a strategic decision support system (DSS) including the management and planning of industrial relations strategies **(Hussain et al., 2007).**

According to **Lengnick-Hall & Lengnick-Hall (2006)**, competitive capabilities arise from an organisation's ability to exploit its technology, build intellectual capability and create a superior knowledge base. There is a powerful linkage between possession of the underlying data in e-HRM and creating a strategic capability based on the greater use of information. Research refers to the 'empowering' impact of e-HRM – for example, **Lengnick-Hall & Mortiz (2003)** note that by allowing employees to control their personal information, organisations make a major statement about their relationship with employees and their culture.

Technology supports improved employee satisfaction - studies have shown that a 2% increase in employee satisfaction can lead to a 1% growth in customer satisfaction **(Rucci et al., 1998). Bhatnagar (2007)** sees e-HRM as providing a powerful brand identity in the external recruitment area which would not be possible with traditional approaches. However, **Marler (2009)** suggests that e-HRM does not in itself make the HR function more strategic and that e-HRM can only become more strategic in the hands of a strategically focused HR function.

c. Employer Branding

E-HRM also presents opportunities for developing the 'employer brand', including certain forms of strategic capability that would not be possible without the technology. As people become increasingly technology-literate and the Internet raises expectations about the quality and method of service delivery in the workplace, those looking at the organisation from outside (such as applicants) will form a view about a potential employer from the way that it presents itself on the internet and the responsiveness of the HR function during the recruitment process. E-HRM can help shape these perceptions in a positive way by providing the ability to access, collect and disseminate information, giving individuals greater access to information about job opportunities, benefits and setting expectations about working for an employer. This creates a powerful external brand identity and competitive advantage in the recruitment market that would not be possible with traditional paper-based approaches. Again, placing a value on these activities is even more complex than in previous categories. Table 5 provides examples of strategic benefits.

Culture Change: AgencyCo

One organisation, a large UK public sector agency, declared that bringing about a significant change in the way that line managers work was a central objective of its e-HRM strategy, with the explicit objective of reinforcing management accountabilities. e-HRM would have two roles, firstly to support the development of a shared services organisation to reduce the administrative workload, and secondly to provide a suite of on-line tools that would emphasise managerial responsibilities and make line managers less dependent on central HR support. These objectives were seen as more important than cost reduction. This organisation described clear cultural changes as an outcome of their project, where managers become more self-sufficient.

TYPE OF BENEFIT	BENEFIT ASSUMPTION	EXAMPLE
A. Improved strategic information: Business Intelligence supports strategic decision making	Better planning results in better employee deployment, better productivity or potentially even the ability to survive in the market.	***1% better deployment of staff leads to value contribution of £725k based on total salary bill***
B. Culture Change and Employee Satisfaction Support for culture change, leading to improved employee satisfaction	Leads to increased productivity, reduced turnover or other forms of competitive advantage. Assume each 2% increase in employee satisfaction leads to a 1% performance	***Improved culture leads to 1% increase in productivity = £1m based on sales of £100m A 0.5% sales increase is worth £200k***
B/C Employer Branding: Technology makes HR more accessible and enhances employer reputation and branding	Assume improved retention of 0.5% for full employee/manager self-service. Assumes £4,300 replacement	***For a 3,000 employee company with 8% employee turnover, reduced turnover = £65k cost per employee***

TABLE 5: EXAMPLE STRATEGIC CAPABILITY BENEFITS

Building the Business Case

The methodology set out below is based on experience of creating a wide range of business cases across different industry sectors. It's a simple, four-stage approach, which involves outlining the assumptions, priorities and potential service delivery models being considered, assessing the value case, developing options and finally preparing the case for presentation. Again, it's based primarily on creating a business case for technology, but the principles are equally applicable for other forms of HR investment. Other methodologies of course exist, but most follow a similar logic - it's based on common sense and attempts to put a structure around what can be a haphazard, tortuous and (often) flawed process. Figure 28 shows the approach in diagram form and the key stages are set out below:

Stage 1: Preparation

Every project is based on a series of assumptions about the nature of the problem to be solved. These are derived from business and HR strategies and typically involve improving the efficiency or quality of an existing operation or creating some new form of organisational capability. In an earlier chapter, the need to understand *"What fire is being put out?"* was discussed, and it's particularly relevant for the creation of a business case. This is the point at which a business case becomes political – is someone simply trying to get post-hoc evidence to support a decision that has already been made or is it a genuine desire to develop a new, innovative solution?

The question is important because it shapes the way a business case is developed. Any good business case will identify alternatives (including the option to do nothing) but the options may be alternatives to a preferred option or genuine alternatives with no particular preferred outcome. There are strong parallels to academic research, where the process involves defining a working (null) hypothesis and identifying the variables that would prove or disprove the theory; sometimes there is no default solution and the business case must focus on exploration, interpretation and generating new theories and solutions. The first stage of any business case is therefore to understand the context of the analysis (who has asked for the business case, why has it been asked for and why now

Organisations sometimes find that the business case analysis quickly becomes blurred with the technology selection process and they are tempted to dive into the technology analysis before defining the overall problem. A further reason for proper definition of the objective of the business case is to ensure that these two activities are kept separate and the business case does not simply seek to compare one technology solution against another. While this may form part of the overall analysis, the focus should be on solving the primary business problem, not just identifying which software to buy. It's all too easy to get down to the level of software comparison without asking some fundamental questions about what the software needs to do, how it will be used, what alternatives exist and the scope of requirements; unless the investigation gets to the root of the business problem, there is a risk of developing a technically efficient solution but failing to meet the central requirement. To continue the academic analogy, it's important to define the research question and frame the decision to be made in appropriate terms.

It's also important to ask 'Who is affected by this project?' Discussion with a wide range of stakeholders is an excellent way of gaining commitment and building enthusiasm for the project. Those affected will include people who are providing the funding, those who will use the system and those that may have a valid contribution to make to its development. Unless there is a strong sense that there is a strong 'burning platform' (that is, a compelling key business reason to go ahead), or that there is a real consequence to failure, the project will never attract enough attention to proceed. Even with a great business case, your project will have to compete with other projects demanding funding. Change management approaches and stakeholders are discussed in greater detail in Chapter 13.

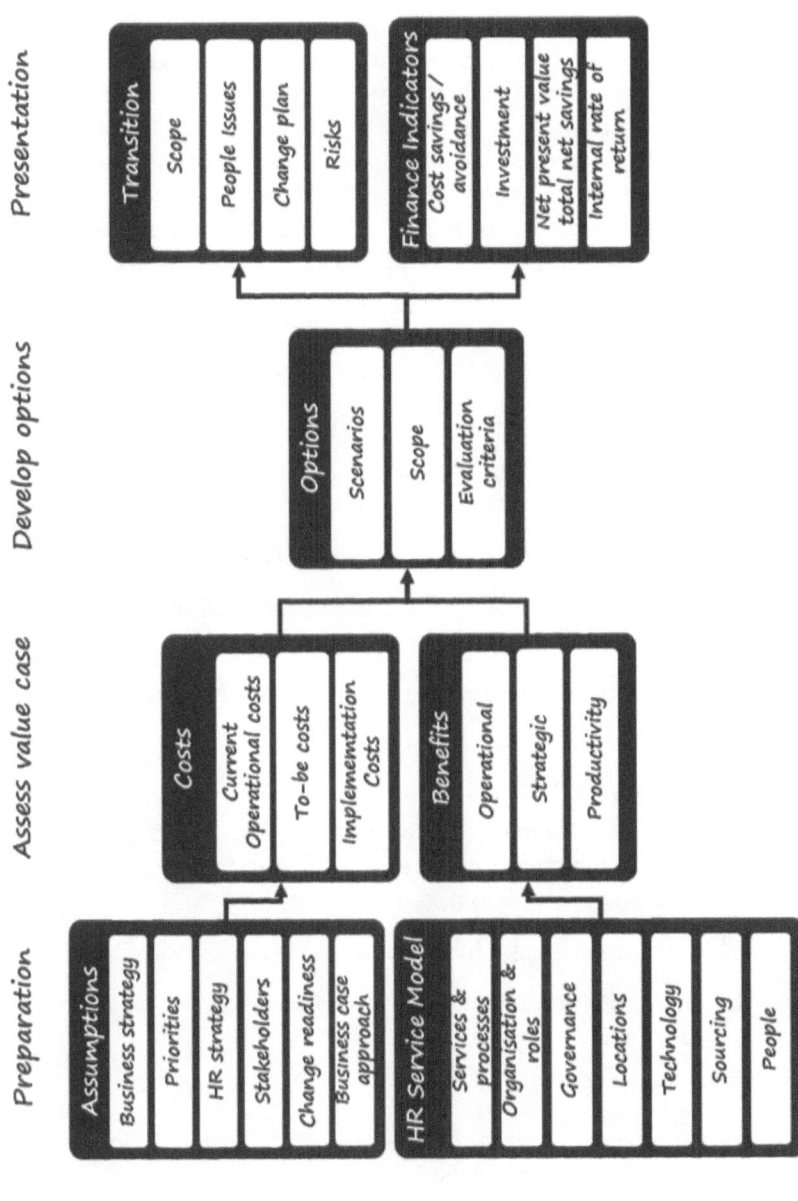

Figure 28: Business Case Methodology

The processes and standards by which business cases are approved vary enormously across organisations. For some, intense financial analysis is demanded; for others, a simplified, high level proposal is acceptable. Some organisations will acknowledge that not all benefits can be easily expressed in financial terms (intangible benefits) and others will insist that only hard cash counts; a risk-averse organisation will require a different business case from one accustomed to taking risks. It's also important to find out the internal rules for proposing a business case and once again, to understand the politics of the business case - what themes tend to work, what has been the approach of previously successful business cases in the organisation, who makes decisions and who are the key influencers?

Key Questions

- What are the business and HR strategy drivers for the project?
- Will existing systems meet these needs?
- What priorities exist or may soon exist that will affect the organisation's ability to thrive or even survive?
- How ready is the organisation to manage the changes needed?
- Who is the customer?
- Is there a 'burning platform' or urgency for a solution? What is the minimum rate of return which is acceptable and over what time period?
- What are the rules for submitting a business case?
- What is the culture of the organisation for obtaining funding?
- What format does a business case need to take?
- Who can provide advice on the technical/financial aspects of the numbers?

Stage 2: Assess the Value Case

The value case is at the heart of the business case – it involves comparing the current costs of the business operation or process in scope to the future costs of running that operation, together with the full range of tangible and intangible benefits that are created. It also takes into account the cost of implementing the new solution, so that costs can be offset against the benefits over a period of time.

1. Current Operational Costs

A thorough analysis of current HR operational costs is an essential part of preparing the business case and will help to shape assumptions, options and the future service delivery model. Surprisingly few organisations have a good understanding of the costs of delivering their current HR and Payroll services, although those that recharge their services back to users typically have better insight into costs. Without this data, it's impossible to create a baseline for the potential benefits of an investment and it will be difficult to measure any improvements it may bring. There are several approaches to identifying current costs:

a. Activity Based Costing (ABC)

Activity Based Costing is based on the work of Kaplan and Cooper (1998) and involves breaking down each business process into discrete components, much like traditional time-and-work measurement process. It requires a detailed analysis of each HR activity to establish total cycle-time (how long each process takes) elapsed time (the actual time spent on each step) plus the fixed operational costs involved. Costs should be based on the fully loaded cost of everyone involved (i.e. including salary and labour burden costs such as benefits provided to HR staff) and the overhead costs of employing administrative staff such as office space etc.

ABC is very much a 'bottom-up' process, where the overall benefits are derived from the combination of many small assumptions and small process improvements. However, for many organisations, it can be difficult to calculate exactly how long each part of a process takes – HR administration is not the same as working in a manufacturing plant because there are so many variables involved, which mean it is not a precise science.

Attempting to define activities to this level of detail may be either too complex or impractical.

b.   'Whole Process' approach

This is a much simpler approach than Activity Based Costing, which at its most basic involves adding up the total value of salaries, facilities, technology and other costs of running the operation in scope. Although this approach is more general in nature, it's a much simpler approach and may be more appropriate should Activity Based Costing seem too cumbersome. However, it risks making sweeping assumptions about how costs are incurred and it may not stand up to deep scrutiny. For this reason, a Whole Process Approach may be used as an initial estimate prior to a more detailed analysis using ABC. Nevertheless, in some case, this approach may meet the needs of the business case and may be accurate enough.

Key Questions

- Are the current costs of delivering HR services understood?

- What is the main driver of these costs – people, facilities, technology?

- What administrative, paper-based, manual processes are currently being carried out by the HR team or other staff?

- How much time and money is spent on providing these activities, including temporary support staff, facilities and equipment?

- What services and processes actually need to be provided?

- What do customers really want?

2. Project Costs

To ensure there is a valid return on investment, it's important to include every item of cost involved in implementing a new solution. Implementation costs are often deceptive and some can easily be overlooked - for example, the introduction of e-HRM may mean that additional IT infrastructure is needed (web servers, new desktop PCs etc.), or it may be necessary to hire additional staff with specialist skills to support the management of e-HRM during the implementation project or in day to day operations.

The analysis of costs should also include the cost of back-filling the project with contractors to enable existing staff to devote more time to the project. Some organisations have special rules about how VAT is handled and this also needs to be factored into the cost calculation. Any redundancy or redeployment costs involved in reducing headcount will also need to be taken into account for the value case.

In simple terms, project implementation costs will either be classed as capital costs or expense. The way the organisation treats these cost items can make a major difference to project economics, so it's important to be clear about how the organisation regards what are capital costs (normally those costs linked to the initial set-up that accountants can depreciate over a defined period) and what are classed as an expense (those costs that come straight from the bottom line and recur over the life of the software or service). Implementation costs are handled in different ways by different organisations – most regard them as an expense but some treat them as capital expenditure. Table 6 provides examples of some of the project implementation costs that typically feature in an HR project.

Key Questions

- Have all implementation costs been included?
- Will realisation costs such as the cost of redundancy be included in project costs?
- How will project implementation costs be treated by Finance?

TYPE	CAPITAL INVESTMENT	EXPENSES
Initial costs	• Application software • Web and application servers • Desktop computers, laptops, tablets • Networks • Anything that will last for several years	• Internal IT support • Project team • External consultancy • Training • Change consultancy • Communications
Ongoing costs	• Software upgrades • Hardware upgrades • License maintenance costs • Software enhancement • Internet fees • Support services • Additional modules • Salaries of HR systems staff	May be capital or expenses

TABLE 6: CAPITAL V EXPENSE COSTS

3. **Benefits**

As discussed at the start of this Chapter, benefits are probably the hardest element of the business case to assess and cause the most debate, because they are predictions of a possible future outcome and cannot be guaranteed. The easiest benefits to define are tangible financial items such as reductions in headcount and operational cost – these are often related to process improvement, resulting in fewer people being needed to provide the service or process. Intangible benefits are by definition, less clear, as they have less direct impact on bottom-line results (at least, using conventional accounting principles – see Chapter 5).

Intangible benefits result from improvements in productivity or strategic capability and are usually based on enabling a transformation in the way that the HR function and line management works. Quantifying these benefits in e-HRM is challenging, in part, because the deliverables of the Human Resources function itself can be quite hard to define – few organisations are able to translate their HR strategy into a hard Return on Investment (ROI), so defining the impact of technology on HR strategy is even more of a problem, unless it relates to hard operational cost reduction. The time period over which the return is made is also important – the faster the return on investment, the more attractive and less risky it is.

Key Questions

- What assumptions are being made about cost reduction?
- Can benefits be defined as Operational, Productivity or Strategic in nature?
- How will challenges to intangible benefits be handled?

Stage 3: Develop Options

The next stage is to set out what options are available to the organisation. Prudent organisations do not like to spend money without good cause and there are two obvious management questions when presented with a business case that asks for money; the first is "*Do we absolutely have to*", quickly followed by '*What else could we do*?' – a sound analysis of options makes the business case stronger. It may be, for example, that the analysis leads to a decision to outsource in order to access technology through a third party provider as part of a 'bundled' offering. Or, the business case may conclude that the technology needs to be much simpler (or perhaps more complex) than originally planned. The evaluation of options should consider a range of scenarios, including details of planned scope and functionality, together with criteria for evaluating the chosen solution.

It's always useful to draw attention to the consequence of taking **no** action and the fact that this may still involve a cost, for example, the rising cost of maintaining an ineffective system or an exposure to legal risk or catastrophic organisational failure. It's often easier to define the specific costs associated with doing nothing than actually taking action, especially if there are consequences for business continuity. As noted in Stage 1, a business case may actually require the generation of solutions rather than simply evaluating a default position For example, this could be a weighted list of evaluation criteria (agreed by the project Steering Group) or a series of benefits targets against which each option can be measured.

One outcome of the business case is the definition of project scope. While this sounds obvious, general references to 'implementing an HR system' or 'Employee Self-Service', can have many meanings. Scope definition is very important even at this early stage, as one of the most common reasons for a project failing to deliver its benefits is 'scope creep', where extra requirements (with implications for cost and time) are added during the design or later phases.

Key Questions

- What business processes are in scope?
- What functionality/modules will be needed?
- Who will use the system, what will be their roles and where will they be located?
- Who will need to be trained and how will this be achieved?
- Does the project include employee or manager self-service?
- What assumptions have been made and how will they be tested?

Stage 4: Presenting the Business Case

Presenting the information is as important as data gathering and analysis. One key reason for the failure of a business case proposal is that it is not presented in terms that the organisation will understand – for example, e-HRM may seem like a great way to make HR life easier (less weekend work for the HR team, but what's in it for everyone else and how does it relate to financial measures?). The final presentation of the business case is in many ways a marketing exercise – it's important to present a vision for HR which senior managers will support and feel inclined to invest in. The inclusion of financial indicators supports the analysis of the overall business case and ensures it is presented in a form and language that the Finance function and other managers will expect. Some typical indicators are:

- **The Return on Investment (ROI)** is a simple figure calculated by taking the overall benefit over a selected time period (say, 5 years) minus initial and ongoing costs over that period then working out the percentage value created. Most organisations have rules about the minimum percentage for payback - in the same way that you would be looking for the most attractive rate of interest at your bank for investing your savings, businesses seek the most attractive Rate of Return. Moreover, the proposal will be in competition with other projects which may have a better Rate of Return.

- Most proposals also expect a **'Net Present value' (NPV)** assessment, which also takes into account the time-value of money invested, making an adjustment for the fact that the cost of capital is relatively more valuable today than the value of the benefits it delivers in the future. The rate applied will be set by Finance.

- There is also likely to be a defined **payback period**, which is the number of years required to pay-off (break-even) the initial investment. For example, if a total investment of £90,000 delivers savings of £30,000 per year, there will be a three year payback period, after which it will make a positive contribution. Payback for technology investment can be between 3-5 years, although some projects can pay back almost immediately. The amount of time required varies across organisations and it's important to check on the right way to handle timescales, NPV, IRR etc.

- Another financial hurdle is the **Internal Rate of Return**, a calculation of the cash flow which quantifies the rate of return on the cash flow over the life of the project.

It's important in any business case to make an honest assessment of how ready the organisation is to embark on the project. Without senior level commitment, the support of managers, the availability of resources (who may need to work on the project full-time) and good project management, there is a strong chance of failure. A typical presentation should start by setting the context for the project – what are the strengths, weaknesses, opportunities and threats facing the HR function? What are its aspirations and what are the business challenges of the organisation? How will technology (or the proposed investment) support or enable the changes needed? How does HR measure itself and what will be the key measures of success for the project? The business case proposal should assess these issues as risks and be clear as to how they will be addressed. The change management aspects of a project are assessed in greater detail in a later chapter.

Finally, a business case should contain an assessment of risks, which can be complex to evaluate and measure. In any project, there will be risks that will need to be dealt with and their identification is as important to the development of the business case as costs and benefits (see the earlier Breakout Box on decision making). Sometimes, the risk of a project might even outweigh any benefits that might be identified. For example, if the business case depends on implementing within a certain timeframe and the variables that might affect the timeframe are too hard to define, then the entire business case could collapse. Even with a less risky plan, it is vital that an early assessment is made of the risks of the project, in consultation with a range of stakeholders, to develop a 'Risk Log'. Potential risks include decreased service quality during implementation, an inability to manage the changes properly, an inability to make staff headcount cuts because of complex employment contracts, trade union or other pressures, resistance from employees and line managers to new ways of working and problems with hardware / software delivery and installation.

Key Questions

- Is the timing of the project appropriate?
- What things need to be in place for the project to succeed?
- Are you clear on the real case for change?
- What is the audience for your business case presentation?

Challenges of the Business Case

Organisations often make a number of errors when developing a business case. One common mistake is to confuse the **indirect impact** of technology with the actual business benefit. For example, reduced errors and reduced data re-keying are part of the automating impact of technology, but they do not in themselves constitute business benefit **outcomes** until a more specific impact can be identified and a value can be placed on this impact. This means that any efficiency improvements must be translated into 'cashable' savings that lead to lower operational costs, improved output/ productivity or have an impact on competitive advantage. 'Cashable' benefits occur when fewer people are needed to deliver the service, paid overtime is no longer necessary, or people are available to be deployed to other jobs. In these cases, 'real' money is involved and the benefits can be converted to financial outcomes. So, in the example given earlier, reduced data re-keying counts as a benefit only if it leads to an actual headcount reduction whose value can be identified. If Human Resources staff are simply able to go home on time or no longer have to work weekends as result of the investment but no money is saved, then it is not directly cashable!

Another related problem is the **unrealised benefit**, where a process is redesigned and automation is introduced, yet the same amount of cost and effort is needed to provide it. This may be because the organisation does not remove excess cost (usually people) from the organisation after the new process or solution is introduced - if this doesn't happen, no real benefit is delivered. This subject is also part of change and transition management, which are discussed in more detail in Chapter 13.

Likewise, business cases can fail because they are based on *'fuzzy' benefits*. For example, *'improving the quality of the HR service'* is not a good business case outcome because it cannot be quantified at that level – it must in some way contribute to reduced cost, improved productivity or strategic capability if it is to qualify as a business benefit. This can be quite a difficult concept but for a Finance Director, making HR more popular will never justify spending money – there has to be a 'so-what?' aspect to it.

Organisations can tie themselves in knots over these issues, but the key point is that true value is created only when it is 'cashable', that is, a positive technology outcome can be converted into a benefit that is as close to a financial measure as possible.

Into the Dragons' Den?

Many readers will also be watchers of the TV programme 'Dragons' Den ©', of which there are almost 25 versions available worldwide. For those of you who are not familiar with this show, people with a business idea are given a chance to pitch to five successful business people (the Dragons) who then decide whether to invest their own money, in exchange for a part-ownership of the business. Some leave with large sums of investment funding, but many leave with nothing except a bruised ego. All have to undergo a series of gruelling questions and rigorous interrogation, where their ideas are robustly challenged, criticised and ridiculed. Inevitably, most give away a bigger share of their business than they would like to, in order to secure the funding they need.

The programme provides some interesting parallels with developing and proposing an HR business case, whether it's for technology, or indeed, any type of HR initiative. Here's how I think Dragons' Den can teach HR some good lessons about building a business case:

1. Everyone that enters the Dragons' Den believes they have a good business idea. However, those who have not thought it through, show no real commitment or have limited potential are quickly found out. So the first lesson is to ask yourself *"If I were investing my own money, would I put it into this idea?"* What are you personally prepared to put at stake (part of your bonus? a promotion? your

reputation?) to show how much you believe in your proposal?

2. Many who enter are hopelessly deluded as to the size of the market for their product, often over-valuing the potential of the idea, so that Dragons demand a bigger share to offset the risk. In HR terms, you should ask whether the idea is actually solving a real business problem and whether the risks involved in the project are offset by the benefits that might be achieved.

3. Others ask for too little, given the scale of the work to be done. This is a sure sign that they do not understand their business or the implications of the idea. Big ideas sometimes need a big investment to get a good return. A common question that many struggle with is *"what are you going to do with the money?"* – it's a good test of whether you actually understand your proposal, what needs to be done and whether the benefits are fully understood.

4. One of the most common reasons for failure is that Den applicants have a poor grasp of the numbers. Many seem to pluck figures from nowhere about potential sales, cost of production, potential customers etc. based on weak assumptions. Often, entrants rely on flimsy information, leading one weary Dragon to say recently *"You seem to know more about the future than you do about the present"*. An HR business case needs to be supported by clear data that will stand up to questions about actual benefits, how they will be delivered, what it will cost to implement and what assumptions you have made.

5. When a really innovative idea is presented, the Dragons usually ask about patents and copyright, because an idea is less attractive if there are other good alternatives. The equivalent in HR business case terms is to make sure that you have considered whether other options are available. If your idea is simply based on doing what everyone else is doing rather than anything genuinely different or original, it won't grab anyone's attention. The only exception to this is where there is a legal or compliance reason for the initiative, but otherwise any investment should give the business some form of competitive edge or unique capability.

6. The Dragons also ask themselves whether the business idea is 'investable' - is there enough substance behind the proposition to make it a higher priority than other opportunities for investment? One Dragon often explains that he is effectively spending his children's inheritance, so each investment has to have a good pay back to make it worthwhile. Just because it's a good idea, it may not mean that it's worthy of investment - two often heard comments are "*It's an interesting idea, but it's not a business I can invest in*" or "*I like you but I don't like the idea*". Make sure your HR business proposal is more than an interesting idea and that it relies on more than your personal charisma to carry it through.

7. One reason why people go to the Dragons' Den rather than to their bank is because they know that having a high-profile investor on board will open doors that would otherwise be closed. It's a clear recognition that sponsorship is important to any business proposal and no matter how good your business idea, it needs to be championed by a significant sponsor. There's a great saying "*The second mouse gets the cheese*" - success tends to go to those who can take a good idea to market, not necessarily those who had the idea. Antonio Meucci, Paul Nipkow and Nikola Tesla developed prototypes for the telephone, television and radio respectively, but the more famous Alexander Graham Bell, John Logie Baird and Guglielmo Marconi produced commercial versions (and got the fame!)

8. There is often a killer moment in each pitch where one of the Dragons spots a 'fatal flaw' that totally undermines the years of development that have gone into the product. For example, baby products that actually put children at risk; egg boilers that don't actually cook the egg; things that fail to work at a crucial moment and so on. This is great entertainment, but don't let it happen to you – check there are no howling errors in your proposition, in particular be aware of the perils of the live software demonstration.

So if you have a proposal for an HR investment, imagine you are about to pitch to the Dragons – check that your idea is investable, that the investment opportunity is real, that you understand the numbers, the assumptions you are making and look for fatal flaws. Otherwise, you might just hear your potential investors tell you "I'm out".

Summary: Building the HR Ready Business Case

The HR Ready Business Case is a key tool for an HR function wishing to gain investment in its initiatives and programmes, although it's a skillset that's often lacking among HR practitioners. Its complexity lies in defining value in terms that can be understood and agreed across the organisation, a task that be very difficult in organisations that resist 'enablers' and 'intangibles'.

This chapter offers two tools to help with this process – the first is the e-HRM Value Model, which provides a framework for looking at how benefits can be identified at the level of operational, productivity and strategic outcomes of a project, together with a simple business case methodology for pulling together the various strands that make up the business case proposal.

Building the HR Ready Business Case: Are you HR Ready?

- [?] Is the basic business problem that needs to be solved well defined?

- [?] Is it clear what is needed to develop a winning business case?

- [?] Are current costs understood and defined?

- [?] Is it possible to define all the potential forms of business benefit?

- [?] Would the business case stand up for an outside investor?

- [?] Is the proposed solution urgent enough or attractive enough that action will be taken?

13 Managing the Changes

Change has a considerable psychological impact on the human mind. To the fearful it is threatening because it means that things may get worse. To the hopeful it is encouraging because things may get better. To the confident it is inspiring because the challenge exists to make things better.

King Whitney Jr.

Why the Management of Change is Important

There's an old English saying that *"You can't teach an old dog new tricks"*, the suggestion being that people easily become set in their ways and are unable to make the necessary changes in their lives to adapt to new circumstances. To some extent, this saying is true, but only partially - we all know people who take comfort in familiar ways of working and fear change because it puts their lifestyle at risk; however, I believe that more people are happy to embrace change, accept and even seek out new ways of working if they perceive the changes will have a positive impact. Change is not always a bad thing.

There are many management clichés about change, including *"The only constant is change"* and *"Constant change is the new normal"*; one of my personal favourites is by J.K. Galbraith – *"Faced with the choice between changing one's mind and proving that there is no need to do so, almost everybody gets busy on the proof"* (cited in Pritchett & Pound, 1990, p17). Given the enormous pace of technical, social and economic change in the past fifty years, of course there is some truth to these aphorisms and their intention is to challenge the status quo and discourage complacency (even though they are often delivered in a patronising manner). Like the Galbraith quote, many are funny and interesting and cause us to reflect on how easy it is to take comfort in the familiar – if nothing else, they remind us that it is easier to stick with what we understand and experience regularly.

Whenever a business project is launched, it will create change - after all, if nothing much changes, there's little point in investing in the new solution. In an HR context, whether a project involves shared services, outsourcing, e-HRM or any combination of these initiatives, change inevitably raises questions about where, when and how people work, the jobs they do, the skills they need and ultimately whether they will still have a job. Change affects not only those affected by new technology or re-structuring, but the customers of HR services, who will also experience changes in the way their services are delivered and will respond positively or negatively as a result.

Most people would agree that the effective management of any transition is critical - it's one of those 'motherhood and apple pie questions', because nobody ever argues that managing change is a bad idea. However, when it comes to investing in a programme of change, spending time and resource on dealing with difficult human emotions, it often becomes an 'optional extra' to a project or is considered too late in the project lifecycle to make a difference. In some cases, the only concession to change management is a few briefing sessions and an e-mail prior to launch. Yet, change and transition management is clearly the most critical part of any project, since without effective change, there is a risk that the full benefits of the project will be minimised or even not achieved at all. One organisation I know of (but I must stress, wasn't consulting for!) spent 12 months implementing an HR/Payroll system and planned a training day for its HR administrators one week before going live; the plan was that the first fifteen minutes of the day would include an overview of the reasons for the change. However, because this was the first real opportunity anyone had to ask questions, most of the training that followed was hijacked by questions about why the old system was being scrapped and what it would mean for their ways of working and of course – would they all still have jobs?. This lack of consultation and involvement in planning the changes almost killed the project.

Why do Projects Fail?

There is evidence to suggest that most change initiatives fail, with potentially around 60% of business re-structuring projects failing to meet their planned objectives. The impact of a failure to introduce effective change can be high: loss of market position, removal of senior management, loss of stakeholder credibility and the loss of key employees.

Technology related projects in particular do not have a good track record of success. One classic report in the 1990s (Standish Group, 1994) studied over 8,000 projects and found that only 31% delivered all their expected benefits and were delivered on-time and on-budget. Around 16% of projects were abandoned and 51% were described as 'challenged'. If you think things have become much better since the 1990s, think again - a 2000 Gartner report found that 40% of IT projects failed to meet business requirements; a KPMG report (2002 noted that in the previous twelve months, almost half of organisations surveyed had experienced at least one project failure and 86% of organisations lost up to one quarter of their planned benefits; only 2% of organisations achieved their targeted benefits. Among the reasons cited for failure were inadequate planning, poor scope management and poor communication between the IT function and the business. More recent studies paint a similar picture (Cited in Tichy & Bascom, 2008) and a 2010 KPMG study in New Zealand found that 70% of companies experienced one project failure and 50% had not achieved their planned benefits As I write this Chapter, news has just broken that the BBC has scrapped a £98m technology project which aimed to transform the way staff developed, used and shared video and audio material, claiming that the initiative had been badly managed and outpaced by changing technology (BBC, 2013).

Although not all the projects in these studies were HR related, the message is clear – IT projects can be problematic and run a high risk of failure without a clear methodology, a sound business plan and a well-defined approach for managing the changes.[21] Figure 29 summarises the common reasons for project failure.

Not surprisingly, the technical aspects of implementation (hardware, software, networks etc.) are not the major determinants of project success – it's the human aspects that matter most, with poor planning, weak communications, badly defined objectives and failure to address key change and people issues making the difference between success and failure.

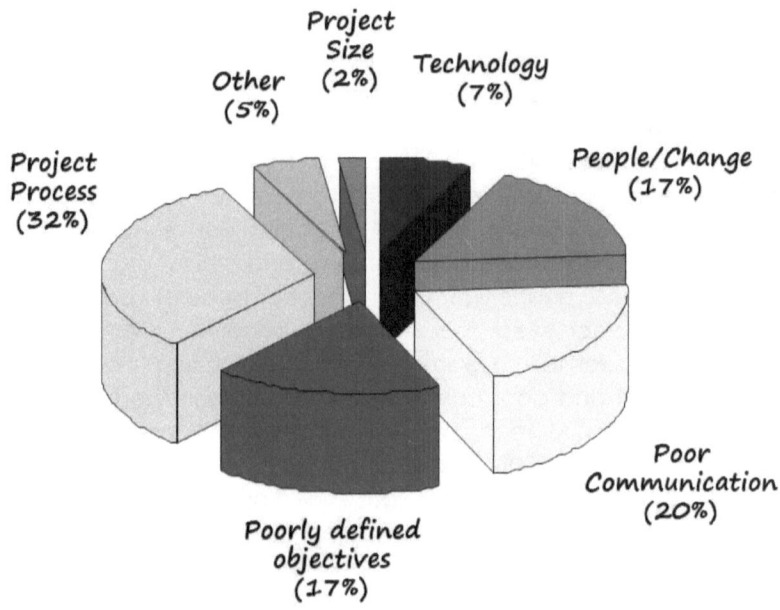

FIGURE 29: REASONS FOR PROJECT FAILURE

---

[21] That is, transition management, rather than contractual 'change control' often required to deal with changes in project scope

Managing Change: The Theory

Many models of change management exist, often based on social psychology, but has its own perspective on achieving change:

Abraham Maslow (1943) argued that individuals will adapt as they pursue 'self-actualisation', which was more likely to be achieved under conditions of openness and personal recognition.

Kurt Lewin (1947) developed his change theories during World War II while investigating how to persuade people to eat cheaper, less attractive meat substitutes such as offal and how to remove racial and religious prejudice. His principle of unfreezing, change and freezing is embedded into social psychology theory.

B.F. Skinner (1957) developed theories of learning, proposing that complex behaviour is learned gradually through the modification of simpler behaviours. Individuals learn by duplicating behaviours they observe in others. Through appropriate rewards, people can learn desirable behaviour.

Theorists such as **Bandura (1989)** proposed Social Learning/Social Cognitive theories, based on an individual's behaviour changing their environment as well as the way the individual thinks or feels.

John Kotter (1996) proposed an 8 stage model for bringing about change. The key steps are: increasing urgency, building the guiding team, getting the vision right, communicate the change vision, empowering action, creating short term wins, consolidating gains and anchoring new approaches into the culture.

Change theories are strongly linked to the technology adoption theories set out in Chapter 8 (page 183) which are concerned with why an individual would choose to adopt a new course of action (or technology) over an existing one. The TAM, TPB and DIT theories set out explain how individuals need to see the relative advantages of proposed new solutions before they will commit to change.

While there's no single dominant reason for project failure (and not even consensus about the top causes), virtually all these issues are people related. Even though many projects have high technology content, weakness in the underlying technology is rarely mentioned as a cause but a consistent theme is that the basic management skills of communication and change management are critical weaknesses in most projects. It's the 'soft' aspects of projects that prevent benefits being realised (it's often said that the soft stuff is the hardest). The conclusion from this is that simply focusing on technology will not lead to project success; people and transition issues must be factored into project planning. Failure to do so may put the project at risk.

FIGURE 30: ORGANISATIONAL READINESS MODEL

Are You Ready for Change?

Long before the planning and implementation work is started, organisations should ask whether the planned changes can be translated from the initial vision to a state where the plans can be shown to work in the 'real' world with 'real' people. However, a change readiness assessment is more than an evaluation of whether people are in a mood for change – it also asks whether the organisation has the resources, infrastructure and leadership in place to successfully deliver all aspects of the planned changes. Change readiness can be defined as *"People's propensity to embrace and use new technologies for accomplishing personal and organisational goals"*.

There are many tools available, but the Organisational Readiness Model presented below (see also Figure 30) is effective whether used for an e-HRM systems project or any other kind of organisational change.

1.   Is There a Clear Vision?

Change management research (for example, Amoako-Gyampha, 2007) confirms that when people feel positively about change, they are more likely to participate positively. People who are ready for change are likely to see the new solution as easy to use and be better able to perceive a smoother transition into new ways of working with minimal effort. The change process is often accompanied by a belief that they will sacrifice benefits if they do not take part in the changes (Walczuch, Lemmink, & Streukens, 2007).

Positive feelings towards change are strongly linked to gaining an understanding of the reasons for change and the planned future state. Although this sounds obvious, it's important to remember that it's much easier to make change happen when everyone sees the long term benefits. E-HRM research reveals that when employees are properly informed about new technology and its impact, they have less uncertainty about the technical changes and will tend to find systems more useful.

Key Questions

- Is the scope of the change clear?
- Has the vision been clearly defined and communicated?
- Is there understanding and support for the vision?
- Has 'what's in it for me' been defined and communicated?

2.   Creating the Case for Change

The idea of a 'burning platform' is a metaphor sometimes used in change management, alluding to the idea that people need powerful reasons to change their ways of working that have previously been normal for them. I believe the origin of this expression is the 1988 Piper Alpha disaster in which 167 men died, where staff on the burning oil exploration platform had to make a life or death decision – to remain on the burning platform and hope to be saved or take a chance that they could survive the 50m drop to the perilous North Sea below. Sixty one men survived the incident.

While organisational decisions are rarely about life or death, every kind of change involves costs, benefits and risks of some kind, whether financial, physical, emotional or otherwise and the investment has to be demonstrably worthwhile. In most cases, there can be no guarantees of a positive outcome either way, but unless there is a strong business case, with a realistic assessment of the costs, benefits and risks, will make it clear why the change is needed and encourage people to take actions that support the end result. Equally, people will need to understand why things cannot stay the same and the consequences of taking no action. See also the Breakout Boxes in Chapter 8 on technology adoption, which stress that if individuals perceive that technology will help them to achieve job related outcomes, they are more likely to use such systems.

Key Questions

- What is the overall compelling reason for the change - is there a 'burning platform'?.

- Is there a good financial case for change (the Return on Investment) as well as an assessment of the feasibility of the project?

- Have the costs and benefits of the project been quantified and are they realistic?

- What are the consequences and risks of taking no action?

3. Clear Leadership and Accountability

Change initiatives can be characterised as 'push systems', where senior managers cause change and put mechanisms in place to support the transition. The introduction of new HR technology, shared services, outsourcing or other HR initiative is typically based on the premise that the change will lead to greater organisational effectiveness and fill a defined performance gap. Leadership is therefore critical and support for the change should come from the top, not only in actively supporting the change but in being seen to adapt to the changes. For example, the arguments for self-service will be diluted if leaders do not themselves use the technology.

Key Questions

- Is the right level of leadership in place to make the change happen and are they adequately empowered?

- Are business leaders committed to the change?

- Do leaders understand the changes required and are they able to translate the vision into clear objectives?

4. Communication and Involvement

In any project, it's important that a robust communications strategy is put in place, whose main aim is to **continuously** inform all those involved about the case for change, especially those most affected by the change. The first step should be to define a communication plan to announce the change and the reasons why it's necessary. At this point, it's important to present a positive image of the change to all those concerned and help them develop a better understanding of the medium and long-term vision and replace rumours with concrete facts.

By involving as many people as possible in developing ideas for the change and how best to implement them, ownership of the plan is improved and the chances of success are higher. For example, when designing new business processes, it often helps to run workshops using established subject matter experts and process leads so they can fully participate in the changes. Of course, certain types of changes cannot be undertaken through a process of involvement (for example, redundancy announcements) and often need to be fully formed before being presented.

Key Questions

- Can the communication plan be implemented?
- Is it easy for people to find out what is going on?
- Do people have to seek out information or is it readily available and easy to find?

5. Stakeholder Management

The communications strategy should focus on specific target groups within the project, usually referred to as 'stakeholders' because they have a vested interest (i.e. a stake) in its outcome. Sometimes, certain groups of people are not even aware that the project will affect them, so they may initially seem disinterested. It's critical that the project team identifies these people early on.

Key Questions

- Who are the key stakeholders?
- Are stakeholders supportive of the planned changes?
- How will the organisation monitor and manage resistance to change?
- Is the stakeholder plan effective at both individual and group level?
- Does the business distinguish between stakeholders who are accepting of change and those who are engaged?

6. Management of Change

At times, organisations can be so damaged by past project failures that they become cynical about future projects. This can lead to a sense of inevitability that all projects will suffer problems and a desire to avoid being linked to failure. Sometimes organisations collectively create cultures that resist change and create negative ways of thinking, such as a belief that change will always be mismanaged, that management will ignore the realities of bringing about change and employees will resist any kind of change that is good for business. An IT Director once told me *"I've seen two HR systems projects fail before now, so I don't hold out much hope for this one"*, a perfect example of an organisation that expects failure.

Good change management becomes critical in these situations and a good project manager is essential. Some organisations hire in an external project manager as a way of breaking the internal cycle of failure.

Key Questions

- Is the business capable of managing the planned changes?
- Does everyone in the organisation have the required ability to deliver the change?
- What has been learned from previous change and how does the business take advantage of this experience?

7. Integrated Planning

This area concerns the role of the project methodology in ensuring that change is managed in a structured manner. Several methodologies are available – including PMBOK, Prince 2, Critical Chain, Event Chain and Agile – the most appropriate depends on the type of project and standards within each organisation. Most methodologies follow a common approach along the lines of: Initiation, Planning and Design; Execution and Construction; Monitoring and Controlling, Completion and Continuous Improvement. A good methodology means that everyone is working to a common plan, ensuring that project milestones are met and that all workstreams are clear as to what is expected of them and when.

Key Questions

- Is the implementation plan sufficiently detailed to enable the changes?
- Is there a mechanism in place for managing changes to scope?
- Are technology, process and people activities fully integrated?

8. People and Organisation

Cultural fit is possibly one of the key change management considerations when contemplating change. John Kotter (1995), writing in the Harvard Business Review, defines culture as "The *shared values, beliefs and behavioural norms that drive the behaviour of the group, although the constituent membership of that group may change*". A more casual definition of culture is *"The way we do things around here"* – it's about the norms, standards and ideals that influence the way a group of people work and socialise together. Every organisation has at least one culture, although in reality, several different cultures are likely to exist in different parts of the business, at different locations or in different work teams. Although easily dismissed as a 'soft' aspect of projects, its power to affect change cannot be underestimated.

Chapter 8 set out the differences between Replication, Enhancement and Transformational strategies for e-HRM and the chosen strategy will have implications for the cultural impact of technology. For example, a very traditional organisation which has changed little over time may choose to build their system to maintain and reinforce the traditional boundaries that exist, such as multiple levels of authorisation, double checking and verifying all information. Alternatively, it could use technology to challenge these ways of working by re-defining each process and actively upsetting the 'cultural norms' that people expect.

Key Questions

- Is the impact on people and culture clear?
- Are the right people involved in change planning?
- What skills and capabilities are required to deliver the project and maintain the solution?
- Are the right mechanisms and policies in place to support the change? (for example, reward)

Summary: Managing the Changes

The following summarises some of the key actions organisations can take to enable change.

1. Conduct a change readiness assessment
2. Conduct a training needs analysis and develop a plan
3. Develop a communications plan that's integrated with the overall plan
4. Run workshops to explain the changes and why they are happening
5. Create a range of training materials – videos, handbooks, user guides, using a range of media
6. Sell the changes positively
7. Make system access easy – install kiosks, consider touch screens instead of keyboards if feasible
8. Conduct surveys to discover what employees actually think
9. Make sure the technology actually works – if people's first experience is poor, they will be reluctant to give you a second chance

FIGURE 31: CHANGE MANAGEMENT TOP TIPS

Managing the Changes: Are you HR Ready?

In addition to the questions raised as part of the Organisational Readiness Model presented here:

- Are there cultural issues that need to be addressed?
- Are there policy issues that need to be addressed?
- Is the organisation ready for change?

Part III: The Future of HR

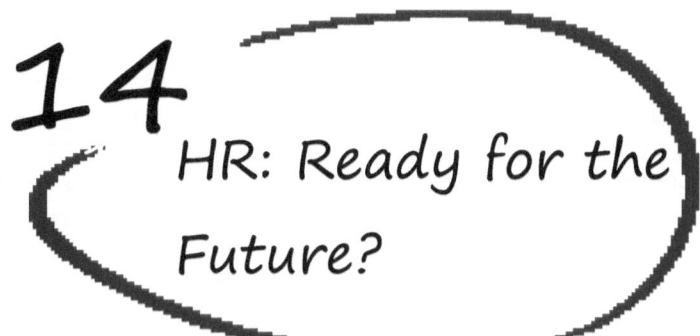
HR: Ready for the Future?

"The only function of economic forecasting is to make astrology look respectable"

J.K Galbraith, Economist

Recent turbulence in the financial markets reminds us that nothing can be taken for granted – the best developed plans for economic growth are at best, one version of the future and organisations need to be ready to change and adapt at short notice. Organisations that plan to be 'HR Ready' will need to consider carefully what future they will be 'HR Ready' for. This chapter crosses its fingers and attempts to give a view on what the future might hold for the HR function. But first, a short health warning: Predictions can go down as well as up, and your HR function may be at risk if you do not make your own plans for the future.

The Economy

At an economic level, we know that (in mid-2013) the global recovery has slowed and prospects are bleak in many economies around the world. Unemployment is rising again and has reached unprecedented levels in the Euro zone, with long term unemployment reaching alarming highs. In some countries, more than one in five young people in the labour market is unemployed and there is a significant risk of a 'lost generation' (European Commission, 2012). However, not all economies are failing – there is slow growth in Asia, Central & Eastern Europe, Brazil, Indonesia, Mexico & Turkey (albeit they are taking a slight detour on the road to economic success).

Organisations appear to be changing in response to structural changes in global economies. One IBM study (2009) asked over 1,000 CEOs and public sector leaders to give their views on the enterprise of the future and found that organisations are hungry for change and keen to innovate. The study identified that future organisations will be 'disruptive by nature', meaning that they will constantly seek to change the mix of products and services offered, borrowing ideas from other sectors and experimenting with new business models. Their loyalty to specific geographies will be strong as long as trading remains economic, but they are prepared to shift their operations in search of the highest return on investment. It's impossible to ignore the impact of rapid expansion and contraction in response to the market, particularly in terms of re-skilling and the transfer of knowledge.

Skills Shortages

Recent years have seen a significant increase in occupational and geographic mobility, with people being highly willing to relocate to areas that offer better employment prospects. During 2010, 3.1 million people migrated into one of the European Union member states, while 2 million people left the Euro zone; the UK, Spain, Italy and Germany accounted for more than 60% of this migration.[22] Despite rampant unemployment, skills remain a major issue confronting many governments. A study by the European Commission (2010) concluded that Europe lacks 20 million skilled workers, especially in key industry sectors such as oil & gas, chemicals, IT, pharmaceuticals, aerospace and health care, where access to the latest engineering and technology skills is critical. The European Commission suggested that workers were simply not being trained quickly enough to meet demand and HR functions will need to play their part in managing training and development programmes to support the demand for up to 16 million technology-based jobs in the years up to 2020. Over the same period, there will be decline in skilled manual jobs (except electricians, reflecting a trend towards computerisation and digital control methods).

---

[22] Source: Eurostat Migration and migrant population statistics. Data includes those that moved between member states

Economic analysis paints a similar picture around the world; one UK research study found that 38% of companies were struggling to recruit the right people, with nearly three quarters citing a lack of technical skills as the primary problem. The German Federal Agency (www.destatis.com) reported that the national skills shortage was becoming worse, with similar reports from agencies in the US, Australia, New Zealand and South Africa. Nearly one in five UK businesses (18%) is concerned that skills shortages will impact its business expansion plans (Grant Thornton, 2012) with 68% of businesses surveyed mentioning this as a significant challenge for recruiting talent. Of great concern is that the UK Commission on Employment and Skills found that two-fifths of employers did no training at all in 2011, most likely due to a lack of confidence about economic growth.

Demographic Change

Most developed nations have an ageing population. This is perhaps best demonstrated by a short anecdote. In the UK, since 1917, every UK citizen has received a congratulatory message from the reigning monarch on reaching the age of 100. In 1917, just 24 messages were sent out; in 1952, 255 were produced; by 2009, 9,640 were sent. The number of people qualifying has grown so much that citizens now have to make a formal request to request a message. It's anticipated that by 2050, there will be around 50,000 people aged 100 or over in the UK, with one in five people currently aged 17-50 hitting the magic age of 100 (UK Department of Work and Pensions, 2011).

It's a similar picture around the world; in most North European countries, an average person can now expect to reach just short of their eightieth birthday, five years longer than in 1987 and twelve years longer than in 1960. The USA and Canada are in a similar position, with 43% of the US workforce expecting to retire in the next ten years. In almost all countries, life expectancy is increasing, which means that many economies face a situation where there will be many more people around who are well past what was once considered to be 'normal' retirement age. When combined with the scrapping by many countries of the statutory retirement age, the result will be a significant impact on succession and career planning, as older workers no longer vacate key positions to create gaps for younger workers. On a more positive note, a major economic benefit will be that an ageing population will create new markets in health care, leisure and travel.

Talking About My Generation

An older workforce means that the workplace will consist of employees with a wide age range, potentially spanning an age gap of fifty to sixty years from the youngest to the oldest employees. The usual categories for these groups, as defined in a joint CIPD/Penna Consulting study (2008) are:

- **Veterans:** Members of the workforce who were born before 1947 and are currently over 66 years old. This group experienced the Second World War in their childhood and joined the workforce when employment opportunities were abundant. Members aspired to a long relationship with one or two employers, often working for more than 20 years with a single employer and in return expecting their loyalty to be rewarded with job security. Movement up the 'corporate ladder' was through invitation as recognition for good work. Although approaching retirement, many are choosing to continue working beyond 'normal' retirement age, especially as legislation increasingly permits this.

- **Baby Boomers:** This group was born between 1948 and 1963 and is now between 50–65 years old. Baby boomers tend to believe that change is possible to an extent that members of other generations do, having seen enormous liberalisation, experienced the push for civil rights, the women's movement, soaring inflation and shifts in trade union power. Members joined the workforce at a time of high competition for jobs and success often resulted from long working hours. Over half have spent the last ten years with their current employer, while movement up the 'corporate ladder' has been through beating competition.

- **Generation X** was born between 1964 and 1978 and its members are approximately 35 to 50 years old. As 'Thatcher's Children' (or Reagan's, Mitterand's, Kohl's, Botha's etc. depending where you grew up) they experienced great economic turmoil, rioting and large scale redundancies. Many graduated into the worst job market since the Great Depression and they have become accustomed to uncertainty. Changing employers became a way of life and the average time with any employer is around five years. This group tends to consist of experienced service knowledge workers with a focus on their 'professional ladder' of employability rather than the 'corporate ladder'.

- **Generation Y** was born between 1979 and 1991 and accounts for around 27% of the UK workforce. During their formative years, they faced higher costs for education, housing and general living, but have grown up in a time of relative peace and prosperity. Generation Y joined the workforce when the economic boom started and until recently had not seen the worst of the effects of a recession. However, they have seen many corporate restructures, mergers and acquisitions and are no strangers to change. Most have spent fewer than three years with their current employer and they tend to see their career not in the form of a ladder – more of a 'scramble'.

- **Generation Z** is just starting to join the workforce. They were born after the fall of the Soviet Union, the unification of Germany and the invention of the internet. They will be the most socially networked generation in history and this is likely to be reflected in their approach to working remotely and collaboratively. During their formative years, they have seen relative global peace, economic stability and the war on terror. They enter the workforce (if they are lucky) in the aftermath of the worst effects of the recession of the late 2000's. Many have not experienced employment and may not do so for several years – some refer to this group as the 'lost generation'.

It's clear that there are potentially many differences between each generation in terms of their economic, political, work and life experience. There is an emerging view that these supposed differences are important because generational differences will need more careful management in the future, especially as different generations will have to work closely with each other and traditional hierarchies break down. The fear is that without proper management, these cross-generational employee groups will lead to problems of alienation, low motivation, lack of productivity and poor employee retention.

At least, that's the theory. The main problem with the generational differences approach is that it makes sweeping assumptions about inter-generational values. Clearly, values are clearly important in an organisational context – they define what people believe to be right or wrong, how they work, what motivates them and how they respond to leadership. Arguably (goes the theory), a 60 year old baby boomer will need an entirely different management approach from an 18 year old Generation Z, with different development, motivation and reward considerations. Yet, even within each generational group there are likely to be differences; for example, early baby boomers born just after World War 2 would have experienced extremes of post-war austerity and would have been the first generation to be labelled as 'Teenagers'. This group is stereotyped as one of the first groups of young people to actively challenge the establishment, whereas previous generations tended to emulate their parents rather than strive to be different. Baby Boomer values were made possible through a combination of post-war economic growth, greater disposable income (and rock & roll) that created a sense of an independent group with its own economic power. However, later Baby Boomers (born after the mid-1950s) seem to be an entirely different group, second generation teenagers with their own icons (The Beatles, Rolling Stones) and a new set of values (feminism, anti-war) although they would not yet have discovered racism and ageism. Late, late baby boomers would differentiate themselves again through the punk movement and political correctness (yes, both at the same time!). The point is that the generational groups as traditionally defined are not only too wide, but within each group there is likely to be wide variance. Some teenage Baby Boomers would have been happy to sit at home, rebelling against nothing and wanting nothing more than to be just like mum and dad.

Another danger of the simplistic stereotyping of people into groups based purely on age is that there are many other important factors other than age that influence values. For example, gender, race and religion play an important part in many people's lives and cannot be ignored as factors that shape workplace values. Regional experience is also important - a generation that grew up in an economically depressed area might feel very different about work than those living in a prosperous area. Similarly, national differences cannot be ignored and it should be noted that much of the research into generational differences stems from the US, as a result of which it's dangerous to generalise that Generation X in the US is the same as Generation X in the rest of the world. As an example, US research tends to see the Vietnam War and the assassination of President Kennedy as defining generational events, but these have far less impact elsewhere. Significantly, world events are now being experienced differently as a result of technology – 9/11 was experienced at the same time around the world and would have influenced a global generation, so potentially the impact of historical events may ultimately lead to more heterogeneous values.

It's also impossible to ignore the effect of life events on workplace attitudes, so at the point employee starts a family, it's likely they will change their expectations with regard to their career, become less mobile and have a different attitude to change. This could happen at age 20, 30 or 40 so it's less likely to be a factor of generational differences, simply a reflection of life progression. There is also evidence that values are not unique to a single generation - one study (Jurkiewicz & Brown, 1998) found that across 15 work related factors, the values held by Baby Boomers, Generation X and Y were very similar. Regardless of the stereotypes, a desire to progress in terms of income, responsibility and influence within the organisation is common to all groups.

As well as gender, religion and regional / national factors, factors such as education, economic background, parental occupation and personality will also have an impact; characterising workplace values based on generational differences therefore carries the risk of stereotyping based on just one variable (birth year); there is therefore a risk that these decisions are 'generationalist'. From an HR perspective, the focus should be on individual factors, taking care not to base assumptions on age and generation.

The Future of HR Outsourcing

HR outsourcing is slowly coming to the top of the agenda of many organisations. Here are some predictions for the HR outsourcing sector - please bear in mind the usual caveats of the dangers of making predictions:

- As outsourcing becomes a generally acceptable response to the need to reduce cost and improve service, more organisations are likely to take the decision to outsource their HR function. According to analysts Everest (2011), the global Multi-Process HR Outsourcing (MPHRO)[23] market has annualised revenue of $3.3 billion, estimated to grow by 24% through to 2015. Although the outsourcing market has levelled off in recent years, it is generally thought that there will be fewer terminations and non-renewals, but there will be an increase in transfers as providers offer robust transition methodologies and creative financing options.

- Analysts predict that the trend to outsource will spread beyond North America and Europe and the adoption of MPHRO will gain further traction in emerging markets such as Asia Pacific and Latin America.

- Recent years have seen a substantial drop in terminations, coupled with a significant number of contract extensions, pointing to a stabilisation of the market and improved buyer satisfaction. At the same time, there has been a decrease in average contract size with a corresponding decrease in the length of multi-process HRO deals.

- Large organisations are currently leading the way in outsourcing their HR functions but outsourcing appears to be just as relevant to smaller organisations as multi-national, multi-process ones.

- The delivery of HR outsourcing services will evolve. Outsourcing will increasingly include technology on a

---

[23] Multi process HRO is where more than one HR process is outsourced to a provider, for example, it may include Payroll, HR Administration and Benefits administration. Single Process HRO is (logically) a single (usually specialist) process such as recruitment

'Software as a Service' basis, where technology is bundled into the overall service offering.

- Continued technological advances will increase web-enabled service delivery solutions. These advances will include increased use of smartphones and tablet technologies to submit routine documents such as expense claims. Increased technology will enable the continued migration towards 'managed service' facilities. MPHRO solutions based on Software-as-a-Service (SaaS) software will be increasingly considered and gradually adopted (Everest, 2012a)

- The range and sophistication of services provided through offshoring will continue to develop. Many organisations have been wary of services being provided by service centres in places such as India and the Philippines, but in most cases it's entirely transparent to the served workforce. Some services are 'data only', as opposed to 'voice' based, meaning that only data entry and processing takes place offshore, using the latest technology to move information around. Offshore locations typically employ highly qualified staff and accuracy and quality levels are very high, with lower costs.

- As more companies outsource their HR, service providers will become more experienced at providing their services. As the scale of outsourcing operations increases and highly trained, professional people join outsourcing companies, service quality is likely to increase as providers become more skilled at tailoring policies and procedures to individual organisations and industries become simpler, again encouraging more outsourcing.

- HR outsourcing will become increasingly strategic. This will impact both on the in-house HR professional and the outsourcing service provider. Where there is a senior HR professional in-house, they will be expected to support and guide their company on people issues at a strategic level. Equally, more outsourcing service providers will be invited to sit at the boardroom table to contribute to the strategic direction of the company.

- Many HR professionals see outsourcing as a potential threat to their personal development. However, outsourcing will increase HR opportunities as outsourcing service providers seek to recruit more HR professionals to fill their skill and experience gaps. This has far reaching benefits for the flexible HR professional who will gain vast experience in dealing with a variety of companies, issues and management cultures that they would never be able to experience when working with just one company. Those HR professionals remaining in-house will need different skills to manage outsourced HR operations, moving more towards project and change management as HR positions become more strategic and consultancy driven.

Technology and the HR Future

In the HR Ready future, organisations will need to understand a great deal about what technology can deliver, not just in terms of *automation*, but in terms of *information*. The effective use of technology is fast becoming an important HR competence, because of its power to enable more strategic forms of HR and support the transformation of the function. As technology develops and is able to provide the tools and data needed to support good management, HR must become a champion for technology, working with managers to define the benefits and demonstrate the 'art of the possible'. The really smart HR people of the future will be highly technology-aware, with a clear idea of what they want from systems, with the ability to manage the changes it brings. Organisations should perhaps consider formalising a role responsible for the development of HR systems technology, not just in terms of systems support, but at the strategic planning level.

By its nature, technological development tends to come in waves – the basic technology for the internet was laid out in the late 1960's, became formalised as the 'web' in the 1980's, but has only truly became omnipresent (and useful to most people) in recent years. Finding meaningful applications for technology is an evolutionary process, as individuals and organisations often struggle to make sense of its implications and find ways of adopting technology into their lives. Often, the technology available is far ahead of the ability of users to turn it into practical applications – indeed, history shows that many technologies existed for long periods before good uses were found (apparently, the Romans had all the ingredients needed to develop the steam engine, but they just saw it as a neat party trick!). There is a parallel here with HR technology – many organisations have good technology platforms, but few properly make sense of them, develop them fully or appreciate their potential to improve people management. Finding practical uses for technology is not a skill that is in abundance among HR professionals and there are few who can straddle the worlds of technology and HR practice; many professionals often disregard the importance of technology in their roles. The issue of technology adoption was discussed in Chapter 8 and it's fascinating to me why HR functions appear to be late adopters, continuing to resist technology until it has become mainstream; perhaps in the HR future, this will be put right.

The transition from process management technology to people management technology, requires a leap in insight and the development of technology champions who will push for new ways of working. A critical skill for the HR professional will be to develop this creative insight into what technology can offer and have the confidence to adopt, adapt and move forward.

HR and Happiness

'Being happy' is fundamental to human experience and it's a highly valued goal in most societies. In general, it pays to be happy - happy people tend to have higher levels of income and are more successful across all aspects of their life – marriage, friendship, work and health. Having spent a hundred years or so looking at what made people neurotic, psychotic, criminal and deviant, research in psychology has now turned its attention to the subject of happiness, under a new branch known as 'positive psychology'. Even governments are now interested in the concept [24] and it seems appropriate as we approach the end of this book to explore the topic from a people management perspective - what does it mean to be happy at work, or indeed, anywhere else?

Although we all experience happiness (or lack of it), there is little agreement on what 'happiness' is. Academic research describes happiness in terms of pleasant judgments (positive attitudes) or

---

[24] "Prime Minister unveils 'Happiness index'", The Independent, 26th November 2010

pleasant experiences (feelings, moods and emotions). Words such as 'contentment' and 'life satisfaction' are often used, whereas dictionaries define happiness as "*a state of mind or feelings characterised by contentment, love, satisfaction, pleasure, or joy*".[25] Because people spend so much of their time at work, the relationship between happiness at work and outside work is likely to be very strong.

One thing is very clear – happiness is not about money.[26] In the last 50 years, average incomes in the Western World have more than doubled, yet these populations are no happier than some of the poorest countries in the world. In fact, in many cases, richer countries are much less happy than poor ones. Richard Layard, an economist interested in happiness, finds that once people's net income rises above $20,000, any additional income has very little effect on levels of happiness (Layard, 2006). Once the basic human needs of shelter, food and warmth are achieved, money seems to have very little impact on overall happiness. In fact, one of the biggest sources of unhappiness in recent times has been the widening gap between rich and poor – it's the social comparison and sense of disadvantage that makes people feel unhappy, rather than the state of being poor itself. If those around you are poor, you're more likely to accept your circumstances and appreciate what you have, while envy makes us miserable. As one writer commented, 'Happiness is not having what you want, but wanting what you have' (Schachtel, 1954). For the record, according to the OECD, Australia is the happiest country in the world.[27]

Many researchers now believe that happiness has a genetic component and that individuals are naturally 'programmed' to be happy or unhappy. Some researchers (Weiss et al, 2008) have suggested that happiness is up to 50% genetically determined, with the balance being 10% environmental and 40% being under

---

[25] Cambridge Advanced Learners Dictionary

[26] Although as Groucho Marx said, "*Money can't buy you happiness, but it can help to put a substantial down payment on it.....*"

[27] Reported in The Guardian, May 28th, 2013

our control. The bad news is that this pre-disposition has little to do with the situation - people who are happy tend to view events quite differently from unhappy people. Happy people are better at avoiding making social comparisons that would disadvantage them, they dwell on success rather than failure, have an optimistic outlook and possess better coping strategies. Some theories even propose that we each return to a set point relatively quickly following events – so whether we win the lottery or experience a terrible loss, we eventually end up no more or less happy than when we started (Brickman, Coates, & Janoff-Bulman, 1978).

There are other factors that seem to make a difference. People who experience greater levels of happiness tend to have a high 'locus of control', that is, they feel that things happen as a result of their own actions, rather than being determined by fate or others, have higher self-esteem and are emotionally more stable. Individuals who show higher levels of gratitude, kindness and forgiveness, are mindful of others and act with a sense of awareness and community are also key factors. Religious and faith-led people score better on happiness ratings, although it's not clear whether this comes from the social support networks linked to religions or something more spiritual. Perhaps some sort of 'cosmic karma' operates, where we reap what we sow.

Those around us can also influence levels of happiness - recent research has shown that we are more likely to be happy if a close friend or colleague has become happier in the last 6 months (Fisher, 2010). Happiness is infectious.

Happiness at Work

For many years, academics dismissed the role of happiness at work, seeing it as too 'new-age', hippy and inconsistent with the more business-like approach of Human Resource Management. However, happiness is strongly related to the concept of employee engagement and has even been described as 'HR's most important metric' (Stevens, 2013). It's an important issue given that employment relationships are changing, people are experiencing lower levels of job security, tenure and loyalty than in previous times and employees are more likely to feel disconnected from their employer and therefore less happy. Although it would be a brave HR Manager that announces an 'employee happiness programme', the benefits of happy employees include:

- Happy workers are more productive, confirming the connection between individual happiness and job performance. Cynthia Fisher (2010) in a review of happiness research going back to the 1950s, suggests that the weight of evidence now supports this view. Interestingly, the relationship seems to work both ways – people not only perform better when happier, but their own perceived high performance actually makes them happier! This 'happiness loop' is more easily accessed by people with complex jobs, who are better able to control and structure what they do and when they do it.

- Happy people have less conflict with their colleagues and are more creative.

- Happy people tend to be more loyal and stay with one employer for longer, with higher levels of job satisfaction and organisational commitment. Perhaps this is because happier people feel a greater sense of control of their own destiny, rather than blaming their employer for bad things that happen. In one long-term study that tracked regular job-hoppers, individuals initially experienced higher levels of happiness in their new jobs, but by the second year, their happiness levels had returned to the same level as before. The grass is not always greener.

Current research is moving away from measuring commitment, satisfaction and engagement and turning its attention to why people are happier or unhappier than others at work and the impact of changing levels of happiness over time.

Although terms such as engagement, commitment and satisfaction have been used in recent years, I propose that ultimately these are really just more formal ways of describing something that ordinary people would define as 'happiness', and that perhaps this is a more useful concept. Of course, employers are not in business simply to make employees happy and the ultimate question is whether 'happy' employees are a source of competitive advantage. If happiness can be seen to lead to better productivity, better retention of skills and business growth, then both employees and employers would benefit. A focus on the conditions that create happiness would therefore be a positive investment for organisations.

Even though a large part of our individual happiness appears to be genetically determined (Weiss et al., 2008), a substantial amount remains in the control of the individual. At risk of sounding like a self-help book, academic research points towards some common themes that can improve levels of happiness:

- Individuals should be encouraged to pursue short-term but challenging goals. At work, this could be involvement with a project or a role that gives a more immediate sense of satisfaction. Good job design remains as important as ever.

- Encourage employees to identify their personal strengths and spend their time applying them. Jobs should provide a good fit with personal strengths and people who are unhappy or performing poorly should be encouraged to change roles or even move to other organisations that are better able to meet their needs.

- Those who sense a vocational 'calling' in their job, where helping others provides inherent personal satisfaction, leads to greater happiness. This idea has long been true for teachers, medical staff and emergency services, but the same principle could equally apply to front-line customer support teams. Again, a good match between the job and person is critical.

- Happy people tend not to daydream – they concentrate on the present, rather than reflect on past mistakes or future problems.

- Organisations can support employee happiness by ensuring all employees have a sense that they will be supported and treated fairly. Clearly, an HR strategy based on promoting these activities might raise a few eyebrows, but creating a culture that supports and promote these qualities may create a unique source of competitive advantage.

However, happiness largely remains in the control of each individual and the key to this seems to be connected to the way we choose to perceive the world and frame each event.

Re-Inventing the HR Function

An implied theme of this book is that many organisations are not (yet) HR Ready; in fact, many are distinctly un-Ready and as a result, put their organisations at risk. Research by the Aberdeen Group (2012) suggests that HR is perceived as being less strategic now than it has been in the past, even among Best in Class organisations. On similar lines, a PWC Saratoga study found that 43% of CEOs say they lack confidence in HR and that European and US organisations are still not making enough progress in human capital management. Once again, Dave Ulrich (2008) has a view on this, based on an assessment of the outlook for the 21st Century HR function, in which he stressed that HR must operate as a *'business within a business'*, rather than performing a set of disconnected and isolated series of HR practices. The emphasis should be on creating value by shifting away from 'activities' to 'outcomes' and focusing on what HR enables, not what HR does. Central to this is a direct challenge to the HR function to define what the organisation wants, structure itself to deliver against those needs and then execute the strategy effectively.

Anita Lettink (2012) refers to the 'consumerization' of HR, a future state where HR is highly technologically capable, where it bases its decisions on data, uses standardised processes and is able to act both locally and globally. In this new world, HR stops acting as the 'middleman' and becomes a function where activities that do not add value are eliminated; in an increasingly consumer-led society, the focus is on what the customer demands and expects, **not** what HR is prepared to supply. It echoes earlier statements that HR should be judged not by what it does, but what it delivers and carries with it the critical implication that HR professionals must not only have a broad technical knowledge of HR, but they must be trained in project management, analytics, business planning, new (mobile) technologies and social media.

This new world may even lead us to question what is really meant when HR people talk about 'being strategic' and whether there is a gap between what HR thinks it should do and what customers – line managers and senior business leaders – actually want from HR. Over the past thirty years, there has been a fundamental assumption that HR and its line customers both want the same thing, that is, a strategically focused HR function. However, research by the Institute for Employment Studies (Lettink, 2012) found that in reality, HR customers definitely do **not** want an HR function that spends much of its time writing strategy documents or conceptualising the future; in practice, line managers want HR people with professional expertise who can help them address their people issues in the context of the business they work in. So, when line managers say they want a strategic HR function, what they actually mean is an HR department that will help them to solve problems that are strategically important for the business, not strategically important for HR. There is a need to re-focus HR's strategic desires towards supporting managers better in delivering their strategies.

Is There a Future for HR?

The people challenges that organisations currently face appear to be getting more, not less, complex and there is a recognition that perhaps the only way for businesses to survive and thrive is through a focus on good people management. However, there is an important distinction to be made between HR as an **activity** and HR as a **function**. We have seen in recent chapters that HR is at a turning point and has to respond better than it has in the past to a new set of challenges. Cost-effective HR service delivery remains a priority for most organisations especially at the transactional level; while good HR services don't automatically lead to better people management, they are a critical part of developing an HR function that can focus on this task. Clearly, HR is learning all the time about how to add value, how to bring about a step increase in performance and how to support line managers in the essential process of managing people.

Despite a steady stream of cynical HR press over the past 30 years, the prognosis for HR appears to be very strong, so let me end on a positive note. Turbulence in the global economy has shown us that nothing can be taken for granted and HR has an important role in building strong organisational capability for the future. Where HR works, it works very well and there are excellent practitioners out there, doing great things for their organisations.

With the right tools, HR can make a difference.

References

Aberdeen Group. (2012). *Human Capital Management Trends 2012: Managing Talent to Lead Organisational Growth.*

Aberdeen Group. (2009). *Intelligent Human Capital Management: Workforce Analytics Drives Profit and Performance.*

Aberdeen Group. (2008). *Web 2.0, talent management and employee engagement.* Aberdeen Group.

Adecco. (2006). Peoplekeeper's survey.

Advanced Performance Institute. (2009). *Delivering Success: How Tesco is Managing, Measuring and Maximising its Performance.* [online]. Available from: http://www.ap-institute.com/media/4312/delivering_success_tesco.pdf.

Agunis, H. (2009). *Performance Management.* Pearson International Edition.

Ahlstrom, P. and Karlsonn, C. (1996). Change processes towards lean production: the role of the management accounting system. *International Journal of Operations and Production Management*, 16(11), pp.42–56.

Ajzen, I. (1991). The theory of planned behaviour. *Organisational Behaviour and Human Decision Processes*, 50, pp.179–211.

Ajzen, I. and Fishbein, M. (1980). *Understanding Attitudes and Predicting Social Behaviour.* Englewood Cliffs, NJ: Prentice-Hall.

Alleyne, C., Kakabadse, A. and Kakabadse, N. (2007). Using the HR Intranet: An exploratory analysis of its impact on managerial satisfaction with the HR function. *Personnel Review.*, 36(2), pp.295–310.

Amoako-Gyampha, K. (2007). Perceived usefulness, user involvement and behavioural intention: an empirical study of ERP implementation. *Computers in Human Behavior*, 23, pp.1232–1248.

Ansoff, I. (1968). *Corporate strategy: An analytic approach to business policy for growth and expansion.* New York: McGraw Hill.

Aon~Consulting. (2010). *One billion man hours lost to sickies across Europe each year.* [online]. Available from: http://aon.mediaroom.com/index.php?s=25776&item=63933.

Appelbaum, E. et al. (2000). *Manufacturing Advantage: Why high performance systems pay off.* Ithica, NY: ILR Press.

Armstrong, M. and Baron, A. (2005). *Managing Performance: Performance Management in Action.* London: CIPD.

Arthur, J.B. (1994). Effects of Human resource systems on manufacturing performance and turnover. *Academy of Management Journal*, 37(3), pp.670–687.

Arvey, R.D. and Murphy, K.R. (1998). Performance evaluation in work settings. *Annual Review of Psychology*, 49, pp.141–168.

Ashford, R.W., Dyson, R.G. and Hodges, S.D. (1988). The Capital-Investment Appraisal of New Technology: Problems, Misconceptions and Research Directions. *The Journal of the Operational Research Society*, pp.637–642.

Bacon, N. (1999). "The realities of human resource management? *Human Relations*, 52(9), p.1179.

Barney, J.B. (1991). Firm resources and sustained competitive advantage. *Journal of management*, 17(1), pp.99–120.

Barney, J.B. (2001). Is the resource based view a useful perspective for strategic management? Yes. *Academy of Management Review*, 26(1), pp.41–56.

Bartel, A.P. (1994). Productivity gains from the implementation of employee training programs. *Industrial Relations*, 33, pp.411–425.

Bath Consultancy Group. (2011). *Making HR Business Partnering Really Work.* [online]. Available from: http://www.gpstrategiesltd.com/downloads/Making-the-move-to-HR-Business-Partnering-really-work-v1.0-June-2011[124].pdf.

BBC. (2013). BBC abandons £100m digital project. [online]. Available from: http://www.bbc.co.uk/news/entertainment-arts-22651126.

Beaman, K.V. (2004). *Out of Site: An Inside Look at HR Outsourcing*. Austin TX.

Beaumont, P. (1992). Human Resource Strategies. In G. Salaman, ed. London: Sage.

Beaumont, P. (1984). Personnel Management and the Welfare Role. *Management Decision*, 22(4), pp.33–42.

Becker, B.E. et al. (1997). HR as a source of shareholder value: Research and recommendations G. R. Ferris, ed. *Human Resource Management Journal*, 31(1), pp.39–47.

Becker, B.E. and Huselid, M.A. (1999). Overview: Strategic Human Resource Management in Five Leading Firms. *Human Resource Management*, 38(4), pp.287–301.

Becker, B E and Huselid, M.A. (1999). Strategic human resource management in five leading firms. *Human Resource Management*, 38(4), pp.287–301.

Becker, B.E. and Huselid, M.A. (2006). Strategic Human Resource Management: where do we go from here? *Journal of Management*, 32(6), pp.898–925.

Becker, B.E., Huselid, M.A. and Ulrich, D. (2001). *The HR Scorecard: Linking people, strategy and performance*. Boston, Massachusetts: Harvard Business School Press.

Belcourt, M. (2006). Outsourcing: the benefits and the risks. *Human Resource Management Review*, 16(2), pp.269–279.

Bersin & Associates. (2011). *Strategic Human Resources and Talent Management: Predictions for 2012 Driving Organizational Performance amidst an Imbalanced Global Workforce*.

Bharadwaj, A.S. (2000). A resource-based perspective on information technology capability and firm performance: an empirical investigation. *MIS Quarterly*, 24(1), pp.169–196.

BlessingWhite. (2005). *Employee Engagement,*. Princeton, NJ.

Blumberg, M. and Pringle, C.D. (1982). The missing opportunity in organizational research: Some implications for a theory of work performance. *Academy of Management Review*, 7, pp.560–569.

Boglind, A., Hallsten, F. and Thilander, P. (2011). HR transformation and shared services: Adoption and adaptation in Swedish organisations. *Personnel Review*, 40(5), pp.570–588.

Borman, W.C. (1991). Job behavior, performance, and effectiveness. In M. D. Dunnette & L. Hough, eds. *Handbook of industrial and organizational psychology*. Palo Alto, CA: Consulting Psychologists Press, pp. 271–326.

Boroughs, A., Palmer, L. and Hunter, I. (2008). *HR Transformation Technology: Delivering Systems to Support the New HR Model*. Aldershot: Gower.

Boudreau, M.C. and Robey, D. (2005). Enacting integrated information technology: A human agency perspective. *Organization Science*, 16(1), pp.3–19.

Brickman, P., Coates, D. and Janoff-Bulman, R. (1978). Lottery winners and accident victims: is happiness relative? *Journal of Personality and Social Psychology*, 36, pp.917–927.

Brown, V.R. and Vaughn, E.D. (2011). The Writing on the (Facebook) Wall: The Use of Social Networking Sites in Hiring Decisions. *Journal of Business Psychology*, 26, pp.219–225.

Buyens, D. and De Vos, A. (2001). Perceptions of the value of the HR function. *Human Resource Management Journal*, 11(3), pp.70–89.

Caldwell, R. (2003). The Changing Roles of Personnel Managers: Old Ambiguities, new Undertainties. *Journal of Management Studies*, 40(4), pp.983–1004.

Cameron, A. and Brion, S. (2010). Overconfidence and the Attainment of Status in Groups. [online]. Available from: http://www.escholarship.org/uc/item/5zz0q2r0.

CareerBuilder. (2012). Thirty-seven percent of companies use social networks to research potential job candidates. [online]. Available from: http://www.careerbuilder.co.uk/share/aboutus/pressreleasesdetail.aspx?sd=4/18/2012&id=pr691&ed=4/18/2099.

Cedar Crestone. (2011). *Cedar Crestone 2011 – 2012 HR Systems Survey : HR Technologies, Deployment Approaches, Value, and*

Metrics 14th annual edition. [online]. Available from: http://www.cedarcrestone.com/media/whitepapers/CC_2011-2012_HRS_Survey_WP.pdf.

Cedar Crestone. (2012). *CedarCrestone 2012–2013 HR Systems Survey: HR Technologies, Deployment Approaches, Value, and Metrics 15th Annual Edition*.

CedarCrestone. (2012a). CedarCrestone 2009–2010 HR Systems Survey: HR Technologies, Deployment Approaches, Value, and Metrics 12th Annual Edition. [online]. Available from: Downloaded from http://www.cedarcrestone.com/research.php on September 30, 2009.

CedarCrestone. (2011). *CedarCrestone 2010-2011 HR Systems Survey*.

CedarCrestone. (2012b). *CedarCrestone 2012–2013 HR Systems Survey: HR Technologies, Deployment Approaches, Value, and Metrics 15th Annual Edition*.

Chandler, A. (1962). *Strategy and Structure: Chapters in the History of the American Industrial Enterprise*. Cambridge, MA: MIT Press.

Chattopadhayay, R. and Ghosh, A.K. (2012). Performance appraisal based on a forced distribution system: its drawbacks and remedies. *International Journal of Productivity and Performance Management*, 61(8), pp.881–896.

Cheese, P., Thomas, R.J. and Craig, E. (2008). *The talent power orgnization: Strategies for globalization, talent management and high performance*. London and Philadelphia: Kogan Page.

CIPD. (2012). *HR Business Partnering*. [online]. Available from: http://www.cipd.co.uk/hr-resources/factsheets/hr-business-partnering.aspx, downloaded January 18th 2013.

CIPD. (2011). *Next Generation HR*. CIPD.

CIPD. (2007). Research Insight: Investors' views of human capital.

CIPD. (2005). *Reward strategy: How to develop a reward strategy*. London.

CIPD & Kingston Engagement and Consortium. (2011). *Locus of engagement: understanding what employees connect with at work.*

Collings, D. and Mellahi, K. (2009). Strategic talent management: A review and research agenda David G. Collings a,., Kamel Mellahi. *Human Resource Management Review*, 19, pp.304–313.

Cooke, F.L. (2006). Modelling an HR Shared Service Center: Experience of an MNC in the United Kingdom. *Human Resource Management2*, 45(2), pp.211–227.

Cooke, F.L., Shen, J. and McBride, A. (2005). Outsourcing HR as a Competitive Strategy? A literature Review and an Assessment of Implications. *Human Resource Management2*, 44(4), pp.413–432.

Coulson-Thomas, C. (2011). World Trade Group Final report. In *Talent management and the high performance organisation*.

Cunningham, I. and Hyman, J. (1999). Devolving human resource responsibilities to the line : Beginning of the end or a new beginning for personnel? , 28(1/2), pp.9–27.

DailyTelegraph. (2013). Office workers irritated by "management speak." *Daily Telegraph*. [online]. Available from: http://www.telegraph.co.uk/finance/jobs/10030834/Office-workers-irritated-by-management-speak.html.

Daniel Kahneman, A.T. (2000). *Choice, Values, Frames*. The Cambridge University Press.

Davenport, T.H. (2000). *Mission critical: realizing the promise of enterprise systems*. Boston, MA: Harvard Business School Press.

Davenport, T.H. (2008). Why Six Sigma Is on the Downslope. *Harvard Business Review*. [online]. Available from: http://blogs.hbr.org/davenport/2008/01/why_six_sigma_is_on_the_downsl.html.

Davis, F.D., Bagozzi, R.P. and Warshaw, P.R. (1989). User acceptance of computer technology: a comparison of two theoretical models. *Management Science*, 35(8), pp.982–1004.

Delaney, J.T. and Huselid, M.A. (1996). The impact of HR management practices on perceptions of organisational performance. *Academy of Management Journal*, 39(4), pp.949–969.

Delmotte, J., Sels, L. (2008). HR Outsourcing: Threat or Opportunity. *Personnel Review*, 37(5), pp.543–563.

Deloitte. (2012). *HR in the cloud: It's inevitable*. [online]. Available from: http://www.deloitte.com/assets/Dcom-Australia/Local Assets/Documents/Services/Consulting/Human Capital/Deloitte_HR_in_the_Cloud_Deloitte_16Apr2012.pdf.

Department of Work and Pensions (UK). (2011). *Number of Future Centenarians by Age Group*. [online]. Available from: http://statistics.dwp.gov.uk/asd/asd1/adhoc_analysis/2011/centenarians_by_age_groups.pdf.

Drucker, P. (1954). *The Practice of Management*. New York: Harper & Row.

Economist, T. (2006). The CEO's role in talent management: how top executives from ten countries are nurturing the leaders of tomorrow.

European Commission. (2012). *Draft Joint Employment Report to the Communication From the CommissionAnnual Growth Survey 2013*. [online]. Available from: http://ec.europa.eu/social/main.jsp?catId=101&langId=en.

Everest. (2012a). *Emerging Markets Driving Growth in Multi-process HR Outsourcing Market, According to Everest Group Study*. [online]. Available from: http://www.everestgrp.com/2012-06-emerging-markets-driving-growth-in-multi-process-hr-outsourcing-market-according-to-everest-group-study-press-release-9773.html.

Everest. (2012b). *What will 2012 Bring to HRO?*

Farndale, E., Paauwe, J. and Hoeksema, L. (2009). In-sourcing HR: shared service centers in The Netherlands. *International Journal of Human Resource Management*, 20(3), pp.544–561.

Fernandez-Stark, K. (2012). *Offshore Services Global Value Chain*. [online]. Available from: http://www.eclac.cl/comercio/tpl/contenidos/offshore_services_global_value_chain_Fernandez_Stark.pdf.

Fisher, C.D. (2010). Happiness at Work. *International Journal of Management Reviews*, 12, pp.384–412.

Fombrun, C.J. (1983). Strategic Management: integrating the human resource systems into strategic planning. *Advances in Stategic Management*, 2.

Foster, S. (2009). *Making Sense of e-HRM: Technological Frames, Value Creation and Competitive Advantage*. Hertfordshire Business School. [online]. Available from: https://uhra.herts.ac.uk/dspace/handle/2299/4511.

Fowler, A. (1990). Performance Management: The MBO of the 1990's. *Personnel Management*, 22, pp.75–90.

Friedman, M. (1953). *Essays in Positive Economics*. University of Chicago Press.

Gagne, F. (2000). Understanding the complete choreography of talent development through DMGT-based analysis. In K. A. Heller et al., eds. *International Handbook of Giftedness and Talent*. Elsevier Science, Oxford.

Garavan, T. (1997). The learning organization: a review and evaluation. *The Learning Organization*, 4(1), pp.18–29.

Gardner, S.D., Lepak, D.P. and Bartol, K.M. (2003). Virtual HR: The impact of information technology on the human resource professional. *journal of Vocational Behaviour*, 63(2), pp.159–179.

Gartner. (2011). *Gartner Predicts 2012*.

Gartner. (1995). Outsourcing – 14 critical success factors. *Business Issues,*, (February).

Gerhart, B., Wright, P.M. and McMahon, G.C. (2000). Measurement error in research on human resources and firm performance: how much error is there and how does it influence effect size estimates? *Personnel Psychology*, 53(4), pp.803–834.

Gibbons, J. (2008). *Employee Engagement: A Review of Current Research and Its Implications*. New York, NY.

Gilley, K.M., Greer, C.R. and Rasheed, A.A. (2004). Human Resource Outsourcing and Organizational Performance in

Manufacturing Firms. *Journal of Business Research*, 57(3), pp.232–240.

Gilley, K.M. and Rasheed, A.A. (2000). Making More by Doing Less: An Analysis of Outsourcing and its Effects on Firm Performance. *Journal of Management*, 26(4), pp.763–790.

Goffee, R. and Jones, G. (2006). *Why Should Anyone Be Led By You: What it Takes to Be an Authentic Leader*. Boston, MA: Harvard Business School.

Gratton, L. and Ghoshal, S. (2005). Beyond best practice. *MIT Sloan Management Review*, 46(3), pp.49–57.

Groysberg, B. (2010). Chasing Stars: The Myth of Talent and the Portability of Performance.

Groysberg, B., Lee, L.E. and Abrahams, R. (2010). What it takes to make "star" lines pay off'. *MIT Sloan Management Review.*, 51(2), pp.57–61.

Grugulis, I., Vincent, S. and Hebson, G. (2003). The Rise of the Network Organisation and the Decline of Discretion. *Human Resource Management Journal2*, 13(2), pp.45–59.

Guardian, T. (2013). World's happiest OECD countries: in full. [online]. Available from: http://www.guardian.co.uk/business/2013/may/28/worlds-happiest-countries-oecd-australia.

Guest, D. and King, Z. (2004). Power, innovation and problem-solving: The Personnel Manager's three steps to heaven. *Journal of Management Studies*, 41(3), pp.401–423.

Hallberg, U.E. and Schaufeli, W.B. (2006). 'Same but different? Can work engagement be discriminated from job involvement and organizational commitment? *European Psychologist*, 11(2), pp.119–127.

Hamel, G. and Prahalad, C.K. (1994). *Competing for the Future*. Boston: Harvard Business School Press.

Hand, J. and Lev, B. (2003). *Intangible Assets: Values, Measures and Risk*. Oxford: Oxford University Press.

Handy, L., Devine, M. and Heath, L. (1996). *360 Feedback: Unguided Missile or Powerful Weapon?* Berkhamstead.

Harris, L., Doughty, D. and Kirk, S. (2002). The devolution of HR responsibilities - perspectives from the UK public sector. *Journal of European Industrial Training*, 26(5), pp.218–229.

Harrison, N. (2008). *How to be a True Business PArtner by Performance Consulting*. Nigel Harrison, ed. Sheffield.

Hempel, P.S. (2004). Preparing the HR Profession for Technology and Information Work. *Human Resource Management*, 43(2/3), pp.163–177.

Hewitt~Consulting. (2008). Hewitt Talent Survey 2008: Building the Talented Organisation.

Hirsch, W. et al. (2008). What customers want from HR. *People Management*, (18 September 2008).

Hunter, I. et al. (2006). *HR Business Partners*. Aldershot: Gower.

Huselid, M.A. (1995). The Impact of Human Resource Management Practices on Turnover, Productivity and Corporate Financial Performance. *Academy of Management Journal*, 38(3), pp.365–672.

Huselid, M.A., Becker, B.E. and Beatty, R.W. (2005). *The Workforce Scorecard: Managing Human Capital to Execute Strategy*. Boston:Mass: Harvard Business School.

IBM. (2009). The Enterprise of the future.

IDC. (2010). *IDC's Worldwide Business Intelligence Tools Tracker Finds the Market Surpassed $4 Billion in Revenues in the Second Half of 2010 with Further Growth Expected in 2011*. [online]. Available from: http://www.idc.com/getdoc.jsp?containerId=prUS22910811.

Janssen, M. and Joha, A. (2006). Motives for establishing shared service centers in public administrations. *International Journal of Information Management2*, 26(2), pp.102–115.

Jurkiewicz, C. and Brown, R. (1998). GenXers vs. Boomers vs. Matures: generational comparisons of public employees' motivation. *Review of Public Personnel Administration1*, Fall, pp.18–37.

Kahn, W.A. (1990). Psychological conditions of personal engagement and disengagement at work. *Academy of Management Journal*, 33(4), pp.692–724.

Kanfer, R. (1990). Motivational theory and industrial and organizational psychology. In M. D. Dunnette & L. Hough, eds. *Handbook of Industrial and Organizational Psychology*. Palo Alto, CA: Consulting Psychology Press, pp. 75–105.

Kaplan, R.S. and Cooper, R. (1998). *Cost and Effect: Using Integrated Cost Systems to Drive Profitability and Performance*. Boston: Harvard Business School Press.

Kaplan, R.S. and Norton, D.P. (1996). Using the balanced scorecard as a strategic management system. *Harvard Business Review*, January-Fe, pp.75–85.

Kearns, P. (2003a). *HR Strategy: Business Focused, Individually Centred*. Oxford: Elsevier Butterworth Heinemann.

Kearns, P. (2003b). *HR Strategy: Business focused, individually centred*. Oxford: Elsevier Butterworth-Heinemann.

Klaas, B., McLendon, J.A. and Gainey, T.W. (2001). Outsourcing HR: The impact of organisational characteristics. *Human Resource Management*, 40(2), pp.125–138.

Kossek, E.E. et al. (1994). Waiting for innovation in the Human Resources Department : Godot implements a Human Resource Information System. *Human Resource Management*, Spring, 33(1), pp.135–139.

Kotter, J.P. (1996). *Leading Change*. Cambridge, MA: Harvard Business School Press.

Kotter, J.P. (1995). Why transformation efforts fail. *Harvard Business Review*, March-Apri, pp.59–67.

Kovach, K. and Cathcart, C.E.J. (1999). Human Resource Information Systems (HRIS): providing business with rapid data access, information exchange and strategic advantage. *Personnel Management*, 28(2), pp.275–281.

KPMG. (2002). *Global IT Management Survey: How Committed are You?* [online]. Available from: http://www.kpmg.com/CN/en/IssuesAndInsights/ArticlesPublicatio ns/Documents/Global-IT-Project-Management-Survey.

Landy, F.J., Barnes, J.L. and Murphy, K.R. (1978). Correlates of perceived performance and accuracy of performance evaluation. *The Journal of Applied Psychology*, 63(6), pp.751–754.

Latham, G., Sulsky, L.M. and MacDonald, H. (2007). Performance Management. In P. Boxall, J. Purcell, & P. Wright, eds. *The Oxford Handbook of Human Resource Management*. Oxford: Oxford University Press.

Lawler, E.E. (2009). Make human capital a source of competitive advantage. *Organizational Dynamics*, 38(1), pp.1–7.

Lawler, E.E. and Mohrman, S. (2003). HR as a strategic partner - what does it take to make it happen? *Human Resource Planning*, 26(3), pp.15–29.

Lawler, E.E.I.I.I., Levenson, A. and Boudreau, J.W. (2004). HR metrics and analytics: use and impact. *Human Resource Planning*, 27(4), pp.27–35.

Layard, R. (2006). *Happiness: Lessons From a New Science*. London: Penguin.

Legge, K. (1978). *Power, Innovation and Problem Solving in Personnel Management*. Maidenhead: McGraw Hill.

Lepak, D.P., Bartol, K.M. and Erhardt, N.L. (2005). A contingency framework for the delivery of HR practices. *Human Resource Management Review*, 15(2), pp.139–159.

Lepak, D.P. and Snell, S.A. (1998). Virtual HR: Strategic human resource management in the 21st century. *Human Resource Management Review*, 8(3), pp.215–234.

Lettink, A. (2012). *The Consumerization of HR: The End of HR as Middleman*.

Lewis, M. (2003). *Moneyball: The Art of Winning an Unfair Game*. New York: W.W. Norton and Company.

Lewis, R.E. and Heckman, R.J. (2006). Talent Management: A Critical Review. *Human Resource Management Review2*, 16, pp.139–154.

Lilly, J.D., Gray, D.A. and Virick, M. (2005). Outsourcing the Human Resource Function: Environmental and Organizational Characteristics that affect HR Performance. *Journal of Business Strategies*, 22(1), pp.55–73.

Locke, E. (1968). Toward a theory of task motivation and incentives. *Organizational Behavior and Human Performance*, 3(2), pp.157–189.

Luhn, H.P. (1958). A Business Intelligence System. *IBM Journal*, 2(4).

Maatman, M., Bondarouk, T. and Looise, J.K. (2010). Conceptualising the capabilities and value creation of HRM shared service models. *Human Resource Management Review*, 20(4), pp.327–339.

Mabey, C., Salaman, G. and Storey, J. (1998). *Human Resource Management : A Strategic Introduction*. Oxford: Blackwell.

MacDuffie, J.P. (1995). Human resource bundles and manufacturing performance: organizational logic and flexible production systems in the world auto industry. , 48(2), pp.197–221.

Maclachlan, R. (2012). London 2012: Britain's Greatest HR Achievement. *People Management*. [online]. Available from: http://www.cipd.co.uk/pm/peoplemanagement/b/weblog/archive/2013/01/29/london-2012-britains-greatest-hr-achievement-2012-10.aspx [Accessed March 21, 2013].

Mansar, S. and Reijers, H.A. (2007). Best practices in business process redesign: use and impact. *Business Process Management Journal*, 13(2), pp.193–213.

Marler, J.H. (2009). Making Human Resource strategic by going to the net: reality or myth? *The International Journal of Human Resource Management*, 20(3), pp.515–527.

Martin, G., Massy, J. and Clarke, T. (2003). When absorptive capacity meets institutions and (e)learners: Adopting, diffusing and exploiting e-learning in organisations. *International Journal of Training and Development*, 7(4), pp.228–244.

Mayo, A. (2006). *The Human Value of the Enterprise*. London: Nicholas Brealey International.

McCann, D. (2009). Memo to CFOs - Don't Trust HR. *CFO Magazine*. [online]. Available from: http://www.cfo.com/article.cfm/13270251.

McKinsey Global Institute. (2011). *Big data: The next frontier for innovation, competition, and productivity.*

Meijerink, J., Bondarouk, T. and Looise, J.K. (2013). Value Creation Through HR Shared Services: Towards a Conceptual Framework. *Personnel Review*, 42(1), pp.83–104.

Mercer. (2013). *It's time for the next generation HR Service Delivery model.*

Mintzberg, H. (1989). *Mintzberg on management: Inside our strange world of organizations*. New York: Free Press.

Moore, G. (1991). *Crossing the Chasm*. Capstone: Chichester.

Morgan, A., Canna, K. and Cullinane, J. (2005). 360 feedback: a critical enquiry. *Personnel Review*, 34(6), pp.663–680.

Morris, B. (2006). Tearing up the Jack Welch playbook. *Fortune*.

Murton, A., Inman, M. and O'Sullivan, N. (2010). *Unlocking Human Resource Management*. London: Hodder Education.

Nehles, A.C. et al. (2006). Implementing human resource management successfully: the role of first-line managers. *Management Review*, 17(3), pp.256–273.

O'Leary, D.E. (2000). *Enterprise resource planning systems: systems, life cycle, electronic commerce, and risk*. Cambridge: Cambridge University Press.

Ohmae, K. (1982). *The mind of the strategist: the art of Japanese business,*. McGraw-Hill.

Parry, E. and Wilson, H. (2009). Factors affecting the adoption of online recruitment. *Personnel Review*, 38(6), pp.655–673.

Penna / CIPD. (2008). Gen Up: How the four generations work.

People Management. (2013). HR: The Damning Verdict. *People Management*, (January), pp.10–11.

Personnel Management. The technologies that will transform learning. *Personnel Management*, pp.38–39.

Peters, T. and Waterman, R. (1982). *In Search of Excellence:* New York: Harper & Row.

Porter, M. (1980). *Competitive Strategy*. New York: Free Press.

Porter, M. and Millar, V.E. (1985). How information gives you competitive advantage. *Harvard Business Review*, July-Augus, pp.149–160.

Porter, M.E. (1991). Towards a Dynamic Theory of Strategy. *Strategic Management Journal*, 12(1), pp.95–117.

Powell, P. (1992). Information Technology Evaluation: Is It Different? *The Journal of the Operational Research Society*, 43(1), pp.29–42.

Prahalad, C.K. and Hamel, G. (1990). The core competence of the corporation. *Harvard Business Review*, 68(3), pp.79–91.

Preece, D.A. and Harrison, M.R. (1988). The Contribution Of Personnel Specialists To Technology Related Organisational Change. *Personnel Review*, 17(1).

Priem, R.L. (2007). A consumer perspective on value creation. *Academy of Management Review*, 32(1), pp.219–235.

Pritchard, K. (2010). Becoming an HR Strategic Partner: tales of transition. *Human Resource Management Journal2*, 20(2), pp.175–188.

Pritchett, P. and Pound, R. (1990). *The Employee Handbook for Organizational Change*. Dallas, Texas: Pritchett Publishing Company.

Purcell, J. (1999). Best practice and best fit : chimera or cul de sac? *Human Resource Management Journal*, 9(3), pp.26–41.

Purcell, J. et al. (2003). Understanding the People and Performance Link: Unlocking the Black Box.

Purcell, J. and Hutchinson, S. (2007). Front-line managers as agents in the HRM performance causal chain: theory, analysis and evidence. *Human Resource Management Journal, 17: 1, 3–20.*, 17(1), pp.3–20.

Ray, G., Barney, J.B. and Muhanna, W.A. (2004). Capabilities, Business Processes, and Competitive Advantage: Choosing the dependent variable in emprical tests of the Resource-Based View. *Strategic Management Journal2*, 25(1), pp.25–37.

Reason, J. (1990). *Human Error*. Ashgate.

Reilly, P., Tamkin, P. and Broughton, A. (2007). The Changing HR Function: Transforming HR?

Reilly, P. and Williams, T. (2003). *How to Get the Best Value From HR: The Shared Service Option*. Aldershot: Gower: Gower.

Remus, U. (2007). Critical success factors for implementing enterprise portals: A comparison with ERP implementations. *Business Process Management Journal*, 13(4), pp.538–552.

Roche, W.K., Teague, P., Coughlan, A., Fahy, M. (2011). *Human Resources in the Recession: Managing and Representing People at Work in Ireland*.

Rogers, E.M. (1995). *Diffusion of Innovations*. 4th ed. New York, NY.: The Free Press,.

Ross, D. and Dicker, S. (2000). How you can add 20% to shareholder value. *Human Resources*, December, pp.52–56.

Ross, S. (2013). How definitions of talent suppress talent management. *Industrial and Commercial Training*, 45(3), pp.166–170.

Ruel, H.J.M., Bondarouk, T. and Looise, J.K. (2004). E-HRM: Innovation or irritation. An explorative empirical study in five large companies on web-based HR. *Management Revue*, 15(3), pp.364–380.

Rummler, G.A. (1996). Redesigning the organization and making it work. *CMA Magazine*, 70(5).

Ruta, C.D. (2009). HR portal alignment for the creation and development of intellectual capital. *The International Journal of Human Resource Management*, 20(3), pp.562–577.

Sadri, J.. and Chatterdee, C. V. (2003). Building organisational character through HRIS. , 3(1), pp.84–98.

Saiyadain, M.S. (1998). *Human Resource Management*. New Delhi: Tata McGraw Hill.

Saks, A.M. (2006). Antecedents and consequences of employee engagement. *Journal of Managerial Psychology*, 21(7), pp.600–619.

Sanchez, A.M. and Perez, M.P. (2001). Lean Indicators and Manufacturing Strategies. *International Journal of Operations and Production Management*, 21(11), pp.1433–1451.

Santhanam, R. and Hartono, E. (2003). Issues in linking information technology capability to firm performance. *MIS Quarterly*, 27(1), pp.125–153.

Scase, R. (2007). *Global Remix: The fight for Competitive Advantage*. London: Kogan Page.

Schachtel. (1954). *The Real Enjoyment of Living*, New York: Dutton.

Schaubroeck, J. et al. (2008). An under-met and over-met expectations model of employee reactions to merit raises. *Journal of Applied Psychology*, 93(424-434).

Schaufeli, W.B. and Bakker, A.B. (2004). Job demands, job resources and their relationship with burnout and engagement: a multi-sample study'. *Journal of Organizational Behavior*, 23(3), pp.293–315.

Schein, E. (1987). Increasing Organisational Effectiveness Though better human resource planning and development. In E. Schein, ed. New York: Oxford University Press, pp. 24–45.

Schuler, R.S. and Jackson, S.E. (1987). Linking competitive strategies with human resource management practices. , 1(3), pp.209–213.

Schuler, R.S. and Walker, J.W. (1990). Human Resources Strategy: Focusing on Issues and Action. *Organizational Dynamics*, 19(1), pp.5–19.

Scott-Jackson, W. et al. (2009). Making the Decision to Outsource Human Resources. *Personnel Review*, 38(3), pp.236–252.

Scott-Jackson, W., Newham, T. and Gurney, M. (2005). *HR Outsourcing: The Key Decisions*. London.

Senge, P.M. (1992). *The Fifth Discipline*. Sydney: Random House.

Sethi, V.W. and King, R. (1994). Development of measures to assess the extent to which an information technology application provides competitive advantage. *Management Science*, 40(12), pp.1601–1627.

Sheehan, C. and Cooper, B.K. (2011). HRM Outsourcing: The Impact of Organisational Size and HRM Strategic Involvement. *Personnel Review*, 40(6), pp.742–760.

Silkroad. (2012). *State of Social Technology and Talent Management: 2012 Latest Findings, Newest Trends, Key Strategies*.

Simon, H. (1983). *Reason in Human Affairs*. Stanford University Press.

Skinner, W. (1981). Big hat, no cattle. *Harvard Business Review*, Sept-Oct, pp.106–114.

Sluis, L. van der. (2008). *Talent Management in Strategisch Perspectief*. Nyenrode:: Nyenrode Business Universiteit.

Smith, A. (1776). *An Inquiry into the Nature and Causes of the Wealth of Nations,*.

Stacey, R. (1993). Strategy as order emerging from chaos. , 26(1), pp.10–17.

Stahl, G.K. et al. (2007). Global Talent Management: How leading multinationals build and sustain their talent pipeline.

Stalk, G., Evans, P. and Schulman, L.E. (1992). Competing on Capabilities: The new Rules of Corporate Strategy. *Harvard Business Review*, 70(2), pp.57–69.

Standish Group. (1994). The Chaos Report. [online]. Available from: downloaded from http://www.ibv.liu.se/content/1/c6/04/12/28/The CHAOS Report.pdf on June 9, 2009.

Stevens, M. (2013). Just because they say they're happy, it doesn't mean they really are... *People Management*, (July), pp.28–31.

Stone, D.L., Stone-Romero, E. and Lukazweski, K. (2006). Factors affecting the acceptance and effectiveness of electronic human resource systems. *Human Resource Management Review*, 16(2), pp.229–244.

Stone, I. (2011). *International approaches to high performance working*. [online]. Available from: http://www.ukces.org.uk/assets/ukces/docs/publications/evidence-report-37-international-approaches-to-hpw.pdf.

Storey, J. (1992). *Developments in the Management of Human Resources*. Oxford: Blackwell.

Storey, J. and Sisson, K. (1993). *Managing Human Resources and Industrial Relations*. Buckingham: Open University Press.

Sullivan, J. (2013). How Google Is Using People Analytics to Completely Reinvent HR. *www.tlnt.com*. [online]. Available from: http://www.tlnt.com/2013/02/26/how-google-is-using-people-analytics-to-completely-reinvent-hr/ [Accessed March 10, 2013].

Sullivan, J. (2011). Talent Management Lessons From Apple ... A Case Study of the World's Most Valuable Firm (Part 2 of 4). *ere.net*. [online]. Available from: http://www.ere.net/2011/09/19/talent-management-lessons-from-apple-a-case-study-of-the-worlds-most-valuable-firm-part-2-of-3/ [Accessed March 20, 2013].

Tansley, C. (2011). What do we mean by "Talent" in Talent Management? *Industrial and Commercial Training*, 43(5), pp.266–274.

Tansley, C., Newell, S. and Williams, H. (2001). Effecting HRM-style practices through an integrated human resource information system : An e-greenfield site? *Personnel Review*, 30(3), pp.351–370.

Taylor, M.S. and Collins, C.J. (2000). Organizational Recruitment: enhancing the intersection of theory and practice. In C. L. Cooper

& E. A. Locke, eds. *Industrial and Organizational Psychology: Linking Theory and Practice*. Oxford: Basil Blackwell.

Taylor, S. (2008). *People Resourcing*. London: CIPD.

Telegraph, D. (2013). One in five jobseekers lie on CV, research shows. *Daily Telegraph*. [online]. Available from: an examination of Wall Street analysts by Boris Groysberg (2010) suggests that [Accessed March 16, 2013].

Thornton., G. (2012). *Global economy in 2013: uncertainty weighing on growth*.

Tichy, L. and Bascom, T. (2008). The business end of IT Project failure. *Mortgage Banking*, March 2008(68.6), pp.28–35.

Timbrell, G., Andrews, N. and Gable, G. (2001). Impediments to inter-firm transfer of best practice: in an enterprise systems context. *Australian Journal of Information Systems*, pp.116–125.

Tjahjono, B. et al. (2010). Six Sigma: a literature review. *International Journal of Lean Six Sigma*, 1(3), pp.216–233.

Tyson, S. and Fell, A. (1986). *Evaluating the Personnel Function*. London: Hutchinson.

Ulrich, D. (1996). *Delivering results : A new Mandate for Human Resource Professionals*. Boston MA: Harvard Business Review Press.

Ulrich, D. (2000). From e-business to e-HR. , 23(2), pp.12–21.

Ulrich, D. et al. (2008). *HR Competencies: Mastery at the Intersection of People and Business*.

Ulrich, D. et al. (2009). *HR Transformation: Building Human Resources from the Outside In*. New York: McGraw-Hill.

Ulrich, D. (1997). *Human Resource Champions : The Next Agenda for Adding Value and Delivering Results*. Boston MA: Harvard Business School Press.

Ulrich, D and Brockbank, W. (2005). *The HR value proposition*. Boston: Harvard Business School Press.

Ulrich, D. and Brockbank, W. (2005). The Work of HR Part One: People and Performance. *Strategic HR Review*, July/Augus(5), pp.20–23.

Ulrich, D. and Smallwood, N. (2012). What is Talent? *Ross School of Business, Executive White Paper*, pp.1–7. [online]. Available from: http://execed.bus.umich.edu/execdev/Includes/MEDIA/whitepa pers/DUlrich_WP_What_is_talent.pdf.

Ulrich, D, Younger, J. and Brockbank, W. (2008). The twenty-first-century HR organization. *Human Resource Management*, 47(4), pp.829–850.

Venkatesh, V. et al. (2003). User acceptance of information technology: toward a unified view. *MIS Quarterly*, 27(3), pp.425–478.

Vroom, V. (1964). *Work and motivation*. Oxford: John Wiley & Sons.

Wagner, E.L., Scott, S.V. and Galliers, R.D. (2006). The creation of "best practice" software: Myth, reality and ethics. *Information and Organisation*, 16(3), pp.251–275.

Walczuch, R., Lemmink, J. and Streukens, S. (2007). The effect of service employees' technology readiness on technology acceptance. *Information and Management*, 44, pp.206–215.

Ward, P. (1997). *360o Feedback*. Londond: Institute of Personnel and Development.

Weiss, A., Bates, T.C. and Licoano, M. (2008). Happiness Is a Personal(ity) Thing: The Genetics of Personality and Well-Being in a Representative Sample. *Psychological Science*, 19(3), pp.205–210.

Wells, G. and Ghuari, H. (2012). *Executive Perceptions of the HR Function*. [online]. Available from: http://www.oracle.com/openworld/lad-en/session-schedule/con30024-enok-1885995.pdf.

Willcocks, L.P. and Lester, S. (1997). In Search of Information Technology Productivity: Assessment Issues. *The Journal of the Operational Research Society*, 48(11), pp.1082–1094.

Williamson, O.E. (1975). *Markets and Hierarchies: Analysis and Antitrust Implications*. New York, NY.: The Free Press,.

Wright, P.M., Gardner, T.M. and Moynihan, L.M. (2003). The impact of HR practices on the performance of business units. *Human Resource Management Journal*, 13(3), pp.21–36.

Yeung, A. and Ulrich, D. (1990). Effective human resource practices for competitive advantage: An empirical assessment of organisations in transition. In R. J. Niehaus & K. F. (eds. . Price, eds. New York: Plenum, pp. 311–326.

Zahra, S.A. and George, G. (2002). Absorptive capacity: A review, reconceptualisation and extension. *Academy of Management Review*, 27(2), pp.185–203.

INDEX

360 performance review....85
9 Box Grid...................... 89, 103
Aberdeeen Group 133
Aberdeen Group....... 21, 101, 105, 265
Absence............................ 123
Accounting for People.... 129
Activity Based Costing..... 283
Adecco 115
Agunis 77, 78
Alleyne, Kakabadse............21
Amoako-Gyampha 303
Analytical Reporting 124
Aon Consulting 124
Appelbaum 86
Apple 61, 103, 181
Apprentice, The 107
Armstrong & Baron 78
Arthur, Jeffrey 55
Ashford, Dyson & Hodges 256
Astra Zeneca........................41
Balanced Scorecards....... 128
Barney 37, 54, 137, 140
Bartel....................................55
Bath Consultancy Group 157
BBC 299
Bearman 37
Beaumont 149
Becker......................... 55, 140
Becker & Huselid........... 54, 72
Becker, Huselid & Ulrich... 141
Beckers & Bsat................... 276
Bersin & Associates... 103, 117
Best of Breed 197
Bhatnagar.......................... 276
Big data............................. 128

BlessingWhite 64
Blumberg & Pringle..............86
Bond, James........................12
Bondarouk 183
Borman 55
Boston Consulting Group 117
Boxall................................. 140
Bridge................................ 117
Britain's Got Talent 93
British Telecom.....................66
Business Case
    Building 279
    Challenges 255
    Operational.................. 263
    Productivity 267
    Strategic Capability 274
Business Intelligence......... 111
Business partner .45, 151, 179, 220
Business Process
    Improvement 238
Business Week 116
Buyens & De Vos.................31
BYOD................................. 133
Caldwell 220
Cameron & Brion.............. 106
Cardy & Miller......................88
CedarCrestone 116, 265
Centres of Expertise............30
Change readiness............ 303
Cheese, Thomas & Craig...94
CIA 160
CIPD 14, 64, 116, 123
CIPD/Penna...................... 318
Cloud technology 188
Collings & Mallahi 97

Collings & Mellahi 92, 95
Cooke 24, 26, 28, 220
Cooke, Shen and McBride 37
COTS
   Commerical off-the shelf
   193
Coulson-Thomas 102
Cranfield University 102
Cunningham & Hyman 271
Customer capital See Human Capital Management
Daily Telegraph 57
Delaney, John 55
Delmotte & Sels 35, 41
Deloitte 34, 149
Dilbert 141
Dragons' Den 292
Drucker, Peter 76
Economist Intelligence Unit
   102
Economist, The 92
e-HRM
   Barriers 184
   Encouraging Adoption 310
   Strategies 178
Employee Engagement 63, 147, 328
Employee Relations 40
Employment Relations 63
e-PM 87, 89
European Commission 316
Everest 38, 323
Expectancy theory 83
Facebook 67
Farndale 31
Flamholz, E.G. 140
Ford, Henry 249, 251
Fowler 79
Future of HR 315
Gagne 97
Galbraith 315
Garavan 65

Gartner 35, 67, 299
Gilley & Rasheed 41
Gilley, Greer & Rasheed 41
Goal setting theory 83
Golden Triangle 153
Google 129
Grint 85
Groysberg et al 107
Grugulis, Vincent & Hebson
   44
Halberg & Schaufeli 64
Hamel & Prahalad 208
Handy, Devine & Heath 84
Happiness 326
Harrison 157
Herzberg, Frederick 62
Hewitt 101
Hope-Hailey et al 220, 271
HR Future
   and Technology 324
   Outlook 330
HR Outsourcing
   Future 322
   Issues 43
   Justification 33
   Scope 36
   Top Ten Tips 46
HR Practices 52
HR Transformation 17
HR Value Model 142
Human Capital
   Management 138, 140
   v HRM 136
Human Capital
   Measurement 111
   Measurement Model ... 121
Human Capital Technology
   170
Hunter, Saunders, Boroughs & Constance 157
Huselid, Mark ... 52, 54, 55, 140
IDC 116

inefficiency 230
Information Week 238
Integrated v Separate HR and Payroll 231
Internal Rate of Return..... 290
Janssen & Joha 26
Kahn 64
Kaplan & Norton 128
Karakanian 271
Klaas et al 43
Klaas, McLendon & Gainey 41
Kochan & Dyer 271
Kotter, John 236, 301, 309
KPMG 299
Latham, Sulsky & MacDonald 78
Lawler & Mohrmon 44
Lawler, Ed 74
Lawler, Levenson & Boudreau 116
Lean Process Design 249
Learning & Development .40, 65
Learning Organisation 65
Lengnick Hall & Lengnick Hall 276
Lengnick Hall & Moritz 276
Lepak, Bartol & Erhardt 31
Lev, Baruch 131, 140
Lewin, Kurt 301
Lewis & Heckman 92, 94
Lewis, Michael 119
Locke 83
London Olympics 59
Luhn 113
Luthans et al 271
Maatman et al 220
Maatman, Bondaraouk & Looise 26
Management Reporting . 122
Marler 276

Martin, Massey & Clarke.. 183
Maslow, Abraham 62, 301
McGovern et al 271
McKinsey 133
Meijerink 31
Meijerink et al 31
Meijerink, Bondarouk & Looise 26
Mercer 219
MHPRO 322
Mobile technology 133
Moneyball 119
Moore, Geoffrey 181
Morgan, Canna & Cullinane 84
Morris 250
Multi-process HRO 322
My Space 67
Nalbantian, Haig 140
NASA 160
Net Present Value 289
Norton, David 141
Offshoring 42
Operational Processes..... 241
Operational Reporting 121
Organisational Readiness Model 303
Outsourced HR 32
Pacioli, Luca 131
Patterson et al 54
Payback Period 289
Payroll 228
  HR or Finance 233
  Integrated v separate systems 231
Performance Cycle 76
Performance Management 74
Personnel 160, 161
Peters & Waterman
  In Search of Excellence 208

Pfeffer 54, 140
Pitt, Brad 119
Porter, Michael 137, 244
Powell 256
Preece 183
Pritchard 159
Process Framework 243
Process Technology 170
Purcell, John 55
PwC 148
PwC Saratoga 140
Ray, Barney & Muhanna .. 244
Recruitment 39, 56
Reilly, Tamkin & Broughton. 26
Resource Based Approach 245
Resource Based View 210
Reward 59
Roche et al 11
Ross & Dicker 31
Ross, Suzanne 97
Rucci et al 54, 276
Rummler 244
Saks 64
Sanchez & Perez 249
Scase 62
Schaubroeck et al 62, 77
Schein, Ed 71
Schmidt & Hunter 56
SecondLife 57
Senge 65
Service Centre 22
Service delivery ... 21, 219, 269
Service Delivery Model 18
Sethi & King 256
Shared Services 23
    Barriers 29
Sickness .... See Absence
Silkroad 67
Six sigma 250
Snell, Stuebner & Lepak 34
Social Technology 57, 67

Software as a Service 323
St. Vincent's Hospital 126
Stahl et al 101
Stalk, Evans & Schulman .. 244
Standish Group 299
Stategic Processes 240
Statutory framework 132
Stone 52
Stone, Stone-Romero & Lukaweski 257
Strassman 140
Structural capital See Human Capital Management
Structure Follows Strategy 210, 245
Sullivan 61, 103
Support Processes 241
Talent Management 91
    Cycle 102
    Strategy 99
Tannenbaum 22
Tansley & Newell 183
Tansley, Carole 92, 93
Taylor 56
Taylor, F.W. 62, 249
Technology Adoption Lifecycle 179
Teo & Rodwell 271
Tesco 82
TGI Friday's 70
Tichy & Bascom 299
Tjahhono et al 250
Truss et al 220
Ulrich & Smallwood 98
Ulrich, David 10, 17, 31, 43, 219, 220, 221
US Air Force 199
Value 130, 138
Value Model 259
Value Processes 240
van Der Sluis 97
Vroom, Victor 83

Wal-Mart 56
Whole Process approach 284
Wikipedia 67
Willcocks & Lester 256
Williamson 37
Woodall et al 33

Workforce Scorecards 127
Wright et al 54
X Factor 105
Yeung & Ulrich 55
You Tube 67

About the Author

Dr. Steve Foster is Business Consultancy Manager at NorthgateArinso (NGA). For the first eleven years of his career, he worked in a range of Human Resources management roles, including roles in compensation, reward, recruitment and as a line HR Manager. After project managing a major HR system implementation and working on a global HR transformation project, he worked as consultancy Practice Lead for The Hunter Group and as Director of e-HR at KPMG. As a consultant, he has worked with a wide range of major clients, helping them transform their HR operations. His specialist areas are HR business process improvement, e-HRM planning and implementation, business case development, outsourcing and change management. He has worked with a wide a range of HR technologies.

Steve regularly presents at HR / technology conferences, has published several articles on technology strategy and human capital management and is regularly quoted in professional magazines and journals. His first degree is in Psychology from the University of Bath, he gained an MBA from Henley Management College, is a Fellow of the CIPD and holds a Professional Doctorate from Hertfordshire Business School, based on his research into how organisations create value through the use of e-HRM.

www.ingramcontent.com/pod-product-compliance
Lightning Source LLC
Chambersburg PA
CBHW031818170526
45157CB00001B/105